**Evaluating
and Improving
Managerial Performance**

VIRGIL K. ROWLAND

Evaluating and Improving Managerial Performance

McGRAW-HILL BOOK COMPANY

New York   St. Louis   San Francisco   Düsseldorf   Johannesburg
Kuala Lumpur   London   Mexico   Montreal   New Delhi
Panama   Rio de Janeiro   Singapore   Sydney   Toronto

EVALUATING AND IMPROVING MANAGERIAL PERFORMANCE

Copyright © 1970 by McGraw-Hill, Inc. All Rights Reserved.
Printed in the United States of America. No part of this
publication may be reproduced, stored in a retrieval system,
or transmitted, in any form or by any means, electronic,
mechanical, photocopying, recording, or otherwise, without
the prior written permission of the publisher. *Library of Congress
Catalog Card Number 72–98488*

ISBN 07-054158-2

2 3 4 5 6 7 8 9 0   MAMM   7 5 4 3 2

To Walker L. Cisler

DISCLAIMER

Throughout this book there are examples of management activities, recordings of management meetings, and stories of customer frustration. All have been disguised so that no company representative can point to a specific instance and properly lay claim to its having occurred in his own company.

It must be understood that many company representatives will think that one or more incidents actually happened in their companies. Because of the basic similarities and the real fundamental situations, it would be strange if a goodly number of companies did not claim the sample stories.

All names have been changed on tape transcriptions, and geographic areas have been purposely altered.

Preface

THIS BOOK is an attempt to pull together the management practices of many thousands of successful managers and to classify, explain, evaluate, and illustrate these practices so that they may be used by other managers who desire to improve their own managerial skills.

One of the difficulties of writing about managerial practices comes from the fact that "managers" are on all levels in the organization charts, and to write of a first-line manager in the same words that are used of a manager on the vice-presidential level leaves many gaps and can cause misunderstanding. Accordingly this book will, on the one hand, show essential differences between the management practices of managers on different levels, and on the other, let the reader decide for himself whether a given technique or skill mentioned in general terms can be applied to his own job specifically. This is necessary to keep from being tiresomely repetitious.

It must be realized that a review of any specific techniques can serve only to stimulate the reader to analyze his own performance on his own job. Merely reading about a need for improvement will not produce improvement. Nor can one dare publicly to censure his own boss's performance (or the performance of those of even higher level) because of failure to measure up to the generalizations brought out in this book.

Hence I can only *hope* to stimulate management people to improve their own performance on their own jobs.

One thing which this book does do, however, is to enunciate by specific directions, examples, and sample working papers just how a manager above the first-line level can go about incorporating the skills outlined into his own section of his company and also how he can get his own managerial subordinates to do the same—and here "authority" can carry weight, for you, the "boss," can direct your own subordinates to improve their managerial performance by using skills they have not been using. It is hoped that these skills may involve some of those listed and amplified in this book.

Basically and chronologically the plan of this book is sixfold. Each of the six parts is a unit in itself, and each of the four middle units takes a managerial need of the manager and illustrates how it can be met. Parts One and Six discuss management philosophies, problems, and the future. Parts Two through Five are devoted to specific management tools or techniques.

Clearly no samples of managerial paper work can be used verbatim from this book—even to translate or modify these examples for use with your own people will not work. This has been cardinal for generations, but unfortunately many management personnel continue to try to sponge off of others for the things they themselves must do if it is to be worthwhile.

I know full well how unheeded the above warning will go, that there will be many who will try to adjust the printed samples to the actual case and will fail—yet, fortunately, there will be countless other management personnel who will recognize that preparing their own paper work with and for their own subordinates will really produce a payoff in the form of improvement of their own managerial performance and the performance of the managers under them.

Some of the materials in this book have been in print in one form or another at previous times. All material has been reviewed for cogency and revised with new interpretations and examples. Two previous books, *Improving Managerial Performance* (Harper & Row, 1958) and *Managerial Performance Standards* (American Management Association, 1960), have served as the original basis for portions of this book. This has been done since these two books are no longer available to the general public and because their material is basic to the structure of this overall approach to improving managerial performance.

Each part of this book will have a few prefacing words at the beginning of the individual section. These could have been made a part of this Preface, but because they relate specifically to the one part only, for convenience's sake they accompany their own parts.

The purpose of this book, then, is to provide an easy-to-follow guide for the management person, regardless of his level in the organization, which will give him knowledge of and an understanding of certain management skills and a way to apply these skills to his own job.

The material in this book is not a panacea, nor is it a magic potion; rather it is a framework for sound, concentrated work by the management person, and when used on that basis, will bring results that are measurable and gratifying.

I owe much to L. A. Appley, J. Walter Dietz, and those many other dedicated management specialists who have added so much to the skills of the professional manager.

The Detroit Edison Company and its chairman, Walker L. Cisler, have given me the "laboratory" to see many of these skills practiced with success and, therefore, have in a large sense contributed to the subject matter of this book.

Grateful thanks are expressed to the persons who have helped in the preparation of this book:

To Alice Smith for her perceptive assistance in the writing and editing of the manuscript.

To Julia Hopf, Ruth Weckmann, and Thomas Sweeney for assistance in preparing and completing the technical aspects of the manuscript.

To J. Douglas Elliott and Gregory Griffith, who have, by their inspection of portions of the manuscript, given me important aid with the text.

To the thousands of persons who, inadvertently or not, have made up the "meat" for the examples cited in the book.

Virgil K. Rowland

"Small deeds done are better than great deeds planned"—*From the last prayer of* THE REVEREND PETER MARSHALL, UNITED STATES SENATE CHAPLAIN, READ TO THE SENATE AFTER HIS DEATH.

Contents

PART ONE

Introduction

CHAPTER ONE

What Is Management?

THE WORD "MANAGEMENT" means different things to different people. One man said to me, "Don't you think management is just a state of mind?" Simple as this definition is, there is some truth in it—though, of course, not the whole truth—since the manager is not a true manager unless he has fully accepted certain fundamental responsibilities. Then there are the textbook definitions, which define "management" in terms of functions. Most commonly they list planning, organizing, staffing, directing, and controlling as the elements of the managerial job. This breakdown may be accurate so far as it goes. Certainly there are other functions that might be added—innovation, for instance.

However, in the case of all but one of these functions—directing—the techniques used will necessarily differ according to the industry, the company size, and the level on which the manager works. So will the extent to which the manager must engage in each of the functions. A first-line foreman, for example, may do very little planning, for the methods to be used and the sequence in which the work must be performed may be largely prescribed by other departments.

But every manager has subordinates and is responsible for directing them and for the results they achieve, regardless of his technical specialty, the industry or the company in which he works, and his position in the organization; directing people is the universal management function. To the extent that the manager can improve the performance of his subordinates, he becomes a better manager, and if he wants to better his performance in this respect he must work continuously at the job of direction.

Unfortunately, many managers seem content to be managers in title only. They do not appear to realize that they are missing an opportunity, that their chances and their organization's chances for growth are being curtailed by their neglect to pay enough attention to the direction and the improvement of the people under them.

Often men have been selected for managerial posts because they have demonstrated ability in specialized fields. Frequently, then, it has been found that their achievements are not so outstanding in their new positions and that their accomplishments leave much to be desired. Because of their professional abilities, their superiors had assumed that somehow, somewhere, sometime through the years these men had "breathed in" a knowledge of, an understanding of, the proper approach to the job of the manager. Too often this is not what really happens.

Observations of thousands of businessmen of all levels—from first-line supervisors to presidents—and consultations with hundreds have made evident the importance of the development of all management people regardless of organizational level. There is evidence also that in many cases individual potentialities are being wasted or improperly utilized. This may be because higher management has discovered no practical approach to the development of its subordinate managers. In some cases top management itself does not realize the need for such an approach. The management techniques discussed herein are geared to be of assistance to *all* management people, but first the highest level of management in an organizational unit must recognize and accept them.

Historically, management as a skill or even as a profession has been cataloged and written about by a host of writers. From the early days of Frederick Taylor and Frank Gilbreth through the activities of countless professional people and practical managers of the last half of the twentieth century a plethora of literature has been published. Much of the material has been sound, because it has explained excellent techniques and skills and presented workable principles and useful tools. On the reverse side of the coin, however, another large portion of this printed matter has been poorly stated throughout and inadequately documented.

Some of the material has been authored by people who have never been managers, and as such has clearly borne the mark of the theoretician and even the dreamy-eyed viewpoint of the cloistered halls.

Then, when an interested and enterprising practitioner of management tries to implement the techniques he has read about, he finds that they just will not work for him. The principles stated so glibly seem to be impossible to apply. Accordingly, the enterprising manager who really wants to improve his own managerial performance finds the going tough, drops the effort, and eventually joins a growing group of disillusioned management people, and this rapidly growing group influences other management people. Thus there is still greater blockage to be overcome when a seriously interested manager really wants to try to improve his own performance.

The ultimate might seem to be a clearing house of top management people who could help determine which articles on management should be printed. This, however, smacks of an infringement of the "freedom of the press" or perhaps, more accurately, the freedom of an editor to print provocative articles to help circulation.

One might say, at this point, that the average management person should be able to recognize what is really useful and what is not. But the blunt fact is that the *average* management person probably will not make the necessary evaluation, because (1) he is looking for a management tool, (2) he figures since it is in print it must be good, (3) he hasn't had broad experience in the practice of basic management skills on his job, and (4) he believes the high-sounding words and promises of the article.

During World War II Channing R. Dooley, one of the co-directors of the Training Within Industry branch of the War Manpower Commission, used to say: "If the manager of today would only *first* try the basic tools of management before attempting to fly off into the higher planes of fancier management, his job would be so much easier." That statement is as true today as it was then. Even if many more managers are practicing better basic management today than were at that earlier time—which is doubtful—industry has created a tremendous group of new managers and, too often, little basic training is given the new ones. Hence the large number who are, as the saying goes, still trying to practice management "by the seat of their pants."

Registrations in management courses, seminars, study groups, survey meetings, and symposiums have been gaining every year. Such activity can only point to an increased awareness of the importance of improving the quality of management in almost every company of any major size.

Then, too, there are the organizations which appeal only to the small company. The meetings are planned by professional groups, management organizations, trade associations, industrial associations, colleges, universities, and, yes, even by a few fly-by-night outfits which deliberately set out to make a quick buck.

Looking at the phrase "increased awareness of the importance of improving managerial performance," one wonders how much awareness there really is. Does it stem from a deeply felt need for improvement on the part of management people or from the fact that attending the meetings is the thing to do?

Does the awareness stem from a well-thought-out policy put forth by top management in a given company, or is it the loner in the organization who feels he needs help?

Does the awareness lead to the registration of the proper people for a given course, those who really need it and can be expected to use it when they get back to their companies, or does it call for a given number of registrations to be passed out on a reward basis? Or is a man sent to a session merely because he hasn't been to one yet?

The writer of this volume has often said in management meetings that much of the information he is discussing has been gained not only from firsthand practical experience but by picking the brains of thousands of management people in many kinds of industries, many different government agencies, hundreds of service organizations, and various incidental types of businesses. He has learned so much from these people's experiences that this book, in one sense, will be just a medium of transmission and bring out some of the things learned from other management people, who came not only from many different companies but from many different countries.

At one time I was assigned to write a paper on the subject "Areas of Knowledge That Management People Need," and in preparation for it I began asking groups of managers and individual managers what it was they needed to know about their jobs that they were having difficulty finding out. When I was speaking to a group, I would ask the members to write down lists, and when I was talking to an individual, I would obtain the answer informally and make a note of it. I continued this practice long after the paper was written, and in the course of a survey conducted over a period of years, I collected answers from more than 8,000 managers at various management levels.

As the answers began to pile up during the first year or two of the continuing survey, they were assembled in categories, which soon numbered thirty-seven. Since this number was too large to utilize intelligently, a committee of specialists in the management field was formed, composed of the head of a department in the school of business of a large and important university, a top management specialist from a top professional management society, and a third-line management practitioner in my own company. With the help of these men, I condensed the answers and sorted them out; and the committee finally determined that the number of categories could be reduced to four.

The question I had asked was phrased as follows: "What areas of knowledge do you feel that you, yourself, need to know more about to do your own management job better, to do your direction-of-people job better?" Answers came from first-line foremen and vice-presidents, and from all points in between, including department heads and plant managers, in all kinds of companies, government agencies, and other types of organizations.

The four areas of knowledge which *all* the listed answers fell into were:

1. We need to know WHAT we are supposed to do as a manager.

2. We need to know HOW FAR we are expected to go in discharging our responsibilities and authorities.

3. We need to know HOW WELL we are expected to do our management job.

4. We need to know HOW WELL WE ARE DOING our management job.

It seems incredible that in all these cases managers had not been sufficiently informed by their superiors of these elementary matters about their jobs, particularly when so many of those who answered had been subjected to a variety of instruction by today's erudite training specialists. When I presented the findings, some high-level managers refused to believe them, but many of the scoffers had to eat their scoffing words when they asked their own subordinates my question. For example:

"Do the management people in your company know what they are supposed to do as managers?" I asked one vice-president. (Among other things, he was secretary of his company's salary board, which had had position descriptions prepared for everyone in the company who was considered a manager.)

He said: "Yes, they do. We have position descriptions right here," and he reached into his desk and brought out a fat loose-leaf binder and placed it in front of him.

I asked him: "Where does it show what they are supposed to do as directors of people?"

He flipped open the book, and started to read a page. Then he tried another one, and kept flipping the pages muttering to himself. Finally, he had to admit he couldn't find anything that answered the question.

Then he said: "I think our folks know anyway. They have been around here long enough." And he called in a subordinate and asked him what he did as a manager.

The subordinate said, in effect, that he didn't know, that the superior had never discussed the matter with him.

(It is encouraging to note that the superior did not reproach the subordinate for embarrassing him in this way, but accepted the fact that he himself had been remiss, and resolved to correct the situation.)

The four areas of which so many managers, from vice-presidents down to foremen, say they need more knowledge are considered in Parts Two through Five of this book, which present techniques that can be used by any manager—regardless of his position in the organization—as a normal part of his job. These techniques work if the manager is convinced that he owes it to his company, his subordinates, and himself to improve his direction of the people under him by ensuring that they get answers to their four questions.

CHAPTER TWO

Changes in Focus

Professional management consultants who are interested in selling some form of management development often use the phrase "change in focus." About every five years, it seems, management needs to "change its focus"—and the particular brand of training offered at the time is the only thing that will accomplish the change.

Actually, a change in focus may be valueless if it is only a change from one narrow focus to another equally narrow. The focus of the good manager has always been broad enough to encompass all the different phases of his job.

Each new development in the management field has been promoted as the cure-all for management ills, and each has in all too many cases proved disappointing as an overall answer to the problem of improving managerial performance. Let me sketch just briefly the more important developments in the twentieth century.

THE EARLY PANACEAS

First, of course, there was Frederick Taylor's scientific management. If this had been presented for what it was—a set of industrial engineering techniques that would make possible improvements in tools, machines, methods, and scheduling—managers would have accepted it as such and would not have felt that they needed to look no further for answers to all their problems. But it was presented as the science of management itself, rather than simply as a new set of tools for management. Certainly, Taylor's differential piecework plan of payment—even with the improvements later incorporated in it by Henry Laurence Gantt—did not produce the "mental revolution" he expected: the wholehearted cooperation of management and labor.

The next big change in focus grew out of the publicity accorded the Hawthorne experiments, which convinced many managers that they must change their focus from financial incentives to nonfinancial incentives if they were to get the production they wanted. This led, eventually, to the view (although the original researchers cannot be blamed for this) that the only thing a manager needed was a pleasant personality. The Hawthorne research did bring out important points about the working environment and its effect on productivity and morale, but again the focus was narrow.

SOME LATER IDEAS

More recently, the changes in focus have come faster and faster. Among the more prominent of those that have evolved has been the doctrine that the manager should concentrate on giving his people an opportunity for self-actualization and creativity. It is true that many people whose jobs provide opportunity for these things are among the most hard-working and sometimes the most effective in the country. But there are others who prefer a job that does not require them to be continually trying new things, and it may be that they are in the majority.

We have also had Douglas McGregor's X and Y theories, which are somewhat related to the self-actualization theory. According to McGregor, management has made its greatest mistake in believing that people don't want to work, that they must be pushed to do so—that is, by acting on what he calls the X theory—whereas most of them would respond if management acted on the Y theory, that people really want to work and be creative. The Y theory has its points, but again, it is not the whole answer. Even people who do want to work and who are capable of valuable creative work require some push at some times, and the manager must know how to apply that push without being a tyrant.

Then there is management by objectives, which is, of course, also a good thing, but it is a sad commentary on management that it has been necessary to make a cult of it. Of course the good manager knows what his objectives are, and of course he has always let his subordinates know what was expected of them. Further, he has always been able to distinguish between true objectives and tasks—between, say, making up a mailing list and making up a mailing list that will produce returns, or between getting out reports regularly and supplying his superiors with the information they actually need. But setting objectives and making sure that subordinates understand them is only one phase of the management job.

We also have the "management grid" theory, which, quite reasonably, calls for the manager to pay equal and maximum attention to people and production. This is, of course, what good managers have always done, although it is questionable whether they have regarded the two fields of attention as different, since, of course, production depends on people. Moreover, it is doubtful whether discussions and meetings based on the managerial grid do much good—apportioning attention in this way may encourage managers to lose sight of the fact that the fundamental management job is to direct people in such a way that they produce maximum results.

Another comparatively new cure-all is "sensitivity training," which is conducted with the laudable aim of making managers more aware of their effect on people, and thus likely to change their ways. Of course, a good manager is sensitive to others and aware of their feelings, but the technique used in sensitivity training is likely to make him crawl into a shell and shun contact with others, unless he has a very thick skin, in which case he will shrug off the training as quickly as he can.

In brief, sensitivity training consists of an unstructured conference in which people are encouraged to light into each other and say exactly what they think of them. This is bad enough when the participants come from different companies and perhaps need never see each other again. But it tends to be pernicious when they are all from the same company, for once they have let go of ordinary courtesy and have brought their true views of each other into the open, it may be impossible for them to work together again. This can be true even if, by and large, they like each other to begin with, for people seldom like each other entirely without reservations of some kind.

One European company president who sat in on such a session without taking part stopped the whole program abruptly. "I will not," he said, "allow my people to be subjected to this."

Finally, we have "management science," or operations research, which resembles scientific management in that it represents an attempt to quantify the factors bearing on management decisions, and in some cases to eliminate the need for decision-making altogether. Management science, and its tool the computer, have been immensely valuable and will be still more valuable in the future. But they cannot free the manager of his responsibilities. There are some situations, of course, in which the mathematical answer is unquestionably the right one, but in a great many cases there are intangibles that must be taken into account in addition to the figures. As just one example, it might seem that if management science techniques indicate that it will be more profitable to concentrate production on products A and B and to expend no resources at all on products C and D, the decision has been dictated by the mathematics. But can one put into figures the possible reactions of customers who have been accustomed to buying all four products from the same company? Or the effect on the labor force, if the changeover requires extensive layoffs? Or the possible effect of putting all the company's eggs into two baskets instead of four?

Management science provides managers with data that will help them make better decisions, but it will probably never make the decisions for them except in routine matters. Like scientific management, management science is a new and valuable tool for management, but it is not the science *of* management.

As one reads the literature produced in the last half-century, one is impressed by the fact that managers have always tended to greet each new development with the same loud cheers, only to find that it falls short of expectations. In cases where the new developments have embodied new tools and techniques, such as industrial engineering and the use of the computer, they have been valuable, but in cases where the attempt has been to focus attention on some aspect of the management job itself— the direction of people—they have been dismal failures. Considering all the training managers have been given in the direction of people, from courses based on the Hawthorne studies to sensitivity training, training in management by objectives, or operation according to the management grid, one would expect to find the majority of employees interested, happy, and productive—no strikes, no apathy, little absenteeism and turnover. Strikes are not as common in some industries as they were, say during the 1930s, but we still have plenty of them, and apathy, poor productivity, and high turnover—despite the immense improvement in working conditions and real wages that has occurred—are more prevalent than ever.

THE NEED REMAINS

Each new idea is supposed to meet the same need—improvement of managerial performance. There is even a sameness in the advertising of the new devices that someone has evolved for training managers, even though each new program has a special title geared to the ideas popular at the time.

The rehashing of the same basic ideas under new names points to only one thing: Top management is dissatisfied with the performance of its subordinates but does not seem to know what to do about it. Hence it is receptive to almost anyone who offers a panacea. Yet the remedy lies in top management's own hands, as this book will attempt to show.

Many of the attempts to change the focus of management have been a response, if an inadequate one, to very real needs. Although the job of the manager is still what it has always been, the social changes that have swept the country in the past generations have made it impossible for management to ignore certain aspects of its responsibilities, as it sometimes could in the past.

Because in the past managers of industry refused to accept leadership in certain respects, leadership of broad social movements fell to others; and management now has been compelled to accept regulations that make its tasks more difficult. But accept them it has, after having dragged its feet as long as it could. Now, happily, many managers appear to be ready to assume the leadership that they or their predecessors once refused to accept.

SOCIAL CHANGES

The social forces that have changed management's conception of its role include, although not necessarily in this order: the great growth of unionism, the demand for welfare programs both public and private, the view that companies must contribute to good causes, the expectation that managers will contribute time to civic service, growing civil unrest, and the increasing number of so-called unemployables who now refuse to remain quietly in the background.

These forces cannot be ignored, although their strength varies in different localities and according to population trends. Together they form an amalgam of creeping change that has flowed over the country much like molten lava, and they cannot be stopped any more than lava can. Gradually, they have changed management's conception of its role and its responsibilities.

Any analysis of the ideas expressed by business management over a fifty-year period will bear out the statement that management philosophy has changed drastically. Everyone knows executives who proudly insist that they have always operated as they do now. Yet many of them were tyrants twenty or thirty years ago; certainly they felt that they had an absolute right to treat their businesses as private provinces in which their word was law. The benevolent and permissive attitude in supervision has grown up so gradually that managers have scarcely realized how much of their old philosophies they have relinquished.

Unions

No management person can deny that the growth of unions has produced changes in management philosophies, even in companies that are not unionized and seem unlikely to be unionized in the near future. Some years ago as management fought a rear-guard action against union encroachments there was much talk of the "management prerogatives" that management had to hold onto at all costs. There is less discussion of the subject today; in fact, many managements have become resigned to the restrictions that they fought bitterly in the past.

It may even be that management has become too accommodating in this respect, and that the pointer on the balance has swung too far toward the opposite side of the scale. There is a school of thought which holds that originally labor was justified in its demands for more favorable management treatment, but that now managements have recognized their own shortcomings and gradually put the relationship between management and labor in better balance. Yet labor has continued to fight for further gains, to the extent that it is now management, rather than labor, that is at a disadvantage. Only when a true balance is reestablished, these management people feel, will there be true statesmanship in labor-management relations.

Government at the federal level has legislated labor gains, and its statutes have been buttressed by state legislation. Changes have occurred that have made these regulations more workable, but the scales are still weighted too heavily on the labor side. Unless legislation in the labor-management field achieves a more reasonable balance, there will continue to be problems, bankruptcies, strikes, and loss of income for both companies and their labor forces. There is need for the "statesmanship" so sadly lacking in many labor-management conflicts.

Welfare Programs

One evidence of the way in which business philosophies have changed is the widespread provision of welfare benefits, and the way in which they are constantly broadened as time goes on, by legislation and new negotiations. No amount of argument for or against the broadening will alter this trend, nor will isolated cries against the changes stem the tide.

The cost of these benefits must now be taken into account in all management planning: when new products are designed, when new plants are opened, and when new businesses are started. And the more widespread they become, the more management tends to accept them as normal and natural.

Contributions

There is yet another type of management contribution to welfare: contributions to civic, charitable, or educational institutions, contributions that stem from corporate largesse, or perhaps from regard for public relations. Once these are made, they tend to become semipermanent, for a corporation that has once contributed to a worthy cause of one kind or another will find it difficult to refuse to do so, or to reduce its contribution, without arousing some bad feeling in the community.

There are some who say that the corporation has no right to dispense the stockholders' money in this way. But there is considerable justification for the practice, even from the viewpoint of the stockholders, and even if the public relations aspects are disregarded. Without aid to the poor, for example, a warped civilization spreads across the nation. Without aid to education, there will be a shortage of trained, skilled people for business. Secondary education is funded from the tax revenues, but many colleges are not, and in both cases many qualified students need aid if they are to attend.

Civic Leadership

Calls upon business for civic leadership are constantly occurring. No longer can a concern hold itself aloof from the needs. It has been said that the top people of a small company are local citizens, those of a larger company are state citizens, those of big companies are national citizens, and those of huge companies are world citizens. This is borne out by the fact that what the small company does may affect the local community in an important way, what the larger company does may have an important effect on a state or region, what the very large company does affects the whole national economy, and what the huge company does may even affect world economy. (There are companies that have grown so vast and spread their operations over so much of the world that some sort of international charter may be necessary.)

But the loan or assignment of personnel to meet civic needs costs the company substantial amounts of money, for often those who are detached from their regular jobs are key men. About the only direct benefit the company receives in return is that the man who takes over a key man's job while he is temporarily absent will receive some training and the key man himself may gain some broader experience.

Civil Unrest and the "Unemployables"

Labor unrest has often disrupted the normal operation of a company, and sometimes strikes have been accompanied by property damage and civil disobedience. Once a settlement has been arrived at, management generally lets bygones be bygones and does not attempt to prosecute those who have caused the damage. And in many companies that have been unionized for a long time, strikes have become less violent; picketing is only token, and takes the form of one or two union members lounging outside each gate.

At times, however, management is confronted with a new type of unrest, civil disorders with racial overtones, disorders that include arson and looting, often by people whom management has considered "unemployable" and who have been rigidly excluded from normal economic life.

To the extent that people were considered unemployable or employable only in menial capacities merely by reason of their race, management in many cases has changed its attitude completely. Often it is now willing not only to hire qualified nonwhite candidates but to seek them out. The change in management's attitude in this respect began during World War II, partly in response to legislation and partly because of the shortage of labor that was experienced at that time, and has accelerated since then.

But hiring qualified people regardless of race presents no great obstacles, once management has overcome its own prejudices and the prejudices of its employees, which it can often overrule by fiat alone. Certainly there is no logical argument against doing so.

It is a different matter, however, to hire those who are considered unemployable by reason of lack of skill, education, and good working habits. And it is in this area that the change in management's thinking—at least in a number of key companies—has undergone a radical change. Some managers have begun to accept the idea that they are responsible for doing something about the civil unrest, not only to protect their own properties but as a civic duty, that as managers they must accept responsibility for leadership in this respect. (This is in direct contrast to management's attitude during the Great Depression, when it opposed government-made jobs but made little or no effort of its own to reduce the great number of jobless who existed at that time.)

The number of "unemployable" people today, however, would be smaller if managers had used better judgment in setting standards for jobs. Often standards have been set too high, as the result of actions on the part of both staff and line people.

The staff—and by this I mean the personnel department—has often tended to set standards for formal education, IQs, and so on, far higher than they need to be, simply in order to reduce the number of applicants and put decisions on applications on as mechanical a basis as possible. One early book on selection even counseled personnel managers to make the formal qualifications so stiff that only two or three applicants could hurdle them. This, the author pointed out, would make the selection job comparatively easy.

But perhaps the line people themselves have been even more responsible for the inflation of job requirements beyond reasonable proportions. These overinflated qualifications have boomeranged, so that starting requirements have risen until a whole new group of "unemployables" has been created. When job classifications and job evaluations are in question, each department head tries to blow up requirements for his own job and for the jobs of the people under him. The more exacting he makes his own job appear, of course, the more important he will seem and the greater his chance for a raise. Also, the more exacting the jobs of those under him are made to appear, the more important his own job will be, and the higher the salaries he succeeds in justifying, the easier he will find it to fill any jobs that become vacant.

Certainly, many companies have required a college or a high school education for jobs that do not require such a background, and often they have passed up good applicants for reasons that were not valid. There is no particular magic in a high school diploma or a college degree—many people get through high school and even through college without acquiring much education that will be of value on the job. Many others quit before graduation for entirely justifiable reasons: family need for money, for example.

When unemployability stems from attitude, however, the case is more difficult. A person who simply doesn't want to work is difficult or impossible to supervise, and some of those in this category actually *are* unem-

ployable. But the group is not so large as it might seem, if proper supervision has been provided. Many of those who have been uninterested in
working may change their attitude once they become accustomed to a
regular paycheck and see how they can, through their own efforts, make
it larger.

It is too bad that some managements have needed a crisis to face these
problems, for the crisis approach is an expensive one. Yet only when crises
recur continually does the average company begin to incorporate the
long-term needs to meet social changes into its planning. Managements
must take some of the blame for creating a major part of the problem.

Social changes are important. We need them, and we must be aware of
them and meet them with constructive action before they turn into crises.

However, most companies can afford the constructive action necessary
only if their managers, all down the line, learn to manage better.

CHAPTER THREE

The Effects of Poor Management

NEVER BEFORE has a country produced such a wealth of goods and services as the United States does today. Proponents of the free enterprise system boast of that fact with justification, and even opponents admit that it is a fact. But both overlook an additional fact: It is becoming more and more difficult for the customer to *get* the goods and services, not because he hasn't the money to purchase them, but because a whole army of people—people who are being paid salaries to facilitate his buying—are actually barring his way to the things he wants.

The sales that are lost in consequence are one of the costs of poor management. If managers all down the line were directing their people properly, the problem would not exist.

At the expense of appearing to be "down" on customer services as practiced in today's retail outlets, I want to cite a few indicative examples of how managements, all along the line from manufacturing to the ultimate consumer sale, are cutting the foundation of their own business progress out from under them. The examples may seem petty, in fact are petty, but they point up a trend, and they really prove a huge need for managerial improvement.

Probably there is no one living in the United States today who has not suffered tortures trying to buy merchandise, procure a service, get a repair or correction made, or perhaps only clear up a misunderstanding over a bill. And for most of us the torture is experienced not in isolated cases but continually. The simplest transaction is likely to take half an hour when it should be consummated in five minutes; it may even take hours and require three or four return visits to the point of purchase. Much of the increased leisure that machines have provided for the American public is being consumed in senseless arguments, exchange of letters, and waiting for deliveries and pickups. And individual American companies are losing a vast amount of potential business to their competitors because many people hesitate to undertake the labor they know will accompany a purchase, and skip or postpone getting the things they want and have money to pay for.

Progress on the way to the top is fraught with more frustrations and delays, but the customer can and does get there eventually if he is persistent. By the time he reaches the "top," however, his efforts have cost the company he is dealing with, or trying to deal with, considerable sums of money. Some part of the higher prices of recent years, in fact, may be chargeable to the fact that the customer finds it so difficult to get what he wants when he wants it at the lower levels. A $4 radio repair eventually snowballs into a $25 rebate on a new radio; a suit is practically remade within a week or two of its purchase because it was not fitted properly in the first place; a hotel is forced eventually to rebate the room rent because the room was filthy and repeated calls to the housekeeper brought no satisfaction; an airline pays the hotel bill for a party of six that was "bumped" off a plane even though the reservations had been made months before, confirmed a few days earlier, and reconfirmed on the morning of the flight. It is expensive, also, to have $100,000-a-year executives working on complaints that could and should be settled by comparatively low-paid clerks.

Top managers, although they will take infinite trouble and go to a good deal of expense to satisfy the customers who take the trouble to get through to them, do not seem to feel much responsibility for the problem as a whole. They are willing enough to put out the fires, but they take little interest in fire prevention. They blame the unions, even prosperity itself, for the situation. Since people are no longer afraid of being fired, they say, it is impossible to control them. With "the kind of people you get nowadays" not much can be done about the poor service customers and would-be customers are getting.

One might point out that this disease is one that afflicts nonunionized companies quite as much as those that are unionized and that—despite the probability that a new job will be fairly easy to obtain—no one likes to be fired; discharge is always a fairly severe punishment because it is a blow to self-esteem. One may also doubt whether people are very much different from what they were in the days when "the customer was always right."

These things are beside the point, however. Whatever the difficulties, it is the manager's job to find solutions, not to drift with the tide and, like so many of his employees today, do as little as he can get by with. If management does not shoulder this responsibility, several things are likely to happen that management will not find pleasant:

1. Markets will be smaller than they might be—in fact, they already are—because more and more people will do without rather than take the time necessary to make a satisfactory purchase.

2. Prices will rise faster than is necessary because of the increased costs of making adjustments on faulty merchandise. (One airline actually employs 2,000 people in its "adjustment" department.) The high prices will encourage foreign competition—they have done so already—and further decrease sales volume.

3. The general public, which up to this point has been largely convinced that private industry is more efficient than government operation, will no longer see a distinction between the two.

4. Life will become more and more uncomfortable for everyone, including the top managers themselves.

Whatever the type of customer, there is something that the customer wants or needs, the desire for which can be elicited or destroyed depending on how he is approached.

A customer wants the help of someone who knows what he is doing, who will help him see more clearly what it is he needs, who directs him so he *gets* what he needs; someone who respects his ideas and knowledge, who suggests ideas to him as well as indicates *why* a particular request cannot be met.

The purpose of a concern is to provide such services as are desired. In short, a concern's existence is contingent on its customers.

Since few true monopolies exist, a customer is generally free to transact his business when, where, and how he chooses. This is true in even the small town or village, for while the number of stores may be very limited, there is the "catalog" method of buying and selling.

The picture is fundamentally the same whether the customer is an individual or a corporation. A few typical examples follow.

INDUSTRIAL EQUIPMENT

In many cases, of course, the customer *has* to buy—a company, for example, cannot do without the equipment necessary to produce its products. Thus it might be argued, even though one company may lose out because of poor service in the past, someone eventually gets the business, and so the general effect on the economy can be considered nil.

But this analysis of the situation takes no account of the cost to the supplier of correcting mistakes. Once the contract is signed, the supplier must ensure that his equipment actually works. And sometimes making the changes that are necessary costs more than his entire profit on the deal.

For example, the X company purchased a $50,000 punch press and found that it did not work. The supplier sent engineers and repairmen to tear it apart and put it together again. But still it did not work. The highly paid crew came back again and repeated the process. No results. In all, it took four visits, and a week's work in each case. If the supplier made 20 percent on the sales price, his original profit would be $10,000. But the salaries of the engineers and repairmen, the travel expenses, and the cost of new parts could easily exceed that figure.

One such case, of course, proves nothing, but from talking with executives from all parts of the country I am convinced that it is not a unique instance, but a very common one. Purchasers of industrial equipment swing a lot of weight, and eventually they do get satisfaction; but the suppliers pay heavily before they succeed in providing it. And, of course, the unprofitable sales cut into their profits—it is not uncommon today for a company to find that it is actually making less profit on greater sales volume than it was earlier on a smaller volume.

DEPARTMENT STORES

Department stores have brought the mistreatment of the customer to a fine art. The attitude of the clerks ranges from complete indifference to actual belligerence. When a customer approaches, all hands may stand by to repel her, and the immediate supervisors stalwartly back them up.

"You couldn't expect to get waited on just standing there," says the floorwalker, whose status has been enhanced by the title "section manager." And if the customer has done much shopping in department stores she knows that he is all too right. Short of shouting and actually laying hands on a clerk, she can't expect to get any attention, and then only the most perfunctory kind.

The best way to make a purchase in a department store, in fact, is to initiate self-service. Find what you want on a counter or a rack, and put the exact change in the clerk's hand. Then—after a considerable wait for the wrapping process, even though it involves merely putting the merchandise in a bag—you can make off with your purchase.

One man picked up six bath towels from a counter, took out a bill to pay for them, and waited while a group of four girls and a supervisor carried on some transactions of their own.

"Shall we put this box there or over here?" asked the supervisor without a glance at the customer.

The girls gravely considered the matter.

"I'd like to buy these," said the customer, shoving forward the towels and the money. There was no answer. No one, apparently, either heard or saw him.

As he was about to walk away, a clerk came back from a coffee break, and explained: "Oh, they're not supposed to wait on customers; they're part of a training squad." Obviously no part of the training inculcated the idea that the staff owed the customer at least the courtesy of a reply.

The hard-to-please customer who compelled the clerk to haul out every possible variety of merchandise before she made a purchase—then perhaps left without making a purchase at all—used to be a byword, and the downtrodden clerk in the case received a good deal of sympathy, both in magazine articles and from other customers. That customer doesn't exist anymore, for clerks no longer make any effort to show the store's wares.

"I'd like a plain blue dacron blouse, size 34," says the customer.

"There they are," clerk replies, with a wave of the hand toward blouses hanging in the case behind her. Only the edges are visible; the customer is evidently supposed to make a choice without seeing the complete article.

Or a customer may be put firmly in her place because she can't describe exactly what she wants; she has the audacity to expect the clerk to bring out several different things and allow her to make a choice.

One woman—not rich, but not poor either by a long shot—had saved up $5,000 to buy herself a mink coat. Backed by the knowledge of this comfortable bank balance, she approached one of the haughty clerks in one of the more expensive stores.

"What kind of a mink coat do you want?" asked the clerk with an air of studied indifference, looking, of course, off into space rather than at the customer.

"Well, I don't exactly know," said the woman. "I thought I would try on a few. . . ."

"If you don't know what you want, how can you expect me to show you any?" said the clerk with satisfaction, turning abruptly away.

It can be seen that a really clever squeeze play designed to prevent sales is possible and frequently used. If the customer knows exactly what she wants, she can be told at once that the store doesn't have it, and one more sale can be averted. If, on the contrary, she is not sure, then it is naturally impossible to serve her.

It is in the provision of services that go along with the merchandise, however, that the stores best exemplify the fine art of annoying the customer.

One young working wife arranged to have the store personnel come and fit slipcovers, and accepted a date three weeks in advance for the visit. The men were to come at 10 A.M., and her boss agreed to let her have the morning off. Twelve o'clock and one o'clock came, but there was no sign of the men. At 2 P.M., she phoned the store and was told they could not come that day, but would show up the next Tuesday. This time her husband took the day off to wait for them, but again they did not appear. Still a third date was set and broken.

Finally, she called the store and laid down an ultimatum: Either the men came at ten o'clock the following day or the order was canceled. She heard the whispered comment, "She's threatening to cancel," then received fervent assurances that the men would be there the very next day and at ten o'clock as specified. They were.

In fact, in most instances involving services, the customer has to get tough to get any satisfaction. One short customer who accepted the sales girl's ultimatum that she "must expect to have to have all her clothes shortened" paid $7 for the shortening of a coat, and also handed in the purchase price in advance. The coat was to be ready the following week.

When she called for the coat, it was not ready; in fact, it appeared that it would not be ready for another week. She visited the store a third time. The coat had been shortened, but the hemline was completely uneven.

The store promised to fix it, and asked her to come back again a week later. When she did, she found that the hemline was still uneven, was worse, in fact, than before. One section hung down in a decided point. She was promised that it would be fixed at once, and the coat was taken away again. Then she waited three hours until it appeared that the store was about to close, and nobody knew anything about the coat. Finally, it was discovered hanging on a rack, untouched. At this point, store personnel began to insist that the hemline was not uneven—had never been uneven—the difficulty was all in her imagination.

The customer lost patience, told them to keep the coat and return the money, both the amount she had paid for the coat and the $7 she had paid in advance for shortening it. No, that was impossible.

It was here that the customer got tough. "I will get the money back," she said quietly, "it's only a question of when, and there will be more blame for everyone if the refund takes longer." Mentally, she was already composing a letter to the executive vice-president of the store, "My mother and my grandmother swore by _____'s [which was true]."

At this point, the clerk weakly observed: "Well, you could take it up to the adjustment department."

In the adjustment department, a courteous clerk agreed that the coat was unwearable in its present condition, but said that the store's policy was to return only the price of the coat, not the money spent for the alteration.

"Well," said the customer, carefully adopting a tone of more sorrow than anger, "all right. This will teach me not to trade at _____'s."

At this the adjustment clerk vanished into the inner office to consult a higher-up, and came back with the good news that all the money would be returned with profuse apologies.

All the incidents so far noted occurred in New York department stores, which have perhaps brought the art of insulting and inconveniencing the customer to the most fantastic levels. Surveys of visitors' opinions reported in the *New York Times* bear this out.

But other stores around the country are catching up. A typical case comes from a Midwest department store. The following letter recounts the customer's difficulties:

On January 13 I took my clock radio into the store for repair work. It should be understood that the instrument had been purchased at least two years before. There was no question raised as to the propriety of its need for repair. It was a straight repair job I was requesting. I was told that it would be several weeks before it would be ready. This was agreeable to me.

The repair card read that the radio had noise in it and that the alarm set was a bit off. I had explained to the lady that the radio played all right, but that after it had been on for a while a tap on its top would eliminate the noise which always began after the radio had been on for a time. I asked for a general overhaul. It needed new buttons on some of the controls. [By the time this letter was written, it was a question of who needed new buttons.] All of this was written down on the card.

Near the last half of March the radio was delivered. I immediately plugged it in, only to discover that it did not play at all. I called the store and was told that if I wanted it fixed rapidly I could take it personally to their radio repair shop on East Street and probably even wait for it.

The next day I took the radio into their repair shop. The man there was very courteous, started making tests, but after about ten minutes I decided it would be better to come back again.

The following day I took a taxi to get the radio. I was informed two tubes had to be replaced, which the man had taken care of. He showed me the old ones. I left very happy since all of the buttons seemed to be on the front of the case.

That evening when I connected the radio it played all right, except that after a bit it started its usual and well-known rattling, but my tap on its top stopped it for a moment. That was the time, however, that I set it to turn off not only the radio but the bed lamp and to turn on the lamp and the radio and the alarm the next morning. To my dismay neither the alarm nor the radio went off. I discovered that the power switch turned off the light as well as the radio. This was a new arrangement! Since the hour was two in the morning, I could not call the store and had to wait until the next morning. When I called the next morning, I was informed that it would be picked up again.

By then I was going into the third month of fussing about this radio and prospects of another three months didn't appeal to me. Thinking better of it, I stopped in the Adjustment Division of the store and talked to a very charming lady to whom I told the story. I told her especially about the problems of the radio and that they should pick it up and have it fixed immediately. I told her also that since I would be out of town for one week that would give them time to fix it and that when I got home it would be working for me. Since I would be away, they were to pick the radio up at the home of Mrs. Kimball, two doors from my own home. This was all carefully written on the order. I saw her writing it. It was to be picked up on the Friday. Friday morning at seven o'clock I took it to Mrs. Kimball and told her the truck would pick up the radio and return it to her. On my return home Mrs. Kimball informed me that the radio was still there and had not been picked up. It was to have been picked up on March 25. This was April 2. On April 4 I called the store again. At first they could find no record of the transaction; later they did find the record. Apparently a mix-up had occurred somewhere, though. Finally the radio was picked up on April 5. On the sixth I called the radio repair shop to see if it was ready, only to have Miss Kay tell me they didn't have any record of it. After some time the order was found, but I was told they couldn't give me any information until the seventh. However, I heard nothing. On Friday sometime during the afternoon this message was taken by my office:

Miss Kay from the store's Radio TV Workshop called. The only thing wrong with the radio is a loose speaker that rattles. However, the clock in it must be sent back to the manufacturer. This will take 2-3 weeks—possibly longer! They won't go ahead without your OK. If you want the work started call Miss Kay—BR 6-5200, ext. 3931.

So far I have been billed for $6 for the first repair and for the price of two tubes on the second repair. Consider the time that I have been without the radio; the telephone calls I have had to make, and the time that has been involved in that; the taxi fare; the use of my car in bringing the article back again.

Frankly, I do not understand how any concern can afford to do business like this, why it takes all this time to discover that the clock has to be sent to the factory. That part of the contraption was all right when we started this deal. Apparently all that was wrong with it was a loose speaker.

The upshot of this was that the customer received a rebate of $25 toward a new radio. Then not long after that her own radio was delivered in perfect condition. The expense to the store, for what was originally a very minor repair, amounted probably to over $200 when all angles of the transaction were considered.

Multiply this amount by thousands—since similar cases are everyday occurrences for the average shopper—and the whole retail price level is affected.

Such a cataloging of typical examples may lead someone to say, "But all department stores are not like this," or "I've had many transactions with department stores which have been entirely satisfactory." Unfortunately, however, in many of these cases the customer has been successful either because he or she was important or well-known to the store or because a clerk of the old school, one who takes pride in giving good service in spite of the boss, gave enough attention to the transaction. But the fact remains that even in the old established businesses, built largely in the past on their fine service policies, laxness has allowed traditionally good service to degenerate to various degrees of poor service.

What is wrong here? Basically, it is definite lack of supervisory activity, from top management down through all subsequent levels of management.

A top management executive who must spend most of his time putting out fires finds little time to direct his subordinates adequately. Issuing ultimatums accomplishes little; threats usually aren't activated. Complacent trust in the work of subordinates allows gears to grow rusty and the routines fall apart. Failure to evaluate performance of subordinates keeps the top man from really improving their performance.

Applying proper managerial techniques to normal operation of the store will help. Department stores basically are *not* different from other types of business. Neither should the type of management practiced be different.

Traditionally, many department stores have been weighed down with outdated systems of operation. But a precarious situation has developed where stores are using electronic equipment. Often middle management is trying to get the more advanced systems to "police" the performance of its subordinates. It doesn't work that way, however, because the average human being resents being bossed by a tape or machine.

The one sure cure is for every management person (once true management responsibility has been properly placed) to go to work as a manager. Then and only then will the customer begin to get the service he is paying for. This, too, could spawn a wholly new (or renewed) kind of customer— one reasonably pleasant because he is treated as a customer. Only when a boss *knows* what his clerks are saying, how they are saying it, how they affect a customer, will he be able to direct that clerk intelligently so that the customer will be better satisfied and consequently become a "continuing" customer.

If undue emphasis has been placed on department stores in this chapter, the reader needs only to translate the types of transactions to his own business to get the ugly similarity of cost, wasted time, undue inconvenience, and frustration of his own customers. No business is so beautifully managed that it does not have some of the types of "goofs" illustrated—the boss who thinks it doesn't is just not realistic.

CHAPTER FOUR

Objectives

MANAGEMENT BY OBJECTIVES, as mentioned earlier, is one of the developments that has been labeled a "change in focus." Under this plan, often the manager sits down with each of his subordinates and together they agree on the goals the subordinate should reach. Then the methods the subordinate should utilize to attain the objectives are up to him, and the manager does not need to supervise closely to be sure that his performance is what it should be.

I believe firmly in management by objectives, but I do not think it is as new as some people believe. Some companies have been practicing it for decades.

Also, I would reverse the way in which the objectives are commonly set. In the usual process, the top man asks his immediate subordinates to set their own objectives, and then they work with the next level of executives on the phases each one should be responsible for, and so on down the line to the rank and file. In one of the most successful applications of the method I know of, however, the top man began by calling his immediate subordinates together, but instead of asking them to discuss their objectives with him, he told them: "We want the setting of objectives to start at the bottom, rather than at the top. Each first-line supervisor should begin by working with his people on their objectives, then the second-line managers should work with the supervisors, and so on up, until finally I will work with each of you on the objectives for the major divisions of the company."

This, it will be noted, is the same method that many companies have found works best in budgeting and in long-range planning. Both budgets and long-range plans can be set by the top men and then parceled out to the various divisions, departments, and sections. But there is much better acceptance of and commitment to both budgets and long-range plans when people at every level have a hand in developing them.

Of course, both the budgets and the long-range plans submitted by the lower levels are modified by higher levels, and so on up to the top. If the original budgets were simply added together, they would be practically sure to total more money than the company could possibly have available. Similarly the long-range plans must be modified at each successive level up to the top if they are not to involve the company in unjustifiable expense and diffusion of effort into unprofitable channels.

In the same way, there are modifications of objectives as managers on each level discuss what they plan to have their people do with their own superiors, for goals so high as to be unrealistic will not only not be met; they will soon be forgotten. And goals so low as to require no effort will exert no influence on motivation.

Now, what is an objective? Everyone knows the dictionary meaning of the word—"something toward which effort is directed; an aim or end of action; goal; object"—but there is some confusion about how much territory an objective should take in. For example, making a profit is an objective for every company, but if the goal is stated so simply, it provides no guidance for anyone. Again, some companies believe they have set objectives because they have set sales and production quotas, but these are insufficient since meeting them may actually work against overall company objectives. A market may be oversold one year, to the detriment of volume in future years, and perhaps loss of good dealers who become soured on the company after being stuck with too much merchandise for too long, and a production quota may be achieved at the expense of running down the plant. Thus, while both meeting sales quotas (provided they are set realistically) and producing the requisite amount of goods and services may be *among* the objectives, they are inadequate for true "management by objectives."

I would define an objective as a condition that should exist, and the objectives for any department or group should cover all the conditions that the manager should be striving to bring about—in organization, in human relations, in control, in production or sales, in customer relations, and so on. More definite examples will be given later, when the technique of setting the objectives is discussed.

THE IMPORTANCE OF METHODS

Another point to consider is how much guidance the manager should provide on methods of meeting objectives. To many people "management by objectives" calls for the manager to leave the methods entirely up to the subordinate. His only check is when he sits down with the subordinate perhaps three to six months or a year later to gauge the progress that has been made toward the goals.

This works very well with some people. In fact, one could as a general rule state that the superior should avoid breathing down his subordinates' necks, checking everything they do. Thus in one of the best-known studies of the effect of supervisory conduct on productivity it was found that one of the main differences between high-productivity sections and low-productivity sections was that the supervisors of the former supervised less closely than those of the latter.

But refraining from constant checking and spying, from parceling out work in little bits and snatches, is one thing, and completely ignoring the methods used to achieve high productivity, say, or low employee turnover, is another. The manager cannot simply ignore how his employees are operating in the interval between checks.

Many people need help on methods as well as clarification of their objectives, and it is the manager's job to know who needs help and of what type. And in speaking of "methods" I am not talking about standard procedures—these are commonly explained to everyone as soon as he comes on the job. "Methods" in the sense that I am using the term here include approaches, attitude, and many nuances of conduct as well as techniques and procedures.

The department store clerks who make life so hard for the customers are undoubtedly aware that their primary job is "to sell," and perhaps they are also told that it is important for them to preserve the store's image as a pleasant place to shop. Some of their very worst behavior, in fact, may be the results of their efforts to help preserve their store's reputation.

For example, take the case of the clerk who told the customer that "no one goes on a cruise now." Probably the store actually had nothing directly labeled "cruise clothes," and the clerk wanted to create the impression that the store was never out of the merchandise it should have. Evidently, no one in charge had ever thought to explain just how one handled a situation of that kind.

Many of the attempts to convince the customer that she is the wrong size or misshapen in some way may also be misguided efforts to excuse the store for being out of some items or sizes.

Or has anyone ever told the clerks that they should look at the customer when she is trying to explain what she wants? I doubt it. I doubt also that any of the managers, from the top man down through the buyer and the section manager, have ever bothered to notice what the clerks are doing or where their eyes are focused.

How can a manager correct these faults—provided he takes enough interest in his people to observe what they are doing? Must he jump in immediately after he witnesses some unfortunate incident and demand: "Why did you say that? Don't you realize that customer went away offended and won't come back?" If he does, he'll probably have a sulky clerk on his hands and the next customer will get the benefit of her bad humor.

But perhaps later, in the course of discussing the objectives, he can inquire: "What should a sales person do, when she can't supply exactly what the customer asks for?" Then he gets the clerk to think of the phraseology that should be used.

Again, consider the equipment that needs overhauling and re-overhauling after it has been installed in the customer's plant. A great deal of publicity has been devoted to the movement called "zero defects," in which employees are asked to sign cards agreeing to strive to do everything right the first time, a program generally introduced with a great deal of fanfare in the form of speeches by executives, presentation of buttons or other souvenirs of one kind or another, and promoted from time to time by awards and public recognition of those who improve their work. Although many companies have reported excellent results from such a program, it cannot, of itself, produce any overall change unless managers up and down the line help their subordinates by showing them how it is possible to avoid many of the common defects and soliciting their suggestions to the same ends. (A suggestion system is good, and so, in many cases, are standard-practice instructions, but there is nothing that can take the place of face-to-face contact between the manager and his subordinates.)

And it is not only rank-and-file employees and first-line supervisors who often need guidance on the methods of achieving objectives as well as on the objectives themselves. Many middle managers are quite as much in need of it; so are many men who are very near the top. (Some chief executives do, too, but there is nothing much that can be done about that. Only the board of directors has the power to make the top man change his ways; and if it is an inside board made up of his subordinates, they are generally afraid to speak up freely, whereas outside directors are seldom in a position to know exactly how he is operating.)

What are some of the ways in which managers may need guidance on methods? To cite just a few examples:

If one of the objectives is "maintaining good human relations" and the extent to which the manager is doing so is to be judged by such things as the number of grievances and the rate of employee turnover, many managers will resort to extreme permissiveness in an effort to ensure that they make a good showing. Others will think that all that is necessary is a pleasant manner—that words speak louder than actions.

Yet permissiveness, when it is carried to the point of excusing sloppy work, actually damages morale. There may be no grievances, no one may be storming out in a fit of rage, but there will be apathy and indifference, which will cause low productivity and errors. No one can possibly take an interest in a job that provides no challenge, no possibility of improvement.

"Ah," says the manager who thinks he should not question methods, "we can take care of that, because another of the objectives is avoiding errors and maintaining productivity." But this may merely make the permissive manager do more of the work himself, and exhaust himself in final checks before the work is passed on to another department or higher up the line. There are high-level controllers, for example, who keep calculators by their desks and check all the work of their subordinates. Then the very fact that the subordinates know their work will be checked anyway leads them to be less careful.

OPTIMIZING

Since the advent of computers, the words "optimum" and "optimizing" have become popular in management circles. No company and no person can achieve everything in an ideal way, for the simple reason that achievement of the ideal in one area makes it impossible to achieve it in another. All that can be achieved is the optimum that minimizes overall costs or maximizes overall gains.

For example, complete "preventive maintenance" of machines so that all unplanned downtime is eliminated is probably possible. ("If you don't believe that," one executive once observed, "you should never ride in an airplane.") But preventing all breakdowns would, in most cases, cost far more than a certain number of breakdowns. The optimum point, in the case of a manufacturing department, is the point where total production costs are lowest. For the airline's flying stock, the optimum may be merely ensuring that the equipment will "fail-safe."

Where the optimizing must be done within one department, it is not too difficult for the manager to recognize the concept. Trouble may arise because the optimum for the company as a whole requires that a given department sacrifice its showing to some extent because better results in another department will more than make up for the deficiency.

It is not in the best interest of the company, therefore, that department and/or section managers always place their own objectives above everything else. They can be induced to be flexible in this respect, however, only if their superiors help them to understand when the department optimum is only a suboptimum from the viewpoint of the company as a whole, and see that they get generous credit when they relinquish some possible progress toward their own objectives in the interest of the general good.

For example, one of the conflicts that may arise is between the sales and the credit departments. From the credit department viewpoint, the optimum would be to have no bad debts whatsoever. The sales department, on the other hand, is interested in volume, and often believes—sometimes rightly—that it is necessary for the company to take a few credit risks in order to get as much volume as possible. It may be that one department should yield entirely to the other on this point, or that each should yield a little in the interest of optimizing total company performance.

Only a common superior—often the top man in the company—can make the decision, but he must do more than arbitrate any disagreements that arise; he must ensure that each department head understands total company objectives as well as his own objectives, and make it clear that the executive who makes a lower score because he has fallen short of his own suboptimum in the interest of the whole company will not only not be penalized but will gain greater recognition thereby. Further, it is not sufficient for him to state this at the time the dispute occurs; he must remember it when it comes time for appraisals or for passing out raises.

LINE ADMINISTRATION

Of course, these things take time, and the chief executive often feels that he cannot spare the time for them. But the fact is that neither management by objectives nor any of the other techniques described in this book will work if the top man does not believe wholeheartedly in them, understand them thoroughly, and work at them day in and day out. If management is getting things done through people, no manager can delegate management of his subordinates to others. It is his primary responsibility; and he must work at it constantly.

Further, he should not attempt to install any of the plans and techniques described unless he really believes they will help him with his work of guiding the company toward success. If he regards them merely as something that can't do any harm and may possibly do some good, a new program to be turned over to the personnel department to follow up, people down the line will begin to forget about them as soon as they feel he is not really interested. In fact, installation of a program of this kind can do harm—if only to the extent of causing a lot of wheelspinning and loss of time that could be put to better use, and perhaps some loss of enthusiasm on the part of managers down the line for any other new idea he introduces.

What the top man really wants done, gets done. Only the line boss really has any influence on his subordinates, for he is the man they must look to for continuity of employment, raises, and promotions. Any technique or program forced on them by a staff department is something to be endured for a time and then forgotten about as soon as the line boss's attention is directed elsewhere.

Whether or not a chief executive—of a company, a division, or a department—should introduce the techniques described in this book depends on the answer to the question: Does he believe that they will help him meet his primary objectives? Does the company president believe they will help him to make the company grow and produce greater return on investment? If he doesn't, doesn't in fact feel that they can further the objectives in such an important way that he can afford to devote a good deal of time to them, he should not attempt to use them. Similarly the plant manager who doesn't believe they will have an important effect on output and quality should not initiate their use. Staff departments can help, as will be explained later. But the techniques described in this book must be used by the line as essential methods of achieving line, not staff, objectives.

PART TWO

Major Segments of a Manager's Job

CHAPTER FIVE

Introduction

A PREREQUISITE to any real improvement in management performance is determination of what the manager *should* be doing. Unless the manager himself knows what he should be doing, any improvements are likely to be made in peripheral areas that actually have little or no bearing on his success as a manager. Yet, as my informal survey showed, many managers have no definite knowledge on this point.

There are, of course, position descriptions for many management jobs. Sometimes they have been intended primarily to facilitate wage and salary administration, and in that case they appear to have served their purpose reasonably well. But more often they are prepared with other purposes in mind as well: to let managers know the extent of their responsibility and authority, for example. Often one finds that they contain such things as objectives, responsibilities, standards and authorities, all under the general umbrella term of "job description." One specialist in the field once observed that descriptions have been prepared to serve so many purposes that they end by serving none of them.

Many of these so-called managerial position descriptions note that one of the manager's responsibilities is the direction of the people under him, but they seldom enlarge on this point. Instead, they list mainly the technical responsibilities of the position.

But the manager himself, when he is actually managing, is not doing the work himself; he is directing the people who are doing it. If he is the sales manager, he should not be trying to do the selling himself—a sales manager who feels that he alone can close a sale might just as well dispense with subordinates and save the cost of having them on the payroll. The sales manager's job is to direct the salesmen in such a way that they sell successfully. If a manager is the controller, he does not keep the books, and he should not have to keep a calculator by his desk to ensure that the figures are accurate. His job is, among other things, to ensure that his people realize the importance of accuracy.

Often, of course, many executives must actually do work that might be classified as technical rather than managerial. A company treasurer, for example, may have to carry on negotiations with banks or underwriters; a production manager in a small plant may have to serve as his own production control man and spend time on the paper work necessary for the chore. Even a company president may have to act as a salesman at times, in the case of a very important customer who will not be satisfied unless he can talk to the very top man. These are not really managerial duties; they are simply the technical parts of the job which, for one reason or another, cannot be delegated in given instances. But since direction of subordinates is the one part of the job that can *never* be delegated, it is the part of the job on which the manager should spend most of his time. It is only reasonable, then, to expect that the manager should be given some guidance in this area so that he may know exactly *what* he should be doing to direct his people and improve their performance.

The lack of any guidance on this point is perpetuated by the tendency of many companies to copy each other's position descriptions. In a previous book,* I illustrated the ineffectiveness of many position descriptions by a critical analysis of the description one company had prepared for its chief financial officer. I did not, of course, mention the name of the company, and further to preserve its anonymity I changed the wording somewhat and altered the sequence of the items which were listed. The description was as follows:

GENERAL RESPONSIBILITIES

Under the direction of the President, is responsible for formulating financial policies, planning and executing financial programs, apprais-

* *Managerial Performance Standards*, American Management Association, New York, 1960.

ing and reporting on the financial results of the operation, supplying financial services, and recommending action to be taken; and is responsible for the supervision of the Controller and Treasurer.

SPECIFIC DUTIES

1. *Organization Development.* Develop and direct his supporting organization and establish the duties and responsibilities for positions reporting to him.
2. *Financial Policy.* Be responsible for the formulation of financial policies and for seeing that they are carried out, making provision for rendering assistance and guidance when needed.
3. *Planning.* Plan the financial needs of the company. Plan programs for meeting these needs and be responsible for carrying out the approved programs.
4. *Accounting.* See that accounting methods and procedures are adequate to control and appraise the financial needs of the enterprise.
5. *Appraisal of Financial Results.* Assist other executives in appraising their activities in terms of financial results, pointing out significant trends in operations as indicated by analysis of the reports; and assist these executives in determining future policies based on applying sound business judgment to the conclusions deduced from such facts.
6. *Capital Expenditures.* Appraise proposed capital expenditures which require the approval of the Board of Directors or the President and advise on their desirability. Approve all permanent property requisitions in excess of $2,000. Review all requests for permanent property budgets.
7. *Inventory Control.* Advise operating departments and division managers on inventory policy.
8. *Insurance.* Be responsible for providing an adequate program of insurance for the company.
9. *Financial Relations.* Be responsible for external financial relationships of the company, including those with banks and financial organizations.
10. *Tax Management.* Be responsible for the determination of tax liabilities and filing of proper returns.
11. *Credit and Collection.* Be responsible for the authorization of credit and collection of money due.

(Several other items follow which have to do only with specific financial operations.)

No mention is made of this officer's duties, other than in item 1, that have to do with the management of people; and yet, conceivably, the people who report to this financial officer, and their subordinates in turn, are human beings who have problems and varying skills and degrees of workmanship. They are people who need direction and sometimes personal advice, who are desirous of being promoted and feel that they should be considered for vacancies, who need to have time off, and who at one time or another have been new on their jobs and have needed induction and close supervision while they were being trained. Certainly they have been considered for salary adjustment, probably periodically, and have every right to assume that their boss gave adequate time to the decision as to what that salary adjustment would be, if any. In short, these and a host of other managerial duties, the adequate performance of which will determine the real worth of this financial officer, have been omitted or ignored. There is apparently no adequate listing of his managerial job.

In criticizing this description I wrote:

> It will be seen that this description is divided into two parts: (1) general responsibilities and (2) specific duties. As in most companies, accounting, controllership duties, the financing of various operations, payrolls, insurance matters, and related items (either wholly or in part) go to make up the bulk of the work. With all this work, it is only fair to assume that there will be people who report to this financial officer. And, in a company of any size, it is quite probable that there will be several levels of managers under his direction. Yet it is clear that every duty listed in this so-called position description, with the exception of No. 1, has to do with the financial aspects of the job rather than with the direction of subordinates.

After the book was published, no less than thirty-four people, all from different companies, wrote me saying, in effect: "I recognized that job description. You've changed it somewhat, but you got it from our organization manual." Also, many of them agreed with my criticism of it; and while others took some small issue with me, none of them claimed that the description had been of value to either the chief financial officer himself or his company. None of them gave any information on who wrote the description—except one, an executive of the company from whose organization manual I had actually drawn the example.

I had answered each claimant by saying that he was only one of many from different companies who had thought they recognized the job description, and I told this man the same thing. He replied that he was not surprised because he had sent a copy to any company that asked for it, and the requests had numbered in the hundreds. However, he added, although he had written the description himself, he had had some doubts about its worth at the time, and he agreed with my critical comments.

I might point out, therefore, that any writer of position descriptions who has any idea of latching onto the one reprinted above will not be wise to do so. This warning would not be necessary were it not for the fact that people are often so unwilling, or unable, to work with their subordinates on the fundamental aspects of the management job that they are ready to copy anything, even a bad example.

Instead of a job description, what managers need is a performance description, a description of what they themselves should be doing. This may cover some actual tasks of a nonmanagerial nature if these are part of their jobs, but it should place the greatest emphasis on what they should be doing, as managers, the different segments of the job that are encompassed by the phrase "directing subordinates."

The following chapters in this section present a step-by-step method of composing a performance description, a method that ensures that both the managers and their boss thoroughly understand the "what's" of the management job and see clearly the way in which improvement can be effected.

At the risk of appearing to be too rigid, I must point out that the techniques described in the succeeding chapters will be successful only when they are used as described. They fail when they are embroidered with extra steps or when variations are used.

The technique of developing a performance description—and the techniques of using it both to set standards of performance and to determine how well the standards are being met—are simple. And because they are simple, the line manager or the staff man who considers himself a professional in the "people area" may be tempted to embellish them. But then whenever a manager tells me that he tried the techniques and they did not work, it invariably turns out that he, or his staff man, added or omitted steps, or deviated in some way from the procedure described.

The possibility that the technique may be vitiated by changes is one of two hazards that must be avoided if the whole process is to be of use. The other certain way to ensure failure and thereby make the process merely a costly and useless exercise is to allow it to be shoved down the throats of the management people by staff men. If the line manager at the top of an organization is sold on the idea only to the extent that he tells some staff man: "OK, you can introduce it. Tell them I said it was a good idea," the techniques will not succeed.

Moreover, the cost of the failure will be high: in time, money, disrupted schedules, and unhappy feelings on the part of those who have been forced into taking part. Some people may get something out of it, but it will not pay its way. It cannot be emphasized too strongly that no management technique will be successful unless:

The top man in the organizational unit *wants* it used, *understands* it himself, *is able to explain it to his subordinates, does it himself,* and *checks on the way his subordinates use it.*

The top man cannot simply give it his blessing. No amount of pushing by staff men will help, because each subordinate knows that if the top man really considered the process necessary, he would take an active part in it. If he cannot explain it to his subordinates, he doesn't really understand it. If he doesn't want to explain it, he really has no interest in it. And if he does not introduce it himself and handle the follow-up personally, he really doesn't think it will contribute much, if anything, to the success of his organization.

When the top man merely gives the idea his blessing and leaves it to staff men to implement it, his subordinates (and for that matter their subordinates) know that what he is really telling them is: "If you have time, the urge, and the inclination, you go ahead and use it." For example:

A college professor in a small Southern college had become quite popular with a technique he had packaged with catchy phrases and workable ideas. Basically, his subject matter was good, and there had been a wealth of use under other beguiling names. The apparent reason for its popularity was its simplicity of application and widespread need. It was fundamentally one of the problem-solving techniques with which current management literature abounds. No aspersions on this package are intended. It was a good technique, well presented, and fundamentally sound.

In one company, all the best techniques were used in presenting the material to the management people. The president himself made the presentation to his corporate officers and told them that he wanted them to take the course, have their subordinates take it, and so on down the line. In addition, there were practice sessions to ensure that each participant would feel at ease when he used the technique with his own subordinates.

Accordingly, the course was presented to all 200 management people in the company. This took approximately three months, since it seemed wise to schedule it at a reasonable rate and not rush it. In this way, it was felt, application of the technique to current problems could begin after the first meeting. Now let's look at the five points again:

First, the top man must *want* it. In this case, the president did want it. Not only did he say so; he was willing to spend a considerable amount of money on it.

Second, the top man must *understand* it. He did, for he had obviously listened carefully to the original presentation.

Third, he must be *able to explain* it to others. Obviously he was, since he made the presentation to the corporate officers.

Fourth, he must *do* it himself. He partially fulfilled this condition by making the presentation himself and by telling his subordinates that he wanted them to work with their own people on it.

Fifth, he must *see that his subordinates do it*. This is where the whole ball of wax melted. He made no effort to follow up. Because of this lapse, a technique that might have become a vital force in the management activities of the company was not used, and a tremendous expense produced little or no return.

One of his vice-presidents was preparing his annual progress report to the president. Looking over the previous year's report, he noted that the course had been conducted. It would be good this year, he reasoned, to report on the use of the techniques by division managers and their subordinates. Accordingly, at his next staff meeting he informed his division managers that his secretary would be around in a couple of days to get a list of the instances in which they and the supervisors under them had used the problem-solving technique in their normal work and the benefits which they felt had accrued as a result.

His secretary dutifully made the rounds about a week later, only to report that not one division manager could find a single example of use of the technique. The vice-president was annoyed and voiced the opinion that he would talk about that at his next meeting with his division heads. He was quite eloquent on the subject until his secretary asked, rather naïvely, "How have you used it yourself, Mr. _____?" That stopped him cold.

He still had nerve enough to tell his president what he had found. Nothing was heard about the conversation between these two. However, very shortly after, a memo to all top officers went out from the president asking each to report examples of the use of the new (and apparently unused) technique. The memo also said that at six months' intervals further reports would be called for.

This attention to the fifth point caused extensive review of the technique, and several of the top officers actually began using it.

It should be emphasized also that the top man in this context need not be the company president, although, of course, company-wide benefits will accrue only if the chief executive works at and with the technique. However, the top man in any organizational unit can introduce the technique and obtain the benefits, whether he is a division head, a department head, or the head of a smaller segment of the company.

The examples given in the following chapters are merely by way of illustration; no one should attempt to use the exact words the managers are quoted as using unless they fit in with his own concepts. It is the steps, the approach, and the general attitude the manager should convey that should be used without change.

Throughout the discussion of the techniques, there will be occasional mention of a "coach," who is a staff man or a line man acting in a staff capacity. His role, which is described more fully in Chapter Twenty-nine, is to help the line men understand and utilize the techniques advocated, not to carry out any of the steps in the processes that are recommended.

CHAPTER SIX

Approaches

THE BOSS MUST, of course, seek the help of his subordinates in developing the performance description, but the question of whether he should use a group or an individual approach then arises. When several managers are or should be doing the same things, the group approach is usually by far the better, but in some cases both approaches may be used with the same person.

THE GROUP APPROACH

In the group approach the boss and his immediate subordinates get together to discuss the components of the subordinates' jobs. For example, take this small portion of an organization whose chart is shown in the illustration. In this case, C, the head of the organizational unit, who reports to D, has eight line subordinates—the B's shown on the chart—and two staff men (the S's). Each of the B's is in charge of a group of foremen (A's) who report to him directly in a line relationship, and each foreman, in turn, directs a group of nonmanagerial people.

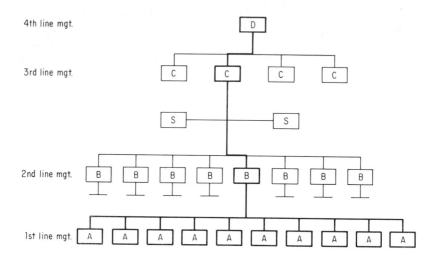

The major segments of the job, managerially speaking, will be practically the same for all the B's. They are all on the same level, all report
to the same boss, and all are attempting to meet the same basic objectives,
and it is the sum of their contributions that enables the boss to meet his
own objectives. Thus each one should be able to contribute to the discussion, although it is possible that some of them have not, up to this point,
been doing all the things that may be classified as their managerial duties.

Should the two staff men be included in the discussion? There is no
point in having them attend the sessions, for their work is entirely different from that of the B's. Also, the discussion will be devoted to the managerial part of the B job, rather than to the technical side. To have the
staff men attend would be to waste their time, and a waste of time is also
a waste of money. (The only staff man who should attend is the one who
is serving as a coach for the line executive. He coaches the line man both
before and after the meeting, as explained in Chapter Twenty-nine, but
while the meeting is in progress he is only an observer.)

Some bosses may have had the staff men attend all meetings in the past,
on the theory that they will feel left out if they are not invited and their
morale will be damaged. But there is no reason why this should be if the
boss explains the plan to them before he calls the meeting.

As a matter of fact, most staff people who do attend find the meetings
uninteresting because the subject matter of the discussion has nothing to
do with their specialties. When they are present at the first one, they
generally ask to be excused from the subsequent meetings because the

discussion does not concern them and they cannot contribute anything to it, because they are too busy, or for any one of a number of good reasons.

This does not mean that the staff people should be exempt from discussions designed to determine the major segments of their jobs. It merely means that the boss will discuss performance descriptions with them individually.

Similarly, the boss may hold individual discussions with some or all of his line subordinates if their jobs include segments that *are* different from those that are common to the entire group. However, basically, a group such as the B's shown in the organization chart above must all direct their subordinates in such a way that their groups have good records in the areas of cost, quality, and quantity. And with the help and the guidance of their boss, they can, through group discussion, come up with a list of what they must do to manage their subordinates so that good records are achieved.

Undoubtedly, each member of such a group will feel in the beginning that his job is different from those of the other participants. Everyone likes to think that he is doing a job that is uniquely difficult and one that requires special qualifications. It is good that people do feel this way, for it adds to their sense of importance, and a sense of the importance of the work one is doing is a vital factor in morale. No right-thinking boss will attempt to destroy this feeling, but he can point out that in directing people there are certain basic actions that everyone—from a top executive on down—must take and certain precautions to be observed.

It is in the identification of these basic segments of managerial work that the group approach has the greatest worth. Certainly, when a group of, say, five to eight or nine people work out a list together more valid ideas will be injected into the discussion than two people could produce. The importance of using the group rather than the individual approach cannot be overstressed if there are several people whose jobs have common elements.

The only justification for using the individual approach in cases of this kind is when the boss realizes that he may put an old-timer in the embarrassing position of having to admit in public that he has not been paying much attention to important aspects of his managerial responsibilities. On the other hand, there are other instances in which managers who are performing poorly need just such exposure and pressure to get them to change for the better. (Of course, no one will be singled out for criticism in front of the group, but the realization that one has been performing inadequately, even if private, will be salutary.)

Should the boss prepare a list in advance, or ask the subordinates to prepare their own lists and bring them to the meeting? The answer is "no" in both cases. Advance preparation of lists by either the boss or the subordinates is not only a waste of time, but has other disadvantages as well. If the boss prepares a list, it sets a pattern, which may not necessarily be a good one; also, members of the group will feel that they will have to accept his list in the end anyway, and will be less interested in advancing their own ideas, perhaps even hesitate to do so for fear of being thought stupid or uncooperative. If the members of the group prepare lists, each one will feel more resentment if one of his ideas is discussed out of existence than he will if his suggestion has been an offhand extemporaneous one. It hurts a good deal to have a carefully thought-out idea criticized or refused, but if a suggestion is merely the result of a moment's reflection, the originator has not really had time to become attached to it, and can relinquish it more easily.

But, although the boss must not prepare a list in advance or attempt to dictate what goes on the list, he *must* lead the group discussion. The line boss may not know as much about leading a meeting or about group psychology as the staff men, but he does know what he wants in the way of managerial performance and he is entitled to get it.

THE INDIVIDUAL APPROACH

The higher the level in the organization, naturally, the greater the variation in job conduct that will be evident. It is true that the direction of people is the same, but the technical and planning portions of the job vary more at each step upward. Policy-making decisions also broaden more and more at higher and higher levels.

Thus at the corporate level there will often be one man in charge of research, one in charge of finance, a third with overall responsibility for marketing, a fourth serving as legal counsel, and so on. In each case, then, it will be necessary for the boss to meet individually with each of his immediate subordinates, but there still may be some common elements that will lend themselves to the group approach.

In the individual approach the basic technique is the same as that used in the group approach—identification of the major segments of the job through free discussion. It differs from the group approach only in that the boss works with just one of his subordinates—who may be either a line man or a staff man—at a time. (If the subordinate is a staff man, the major segments of his job may be technical rather than managerial, although if he is the head of a staff department he will stand in a line relationship to his own subordinates, and in that case will need the same managerial skills that the line executive must employ.)

In the individual approach, only two brains can be drawn on for ideas. Granted that in the case of a high executive and his superior, those brains may be considered of exceptional quality; still it may be more difficult to obtain suggestions. For this reason, the boss may have a greater tendency to jump into the act, since he may get impatient when he has to wait for his subordinate to identify the segments of his job. But if he does begin to dominate the meeting, the major value of the technique will be lost.

On the other hand, if the boss can suppress his impatience, draw out the thoughts of his subordinates, and then, by judicious guidance, get agreement on a good list of the major segments of the job, the subordinate's performance may be expected to show improvement. In fact, the boss himself has already improved his own performance in the managerial area by virtue of the fact that he has probably learned more about conducting a meeting than he knew before.

One of the chief reasons for using the individual approach, especially at the higher levels of the organization, is that the process allows, even calls for, a thorough discussion of ways in which actual performance can be improved in the future. In the group approach, of course, it is not possible to pinpoint areas in which individual members of the group need to show improvement, for to do so would embarrass those who were singled out. It is expected that those who have been neglecting some portions of their jobs will realize that fact and devote more attention to them in the future, and this generally happens. However, the realization may not be so acute as it is when the individual approach is used.

PHYSICAL REQUIREMENTS

Where should the meetings be held? What equipment will be needed for the sessions?

If the manager has an office with a table and room for as many chairs as there will be participants, his office is entirely suitable, providing that he can shut off interruptions. Telephone calls should not be routed to him while the meeting is in progress, nor should people be allowed to barge in.

If the boss's office is not suitable, then a quiet conference room will be a good place to hold the meeting. Here, too, interruptions should not be allowed.

If the boss's office is not suitable and there is no conference room available, then the next best place will have to do. But because of the nature of the subject matter, the meeting should not be held in any spot where passers-by will be able to eavesdrop. This is not because the subject matter is so hush-hush or private, but because it concerns only the boss and his subordinates. It just isn't anyone else's business; so why air the discussion for everyone to hear?

The only equipment needed in addition to a room that provides adequate privacy and comfort is a paperboard, some light adhesive tape (transparent or masking tape will do very nicely), and a crayon or a felt marking pen. If the conference room has a board on which papers may be attached by means of metal strips or small magnets, then the tape will not be needed.

The paperboard must be placed so that all members of the group (the leader excepted) can easily see the writing on it. Since the boss will be moving around, and writing on the paperboard, any place the board may be set up will be satisfactory for him.

It is also important that there be a clear wall area within easy view of everyone in the group, so that the completed sheets from the paperboard can be placed on it.

The boss will be on his feet during most of the meeting, but he may find it well to have a high stool available somewhat to one side of the paperboard. Then he can perch on it at times when discussions are going on and there is no need for him to write anything.

Where the individual approach is used, the discussion can usually be conducted in the boss's office, but even here a paperboard may be of value since it will enable the subordinate to see immediately what the boss is writing down without looking over his shoulder.

Chapters Seven and Eight of this section will illustrate the technique used in the group method to draw up a list of the major segments of a managerial job at any level in the organization.

CHAPTER SEVEN

Preparing a Performance Description: Step 1

A PERFORMANCE DESCRIPTION, as was pointed out in previous chapters, differs from a job description in that it does not list responsibilities or authorities but the things a manager actually does himself, not the duties he delegates or supervises. And, of course, the more he delegates, the more the segments of his job are the things he does in directing his people.

The technique used in determining the segments of the job is not only simple; it is one that is familiar to every manager in other contexts. It has been applied to the preparation of many types of plans and projects, and to the solution of problems. A variety of names have been applied to it. The only new thing about it is the application of it to the preparation of performance descriptions.

Institution of it could be called a "program," but this term implies that it is something extraneous to the manager's real job, something imposed from without, perhaps by a staff group. Therefore I prefer to call it a technique used in the on-the-job man-boss relationship. The most important point is that it is *always* employed by the line boss in a meeting with his immediate subordinate or subordinates.

If anyone other than the boss attempts to use the technique, the benefits will fall far short of the possibilities; in fact, they may be nonexistent, or so temporary as to make little difference in the overall performance of the managers. No matter how skillful in conducting meetings a staff person may be, the line managers do not report to him, and therefore, they do not feel that satisfying him is their real job. Consequently, he may cajole, plead, or even beg, but the results he gets are at best tepid. (In this case at least, it is better to have the right man do a poor job than to have the wrong one do a good job.)

The staff man will be well advised to avoid attempting to play this role in which he cannot, in the nature of things, achieve success. How can he avoid doing the job if his boss, the line man, or some other high-level executive asks him to do so? There is one phrase I have found very effective under these circumstances. If I say I cannot do it, and the line man asks me why, I say: "They just don't report to me." He may have to think the matter over for a time, but eventually he nods.

Let us assume that the line boss wants to work with his immediate subordinates on preparation of their performance descriptions and has asked them to meet with him at a designated time and place. For this first meeting he has made no preparation other than to review mentally the technique he will use in leading the meeting and his own feeling about the proposed subject matter. But he has been very careful *not* to write down any of his own ideas about what the descriptions should cover for fear that he will let his preconceptions show as the meeting progresses and so fail to get the best from his group. Nor has he told his subordinates the purpose of the meeting; thus they will come to it without any preset convictions and perhaps with a healthy curiosity. (There may be such comments as: "I wonder what he's up to now," or "What new idea has he got up his sleeve?" or "Do you suppose he's read another book and wants us to start doing everything differently?")

STARTING THE MEETING

As an example, let us use a meeting conducted by a vice-president for the managers who report to him.

Much of the success of the meeting depends on the introduction of the subject matter, the opening remarks the boss uses to get the discussion off the ground. Here his sincerity, and the extent to which his subordinates recognize that he is sincere, are very important.

For this reason the boss should not try to make a drastic change in his own manner. For example, if he has been in the habit of conducting meetings autocratically, and tries to change his approach completely this time, his subordinates will not take the transformation seriously. ("He must have read another book or heard something at a meeting somewhere.") In fact, if the boss—whether or not he has been autocratic in the past—uses permissiveness to the point where nothing is said, the meeting can become quite pointless.

Again, if the boss starts out by "passing the buck," by stating that the boys upstairs have asked him to conduct the meeting, he is not doing his job, and his subordinates will recognize that he is speaking out of ignorance, fear, or bluff. And if the boss meanders through his opening remarks, using obviously planned and stilted phrases, the subordinates may feel that they are being unjustly criticized and become defensive and argumentative.

Poor starts of this kind, along with others that have to be heard to be believed, have ensured failure from the beginning. Then, no matter how sincere the boss really is or how hard he subsequently tries, he will have uphill sledding.

It may be assumed that the boss is actually sincere in his belief that use of the technique will produce improvement in his subordinates' performance and help him to achieve his own objectives. If he isn't convinced that it will, he shouldn't hold the meeting at all.

Perhaps the boss has been somewhat autocratic in the past, and this is the first time he has seriously approached his subordinates with a request for cooperation in their joint management effort. If so, always providing he is convinced that their cooperation in the preparation of a performance description will help him with his own management job, the meeting may mark the beginning of a new type of relationship that will make his work easier in the future.

No one can write the opening remarks for his boss, for he must use his own natural style. The following words, therefore, are not prescribed for anyone; they are included merely to show the points that it is often useful to cover. Some bosses may want to omit some of the ideas incorporated or include others.

Thanks for changing your schedules so you could get to this meeting with me today. I'm certain that some of you have been wondering what it was to be about. Frankly I am enthusiastic about what I want to discuss with you.

First, I want to make it clear I am not being critical, but rather am very proud of what we all have accomplished so far, but I do want to talk about some possible ways we can all do even better.

In the first place, the old, long-held opinion that as long as we are making a profit everything must be all right. This is not the time to rest on our oars. When things are going well is the time for us to look to the future and see what we can do to make things better.

This is not an idea of mine, though I must say I agree with it. [If appropriate, one could say in addition, "I have been through some meetings with my boss, and I want to bring some of the things I learned in those meetings to you."]

I have learned a simple way for us all to look at our jobs, see just what we are doing on them as managers, and to discuss what other things we should be doing to make our own performance better. It must be obvious to us all that better performance on our part will pay off both for our company and for us, too.

There is nothing which we are going to talk about today which will point a finger at anyone in particular—rather, if this meeting is like the ones I attended with my boss, it will point out to all of us that there are worthwhile things which some of us have not been doing that we all should be doing.

To illustrate what I mean, I would like to have you tell me the things you do as a manager. I will list them on the paperboard. Each one can think of things which you do as a manager; so let's all join in while I write them.

Preparation of the performance description starts when the leader, in this case the vice-president, asks his subordinates what they do as managers in their own jobs.

The verb "do" means action. In the light of this, just what does a given manager actually do? He may open his own mail, answer his telephone, or dictate letters to his secretary, but these are not major or even minor segments of his job. In each case, they are simply some of the means he uses in handling some segment. In conducting a telephone conversation or writing a letter, for example, he may be keeping a subordinate informed of what is expected of him, helping a subordinate solve a problem, or handling any one of the major "what's" of his job.

On the other hand, if he is filling a vacancy in the ranks of his immediate subordinates, he is actually *doing* something. There are certain steps he must go through, certain actions he has to take. If his company practices long-range planning, he must make the plans himself; he can't pass the job to someone else. He can *tell* his subordinates to make their own plans, but he himself must judge them and coordinate them. Again, when the manager conducts a meeting of his subordinates, on long-range planning or anything else, that is something he does. Or if he evaluates the performance of his subordinates—and every manager does, formally or informally—that is another "what" of his job, something he himself does, something he cannot delegate.

The foregoing is by way of illustration of the type of thing the leader should eventually get on the list of major segments of performance, but he should not offer illustrations at the start. In this first meeting, he must maintain a questioning attitude, and not allow his own ideas to show, through his words, his gestures, or his facial expression.

The boss may find at the outset that the subordinates are somewhat hesitant about suggesting the things they actually do. The idea is new to them, and they have to mull it over for awhile. The delay may seem long to the leader, but usually the interval is no more than a few seconds. (In one case in which the boss felt that there had been complete silence for ten or fifteen minutes, the interval, as clocked by a stopwatch, was actually twenty-two seconds.)

The interval may seem long to the subordinates also. It is a little embarrassing for a man to realize that he is being paid for doing a job and yet he can't think of a single thing he is doing to earn the money. For this reason, someone is sure to come up with a statement of some kind before too many moments have passed.

The delay may make the boss want to break the silence with a thoughtful hint, but he will be much smarter to repeat the question, perhaps in different phraseology. In order to avoid simply standing there looking hopeful and feeling foolish, he will step up to the paperboard and write a heading at the top of the sheet. If he is a vice-president, his subordinates could have the title of manager, and he can write:

"The major segments of a manager's job are:"

Then turning back to the group, he can ask again, "What do you do as managers?"

When some member of the group states some one thing he does, the boss writes it on the paperboard, *just as the subordinate phrased it*. It must be stressed at this point that regardless of what is said, the boss writes it down. He may not believe that it should be included, he may even be violently opposed to including it, but he makes no comments either audible or visible. He simply turns back to the group and asks: "What else do you do?"

In addition, at this stage he should permit no discussion from the floor. Many of those present may not believe the suggestion is pertinent, but they should not be allowed to express their disagreement during the initial listing. The time for discussion comes later, and the boss can tell them so.

What happens if discussion is allowed at this point is illustrated by a case reported to me in a letter from an assistant nursing administrator of a number of hospitals in a major city. Both administrator and the assistant believed they had thoroughly mastered the technique of conducting this kind of a meeting, and the administrator had conducted a meeting of those in charge of hospital administration in twelve different hospitals. The assistant administrator had been assigned the job of critiquing the administrator's performance. (It is probably unchivalrous to state that all those taking part in this meeting were women. It is also irrelevant because many meetings in which the participants are men have had the same unfortunate results.)

After starting the meeting in her own way, the administrator moved to the paperboard, wrote the heading, and turned for an answer to the question: "What do you do as directors of your hospitals?"

One of the directors named a duty, and while the administrator was writing it down, bedlam broke loose. Every one of the directors had a comment, and many tried speaking at the same time. In an attempt to restore order the administrator asked that people speak one at a time. This they did, although there were many interruptions. One gripe after another was aired, comments and opinions long suppressed sought fresh air, and the discussion and the arguments continued until all the allotted time had been used up and the meeting had to be adjourned.

In her letter, the assistant administrator asked me whether she could discuss the matter with me further and find out why the meeting had gone wrong. Since I happened to be in her city a few days later, we met. When she had given me a fuller description of the meeting, I asked what she felt has been accomplished. She replied that it had been a good gripe session—many dormant complaints had been brought into the open, and as a result several controversial policies were being reviewed. But no progress at all had been made toward the preparation of performance descriptions. Somewhat sheepishly she admitted that in allowing comments while the first list was being drawn up, the administrator had deviated from the rules of the technique. After some discussion, she was convinced that all the trouble had occurred because this rule was ignored, and determined to try again. A few weeks later I receiver a letter from her saying: "It works. Thanks."

In another case, the leader of a meeting—a man this time and a production vice-president—couldn't help expressing his own displeasure at some of his plant managers' views of what they did. As a result, the meeting broke up on a sour note. But the boss was anxious to eradicate the bad impression he had made, and he still wanted to use the technique. The only advice I could give him was to try again, and this time to keep his own mouth shut and his face "poker." He did, and it worked, although he admitted that it took a lot longer to win back some of the lost good feelings.

The moral: Don't lose ground by changing the tried and proved techniques. It's harder to regain lost ground than to do it correctly the first time.

When enough items have been suggested to fill one sheet, the leader places it on the wall or the magnetic strip so that it is visible to all. Then he starts a second sheet (without the heading) and continues, using as many sheets as necessary and transferring them to the wall as soon as they are filled. When the process is completed, all the sheets have been placed where they are visible to everyone.

This step is concluded when repetition becomes evident and someone in the group insists on pointing it out or the leader himself feels that enough major segments of the job have been suggested to make it profitable to go on to discussion of them. (Probably at this point his arm will be too tired from writing on the paperboard anyway.)

If repetition shows up very early in the process, however, the leader should call for more items that are *different*. But if a list of some ten, fifteen, twenty, or more items has been suggested, then repetition may be a valid reason for concluding this phase. Just how many items there should be will depend partially on the nature of the job, but there should be enough to fill several large sheets of paper and supply plenty of material for discussion. The items suggested, even though they may not be phrased as they should be and some of them may not be valid, should cover a good cross section of the job duties before the first step is concluded.

It is the leader's responsibility to determine when enough is enough, and the simple criteria above will help him decide when he can safely end this part of this discussion and still have enough material for the second step in which the list will be modified and brought closer to reality.

All of the above part of this chapter merely serves to illustrate the first part of the technique used to determine performance description by the group process:

STEP 1.   Write down every item each individual suggests until an appropriate list is compiled.

The production vice-president has called his seven plant managers together. He told them that for purposes of studying his techniques of leading this meeting a tape recorder was running, but he hoped that it would not affect them. The resulting tape shows that apparently soon after the meeting started they forgot all about it. Here follows a portion of the tape transcribed:

VP THOMPSON: I called this meeting so that we could make a list—together—of the things you all do as plant managers. We can call this a performance description. To do this I'm going to head this sheet (*he writes at the top of the first sheet of paperboard, talking as he writes*) The major segments of a plant manager's job are, colon, number one, period. (*He turns to the group.*) What do you do on your manager's job? (*Since he receives no immediate answers, he tries another tack.*) What are the things you do as you run your plant?

HARRY WHITE: That's an easy one to answer. I run the plant according to the objectives set up by the company.

THOMPSON: (*Writes*) Run plant according to company objectives. (*Turning back after placing a number 2 next on the sheet*) What else do you do?

RALPH BECK: Meet all production quotas.

THOMPSON: (*Writes*) Meet all production quotas. Number three (*placing the next number, 3, under the last item*). What else?

WHITE: That's implied in what I said.

MANUEL LAMBARZI: No, it's not. It's a specific thing.

PETER BUCKLEY: Yes, it is—it seems to me that unless we do the second thing consciously, we don't accomplish the first . . .

THOMPSON: (*Interrupting*) Please. You fellows both may have a point, but for now I want to list our ideas. We'll talk about them later.

BUCKLEY: OK, if you say so, but I didn't want to let that slide by.

THOMPSON: What else?

MIKE HANOVER: I think we should put up that we measure the performance of our supervisors.

THOMPSON: How do you want me to put it—"Measure performance of supervisors"?

HANOVER: That's OK, or maybe to use a fancier word, "Evaluate performance of subordinates," would be better.

THOMPSON: (*Writes after 3*) Evaluate performance of subordinates. What else? (*Placing a 4 next*)

WESLEY RICH: I'm sure we also ought to have "Give raises" on that list.

THOMPSON: (*Writes after 4*) Gives raises.

GEORGE ROTH: Wouldn't that all come under salary administration?

THOMPSON: Could be, but let's go on; we can pick up on our discussion later.

ROTH: It seems to me that all we have said so far is covered by the list of duties we all talked about last year when we had those management meetings.

THOMPSON: What do you mean?

ROTH: Planning, organizing staffing, directing, and checking results. It seems to me implementing is in there too, somewhere, but I'm not sure where.

THOMPSON: (*Placing a 5 on the paper and writing*) Five. Planning. (*Then placing a 6 on the paper and writing*) Six. Organizing. (*The sheet being full, he tears it from the pad and places it on the wall with temporary fasteners and in view of all members of the group. Then, placing a 7 on the next blank sheet and writing*) Seven. Staffing. Eight. Directing. Nine. Checking results. Ten. (*writing the number 10 next*).

LAMBARZI: Yes, but . . .

BUCKLEY: That can't be right, from what we've been talking about . . .

THOMPSON: (*Interrupting*) I know you all want to get into this conversation, but, please, let's hold it a while until we get up some more things that we do. What shall I put up here for ten?

RICH: I fill vacancies when someone retires.

THOMPSON: (*Writing after 10*) Fill vacancies after retirements. What else?

BECK: I try *not* to fill vacancies after retirements.

THOMPSON: (*Laughing as he writes*) Try *not* to fill vacancies after retirements. (*Then, tearing off the sheet*) That fills this sheet. Just let me put it up here with the other one. (*Fastens it up on the wall. Turns back to the board and starts the third sheet with the number 11.*) What else?

The group continues to supply the boss with items until he has enough to use for a good discussion (this discussion will be continued in the next chapter).

The paper work so far posted will show the following:

The major segments of a plant manager's job are:
1. Run plant according to company objectives
2. Meet all production quotas
3. Evaluate performance of subordinates
4. Give raises

5. Planning
6. Organizing
7. Staffing
8. Directing
9. Checking results
10. Fill vacancies after retirements
11. Try *not* to fill vacancies after retirements

It should be evident that the boss will not agree with all of these items of performance, but at this time it does not matter. The real agreement on just what they do or should be doing will come in the discussion phase. It is unfair to judge *any* of the group by the first list. This list, incidentally, is a reasonably good representation of most first lists; differences between organizational levels are evident only in that higher levels use a more "tony" vocabulary, and even that is not always true.

ANOTHER TYPICAL SESSION:
SECOND-LINE LEVEL

To illustrate further the use of step 1 of the technique of preparing a performance description, a tape recording of a session conducted by the manager of a small plant for his foremen and forewomen is used. This particular plant manager was the same Harry White who was in the session previously described.

Space here also allows for only a portion of the proceedings of the actual meeting to be shown. Also, some of the discussion was repetitive in nature and for the purposes of this example can be omitted.

HARRY WHITE: Today I have asked you to spend some time with me to see if we can work out together a listing of the things you do as managers, as directors of people, as foremen and forewomen, as it were. The technique I want to use to do this will be to write down on this paperboard the things you tell me are the things you do as supervisors. As the list grows, I'll place the filled sheets on the wall so that we can all see them. Now, for a start, I'm going to put this sentence on the top of the first sheet. (*He writes as he says*) The major segments of foremen's and forewomen's managerial performance are, colon, number one, period. (*He turns back to his subordinates.*) What are the things you do as a supervisor?

TOM: Well, for one thing, I handle the complaints of my people.

HARRY WHITE: (*Writes*) Handle complaints (*and then places the number 2 on the sheet and turns back to the group*). What else do you do?

TOM: I also get the work out.

HARRY WHITE: (*Writes*) Get the work out (*and adds the number 3*). (*He continues writing what is said and putting down the next number.*) What else?

JOE: My job is to see that everyone is on time. I suppose you could say I enforce punctuality.

BOB: Well, we all do that, but I think there are more important things than that.

HARRY WHITE: Such as?

BOB: Well, enforcing production standards. It seems to me we all should be doing more of that. There is too much scrap now, and the reports say it is getting worse all of the time.

HARRY WHITE: You said two things then. (*Writes after 4*) Enforce production standards (*and, for number 5*) Reduce scrap.

BOB: I didn't see it as two things; they are part and parcel of the same thing, I think.

HARRY WHITE: You may be right. We'll come back to that in a moment. Now, what other things are there to go on this list of major segments?

MARY: Mr. White, I don't know if this is what you had in mind, but it seems to me that a big part of our work is to keep the girls happy on their job.

HARRY WHITE: How'll we say that?

MARY: Well, I suppose you could say it is promoting amiability, though that sounds a bit unbusinesslike.

RUTH: How about "Get better human relations"?

HARRY WHITE: Suppose we put it, "Improve personal relationships"? (*He writes this after 6.*) We'll all know what we mean by that for now at least. What else? What are the things you actually do as you direct your people?

BILL: I fill out all the reports.

HARRY WHITE: (*Writing*) Fill out reports.

JOE: That's not directing people; that's just paper work.

HARRY WHITE: Before we debate that, let's get some more major segments on the list. What else do you *do?*

WALT: This may be wrong, but I have always felt that we should grant time off to our people ourselves.

HARRY WHITE: (*Several start to talk, but the plant manager interrupts.*) All right, for now at least let's put "Grant time off" on our list. We'll discuss it thoroughly a bit later. (*A muttering continues as two people privately argue the last point, but the plant manager again calls for additional items to go on the list.*)

JIM: I personally feel that we supervisors have a big responsibility in improving the morale of our employees. I think we need to do more in that field. If we don't do it, no one else will, and it is getting so low now that we should do something about it. (*Again a muttering of words from several persons*)

HARRY WHITE: (*Cutting through the undercurrent as he writes and says*) Number nine. Improve employee morale. Now, what else?

JOE: You know, it's funny that no one has suggested that we fill vacancies in our own groups. We all have to interview the candidates personnel sends us. I've had to do three sets of interviews in the last month.

HARRY WHITE: (*Writes*) Ten. Interview applicants.

BILL: Well, for that matter, we have to evaluate the performance of our people by the annual rating.

HARRY WHITE: Evaluate performance for number eleven (*talking as he writes*).

WALT: I don't think that last one is our job. We only do what personnel tells us to.

HARRY WHITE: Well, would you agree that it could be your job?

WALT: I suppose so, but we've never really done it.

HARRY WHITE: For now, then, let's leave it on the list. What else goes on?

VINCE: I have kept pretty quiet till now, but it seems to me that we are just now getting to the important things we do as managers. I'd like to add that we train our employees, we determine pay adjustments, and we make recommendations for promotions to other jobs.

HARRY WHITE: Let me get all of those down now (*writing*): Twelve. Train employees. Thirteen. Make pay adjustments. Fourteen. Recommend promotions.

WALT: Now, wait a minute; we don't all of us do those things. As a matter of course, I always turn my new employees over to an old-timer to train. And I know most of us wait for personnel to tell us what the raises should be.

MARY: That's right, and I don't think I have ever made a recommendation to promote one of my folks—I need them myself. Anyway, my girls would resent it if I did.

HARRY WHITE: We have the makings here for some real discussion, but first, are there any other things you want to put on this list?

BILL: Yes, I think we should have something on that list about cutting or controlling the cost of the work in our groups.

HARRY WHITE: All right. For number fifteen, (*he writes*) control costs. Anything else? Remember, we are listing the things you all do—or perhaps should be doing—as you direct your people.

VINCE: This may be something most of us don't do much of, but it seems to me we all should be looking to the future about organization of our own group.

HARRY WHITE: Could we call that "organization planning"?

VINCE: That's good. I know I haven't done much about it, but I think I should.

HARRY WHITE: (*Writes*) Organization planning.

WALT: That's all right for you to say, but how can I make any plans to change my operations? They all depend on the rest of you.

HARRY WHITE: We'll get to that. Now, how about it, any more major segments?

TOM: This all seems pretty complicated. I think we're getting a phony list up here. We now have three sheets on the wall. Most of them are things we don't do much of. I dunno . . .

HARRY WHITE: Anything else?

JOE: Yes, I think we should have "Correct mistakes" up there.

HARRY WHITE: (*Writes*) Correct mistakes. What else?

WALT: I have the feeling that we should try to get our people to appreciate the importance of their job as it relates to the other operations in the plant. One wrong temperature reading can ruin a whole batch of cereal.

VINCE: That comes under—which one is it? Oh, there it is—number two, "Get work out." Or is it number twelve, "Train employees"? It's part of both of them. It seems to me we are now repeating ourselves.

HARRY WHITE: Let's leave it on as number seventeen, just so we won't lose it. Perhaps you are right, though, Vince, when you say we seem to be repeating ourselves. Actually we have put several things up there which someone has said that perhaps you should be doing, other items which only some of you do, and also some items which a few of you feel are questionable.

The resulting first list of the major segments of their job looks like this (actually this is only part of the list):

The major segments of foremen's and forewomen's performance are:
1. Handle complaints
2. Get work out
3. Enforce punctuality
4. Enforce production standards
5. Reduce scrap
6. Improve personal relationships
7. Fill out reports
8. Grant time off

9. Improve employee morale
10. Interview applicants
11. Evaluate performance
12. Train employees
13. Make pay adjustments
14. Recommend promotions
15. Control costs
16. Organization planning
17. Correct mistakes
18.

The next chapter will deal with steps 2 and 3 of the technique for preparing performance descriptions.

CHAPTER EIGHT

Preparing a Performance Description: Steps 2 and 3

THE REAL WORTH of the technique begins to appear once the preliminary list is completed by the process described and illustrated in the last chapter, for it is in steps 2 and 3 that the subordinates begin to understand what they, as managers, should be doing.

While the first list is being made, the process flows along with reasonable smoothness, for any disagreements are shunted aside until a sufficient number of segments have been listed. In step 2, the subordinates discuss each item on this list in turn, and in step 3 they reach a common understanding of the "what's" of their job. In the process they may discard some items, combine others, and perhaps rephrase still others.

Steps 2 and 3 are used concurrently. The discussion of the first item continues until understanding and agreement are reached. Then the process is repeated for each item on the list.

LEADING A MEETING

The term "discussion" as used here means a free, nondirected play of ideas involving all members of the group, a discussion limited only by the subject matter of the major segment under consideration. A *free* discussion is one in which *all* members of the group get into the act without feeling that they are on dangerous ground. Creating and maintaining an atmosphere that makes this possible are the responsibility of the boss as he leads the meeting. To say that the play of ideas is "nondirected" implies that the boss will not, by statement or attitude, steer the meeting to conclusions that smack of his own ideas. If he does, the real value of the meeting will be lost, and the whole operation will degenerate into boss-back-scratching and an exercise in semantics.

The boss, however, does more than simply listen and write down the conclusions. He is the leader of the meeting and he must lead it in order to ensure that everyone present gets a chance to present his ideas and that everyone is encouraged to think through his conception of what he should actually be doing on the job.

If the quiet members of the group are outtalked by the more aggressive members, the results will be slanted; and the boss must prevent this from happening. He is responsible for seeing to it that the quieter members of the group are drawn into the discussion but not forcefully pushed into it. Perhaps the best way to describe the role of the boss is to say that he should never make statements (which are easy to misconstrue) but should always ask questions (which have to be answered). Further, the questions should not be worded in such a way that they indicate the answer the boss expects or wants. For example, he should not say: "Wouldn't you all agree that this [mentioning an item] is one of the major segments of the job?" Instead, he should ask: "How do you feel about including this item?"

During the discussion, someone may suggest a new major segment of the job. This may indicate an item to be added later or make it clear that ultimately one of the major segments should be split into two or more, or that some of them should be combined. But until there is a clear understanding of the segment under consideration, the discussion should be kept on that one point. This can be done by questioning rather than by making statements. For example, the boss can say: "Do you think that is part of this segment? If it is, we can discuss it now; if not, we can postpone it until later."

However, suggestions of new major segments should not be discouraged. Rather, it is standard practice to encourage them, for often some of the best segments appear only after the discussion has started. But the leader should confine the discussion to the major item under consideration until the group has thoroughly talked it out. If a new segment is suggested, he simply adds it to the first list and assures the person who proposed it that it will be discussed at the proper time.

Experience often shows that a simply stated major segment, such as "Train my subordinates," can mean something different to each member of the group. When step 2 starts, someone may state he delegates the training to experienced old-timers. Then the boss may ask, "What training do you delegate?" and practically always the man will reply that he delegates job training. In that case the boss can ask the group: "Do you all delegate your job training in the same way?" and the discussion will be off and running. In the end, members of the group will all understand that job training is only one of the various kinds of training that may be needed. For example, some erudite member of the group may say that he means "vestibule training," which *he* delegates to the training specialists. Or one of a group of third-level managers may say he means "supervisory training," and so on.

This type of analysis goes on until the leader (the boss) finally queries: "Then just what type of training are we talking about here? What kinds of training, if any, are part of your own job?" Once the subordinates understand what the term means and agree on a common definition of it, the item can be placed on the second list.

Perhaps as a result of the discussion, the statement "Train subordinates" might be discarded, and several specific types of training placed on the list in its stead.

When a boss and his subordinates talk about such elementary segments of job performance and the subordinates work to determine what the terms actually mean, all kinds of pertinent new ideas often develop, and all participants gain a better understanding of the difference between the things they delegate and the things they must do themselves. In addition, the boss gets a clearer insight into the ways in which his subordinates think (or perhaps do not think) and a better understanding of how he himself interprets some of the taken-for-granted terms that are bandied about so easily.

So far in this chapter, stress has been placed on the job of the leader. Too often those who coach managers in the use of the three-step technique tend to minimize the role of the leader by saying that the process is simple and easy to learn because, after all, it is really only management in action and the boss has been managing for some time.

The process *is* simple, but it is not necessarily simple to use. So much depends on the way in which the boss has conducted meetings in the past.

If he has been accustomed to dominating meetings of his subordinates, he may have a tendency to revert to type which should give his coach concern. But the thoughtful boss, once he becomes aware of this, will probably attempt to improve. When a boss has familiarized himself with the application of the three-step technique, has practiced it in successive meetings, and has been adequately coached in it, he does become adept at it. When he has reached this point, then he does find the process simple and easy.

THE BOSS'S IDEAS

Ideally, the entire list of the "what's" of the management job is drawn from the suggestions of the group. But many bosses find it impossible not to inject their own ideas at some point in the discussion. After all, so the argument runs, the boss has probably had more experience in management than most of his subordinates; and undoubtedly he has better knowledge of overall company objectives. But, and it is a very big "but," if the boss feels he must present his own ideas he should withhold any indication of what he thinks until his subordinates have exhausted their suggestions. And even then he must be careful not to sit on anyone or blatantly force his views on the group. His aim should be to help everyone in the group understand what a manager should do, not to have his group learn a list by rote.

As a matter of fact, if the boss uses the questioning procedure skillfully enough, he need have little fear that the second and final list will not include most or all of the things he himself feels important. Critics have suggested that this could happen, and sometimes they have been right. However, it generally occurs only when the leader is too impatient to elicit all the ideas of his subordinates, for it is unlikely that every member of the group will be totally unaware of an important segment of the job.

Let us say, however, that no one has suggested some segment of the job that the boss believes it is essential to include, and he feels the omission cannot be allowed. In that case, he will undoubtedly suggest the item himself—under the circumstances, it is too much to expect that he will keep silent about it.

But suppose the discussion shows that the group strongly disagrees with him, that the members feel that the item in question emphatically does not belong in their performance description. What then?

In that case, I believe, the boss should go along with the group, and agree to the omission, for the danger of doing so is less than might appear.

Since the item has been thoroughly discussed he can rest assured that his idea is firmly embedded in the minds of the subordinates, and their subsequent day-to-day performance will be affected by it. An example will illustrate how things work out.

One group of second-line managers had completed step 1 and was well into the discussion of the items—one of which stated that it was part of their job to check with their superior on the factors to be used in selecting first-line supervisors. One member of the group, Wes Hamilton, strongly disagreed. "That checking-with-the-boss bit is entirely unnecessary," he said. "We included 'selecting supervisors' as one of the items of performance, and if we're really going to select them, we have to decide what we want."

The boss, on the other hand, liked the idea of the check; if he could see the lists of qualifications they prepared, he felt, he could help them ensure that it was complete. But he asked the other members of the group how they felt about it.

Most of them accepted Wes's reasoning, and many of them made such comments as: "After all, if we're responsible for first-line supervisors' performances, it's up to us to get good ones." And "We're much closer to the first-line supervisors than Mr. Blank is; he can't know all the details of their job the way we do."

The boss said no more about the matter at the time, but later on at the end of the session he came back to the subject and asked whether the group didn't feel that he might give them some help when they had to draw up a list of qualifications for a new supervisor. No one in the group agreed except the man who had originally suggested the item, and the boss dropped the matter, although, as he later told his coach, he felt somewhat disappointed with the outcome of the meeting because of the omission.

By a coincidence, it happened that a week or two later Wes himself was faced with the job of selecting a new first-line supervisor, and he dropped by the coach's office, ostensibly to show him the list of qualifications he had drawn up. The coach was a little puzzled. Why, he wondered, was Wes showing him the list? Drawing it up was a line job in any case, and Wes had insisted that he, and only he, should decide what it should include.

But Wes seemed reluctant to leave. He continued talking about extraneous matters for quite some time. Finally, he asked, somewhat hesitantly, "Do you think the boss would like to see this list before I start to use it?"

The coach, who had been present at the discussion meeting, had a little difficulty keeping a straight face, but he admitted that he thought the boss might be quite willing to look it over.

So Wes went on to show the list to the boss, and as they talked it over, the boss was able to suggest an additional qualification that Wes had not thought of, and this factor was the one Wes used eventually in deciding among the three top candidates for the job, who appeared to meet all the other qualifications equally well.

Moreover, the boss will have other opportunities of getting his ideas onto the list. The setting of standards is the next step after the list of "what's" has been developed, and while the standard-setting sessions are in progress, normal activities will continue and there will be many occasions when the boss will have informal meetings with his subordinates.

For example, during a discussion of some problem that arises, it may become evident that an item or two can be added to the list. Then the boss can say casually in the next meeting: "Would you agree that, under these circumstances, we should add this to the list?" Or, "I was discussing the problem of _____ with _____ [naming one of the group] the other day, and it occurred to me that you all have to meet it at one time or another. Let's add it to the list."

By the time this stage has been reached, members of the group will be past the point where it is necessary to handle them delicately to avoid choking off their ideas, and usually they can be depended on to realize that the boss is seriously trying to help them, not attempting to force his ideas down their throats.

Domineering management people often assert that they cannot relinquish control lest they be considered spineless. But consultative supervision and cooperative decision-making on these matters do pay off. After all, if a subordinate has not accepted the idea that certain things are part of his job, he will neglect them whenever there is little chance that his neglect will come to his boss's attention.

MAKING THE SECOND LIST

Now let us say that the boss has worked through step 1 of the technique of preparing performance descriptions. Here, it will be remembered, the subordinates prepared a *first* list of the major segments of their managerial jobs.

When the list was completed, the vice-president might say: "We now have quite a few major segments listed, and judging from the comments and some of the undertone remarks, some of you appear to disagree with some of the items or at least want to clarify them. So let's start a new sheet with the same heading." Then he writes the same heading on a blank sheet on the paperboard, perhaps abbreviating the words so that no time is lost unnecessarily.

Next, he turns to the group and reads the first major segment aloud. This is important because it helps to focus everyone's attention on the same thing. Then in order to stimulate discussion he asks such questions as:

"Is this something we all do? Or perhaps *should* do?"

"Is this activity within the scope of the job?"

"Will this add too much to our job if we try it?"

"Is it fair to expect you to do this?"

"Will the fact that some of us do this and others don't be important?"

"What do we mean by this?"

"How do we interpret this segment?"

"What problems do you think might occur if we do this?"

Naturally, the boss does not fire all these questions at the group at once; one of them is usually sufficient to start the discussion. Most management groups will not need much stimulation, because they are concerned about doing a good job and want to know what they should be doing as managers. Also, as the first list has been taking shape and the items have been written down, each member of the group has generally been forming an opinion about each item.

The boss keeps the discussion of an item going until he feels that most members of the group understand its meaning and are in agreement that it should be accepted or rejected. One way of discovering the extent to which there is understanding is to ask one or more members of the group to state their interpretations.

In every group, of course, there is likely to be at least one holdout, if only for the reason that some people enjoy being holdouts and are prepared to argue indefinitely. In handling a situation of this sort, the boss must use discretion. He can, for example, use his authority and say flatly that since most of the group are agreed, the item must appear on the second list, but in doing so he is to some extent admitting his failure as a leader. It is often more advisable to say something like this: "Well, since so many of us do agree, perhaps those who disagree will let it go for now, and if necessary we can come back to the matter later." This seems to work, for often the dissenter is not as positive as he seems, but has reached the point where he cannot relinquish his stand without feeling foolish. The boss's statement takes him off the hook, and makes it unnecessary for him to admit that he was wrong. Generally there is no need to go back to the item later; the holdout is only too glad to let the matter drop when he can do so without losing face.

As each item on the first list is discussed, one of three things will happen:

1. The group will agree that it is something they all do or should do, and therefore it can be placed on the second list.

2. The group determines that the item is *not* something they should be doing, and accordingly, it should be discarded.

3. It is agreed that the item should be rewritten to convey a meaning somewhat different from what the wording on the first list implied or that it should be stated as two items or combined with some other item.

When the decision on each major segment has been reached, the leader either copies it onto the new list, writes it down in its changed form, or if it is not to be used, goes on to the next item. In each case, regardless of the way in which the item is treated, it is crossed off the first list.

There is no such thing as a complete first list. Often it is filled with platitudinous items drawn from textbooks. Only as each member of the group considers each item in relation to his own job does a realistic list appear.

If the group is composed of people who have had a course or two in management, some—perhaps all—of them are likely to say that their job consists of planning, organizing, staffing, direction, and control. This is a good abstract description of the management job, but it is not of much use to managers in their day-to-day work. However, the boss can easily bring it—and the group—down to earth by asking such questions as:

"What do you plan? How do you do it?"

"In staffing, what positions do you fill? What steps do you have to take to fill them?"

"What controls must you use?"

Someone once said that the test of a good major segment is whether or not a standard of performance can be set for it. In other words, if the manager is supposed to do something, it should be possible to determine how well it should be done. And one cannot set a standard for "planning" in the abstract—everyone plans to some extent, both on the job and off it.

To develop a meaningful standard, one must know *what* the manager plans and the steps he is supposed to take in order to develop his plans.

Planning, organizing, and so on, are skills the manager uses in handling *all* aspects of his job. They are not separate major segments.

Even the second list is not always complete, for normal day-to-day activities may suggest new major segments that no one—including the boss—has thought of. Also, no list is "final." Conditions change, and what may be important at one time may be unimportant at another. The major value of the second list is that it provides a starting point that makes it possible to set standards.

But an important caution should be mentioned here. As the group discusses the major "what's" of the job, it may take a side trail and attempt to bring in units of measurement and determination of responsibility and authority. The leader must realize that these two steps come later and keep the meeting to the subject at hand: determining *what* the manager does.

The final technique the leader uses in the last part of the meeting is to review the entire second list orally with the group and ask the members if they all agree on the list of major segments that they have themselves hammered out in the discussion. Then, if it seems appropriate because one or two people have been in noticeable disagreement with the conclusions of the majority, he may ask: "Does anyone still feel that this list should be changed? If so, let's try to resolve the matter now." Usually, however, experience shows that most of the earlier disagreements fade into nothing by the end of a properly handled session, and it is not even necessary to raise the question.

If one man is conducting a series of meetings with several groups of subordinates, or if the plan is to have his immediate subordinates conduct similar meetings with *their* immediate subordinates later, for the sake of uniformity it is helpful to start both the first or temporary list and the final list with a standard sentence: "The major segments of the _____'s performance are:" The blank will be filled in with the title appropriate to the group: first-line supervisor, department head, plant manager, branch director, vice-president, or district superintendent, for example. This is the only sentence the boss will need to memorize in preparation for this meeting.

Someone has facetiously said that it is easy to be a leader in such a meeting. The only things the boss needs to be able to do are to *write legibly* on the paperboard, to be able to read (in this case his own writing), and to be able to ask questions, not to answer any, the implication being that the boss can get by with little effort. But those who have actually conducted such a meeting know that it requires a high degree of leadership, also that they improve their leadership as they continue to use the technique.

Now let us recapitulate the three steps of the technique in chronological order:

1. Write down every item each individual suggests until an appropriate list is compiled.

2. Let the group discuss each item and either discard it or accept it—in its original form or in a new form.

3. Make the agreed-to new list of major segments.

AN EXAMPLE

In the preceding chapter transcripts of two performance-description sessions were recorded through step 1. Now follows a continuation of a portion of the steps 2 and 3 parts for the same groups.

The portion of the first list used previously is repeated for ease of following the discussion as taped, although the group had extended it to thirty-one items.

The major segments of a plant manager's job are:

1. Run plant according to company objectives
2. Meet all production quotas
3. Evaluate performance of subordinates
4. Give raises
5. Planning
6. Organizing
7. Staffing
8. Directing
9. Checking results
10. Fill vacancies after retirements
11. Try *not* to fill vacancies after retirements

Now for more of the transcript of the meeting the vice-president had with his plant managers. The transcript for the rest of the meeting between one of the plant managers and his foremen and forewomen will follow the vice-president's transcript.

VP THOMPSON: Now that we have decided that we have enough items of major importance in your performance to give us a good basis for discussion—a total of five sheets and thirty-one items—let's start with a clean sheet and talk about these major segments. Let's put up here the same heading we started the first list with (*writing on a new sheet of the paperboard*): Major segments of a plant manager's job are, colon, number one, period. (*Turning back to the group*) Let's read the first item we have on our first list. (*He reads*) Run plant according to company objectives. Is that something you all do?

HANOVER: Of course we do.

LAMBARZI: Sure.

RICH: I hope I do.

THOMPSON: How do you do it?

RICH: I measure all I do against the objectives.

THOMPSON: Then are you saying that one of the things you do is measuring the work of your plant, an actual measurement? That is a real action point?

RICH: Yes, you could say that, though now it seems a bit vague to me.

THOMPSON: What we want is an agreed-to list of actual things we all do or *should* do in running our plant.

RICH: Well, in that context, maybe I don't really measure everything in terms of the company objectives—that is, all of the time.

THOMPSON: How do some of the others of you feel about this?

BECK: I suppose we all do this in general, though I'm sure I don't consciously do it all of the time.

BUCKLEY: I like to think I do it from the negative approach—don't misunderstand me, I'm not a negative manager, it's just that I keep myself geared to spotting when things go wrong. If they are right I don't fuss, but I'm tuned to mistakes. It's when we slip from meeting our objectives that I go after someone.

BECK: That's true for me too, I guess.

RICH: Yeah, I guess that's what I had in mind.

THOMPSON: Then are you saying that this first item (*reading*) "Run plant according to company objectives" is really not something that you actually do but rather it is an overall balance wheel for your general performance?

WHITE: It looks to me that that first thing is one of our responsibilities.

LAMBARZI: What's the difference?

THOMPSON: Is there a difference?

BECK: Sure there is.

THOMPSON: How?

BECK: What you do is one thing, what you are responsible for is another.

LAMBARZI: They look like the same to me.

BECK: Oh, don't get hepped on semantics. It's really simple to see the difference if you look at it right.

THOMPSON: How is that? What is the right viewpoint?

WHITE: It's like this—when you [*Thompson*] tell me I am responsible for operating my plant according to company objectives that tells me that I had better *do* certain things, take certain actions to see that I discharge my responsibility as I said.

HANOVER: That's right. I have to *do* things like, oh, number two up there, meet production quotas.

LAMBARZI: No, that's the same thing, it is your responsibility to meet quotas. You must *do* things, take actions to meet quotas.

WHITE: Well, maybe you are right on number two, maybe I didn't pick a good example—but look at numbers three and four. Those things you do—and sure you, or rather we, are all responsible for them and each one of them is *done* by doing different steps, but I still maintain that we do these things.

THOMPSON: Could we determine how well we should do these segments you mention?

WHITE: I think so—(*thoughtfully*) look, do you want a step-by-step listing of how we do everything?

THOMPSON: Do you think I should?

BECK: No, I don't think so. Certainly our own area of freedom should allow us to know how to do some things.

RICH: That's right, you shouldn't have to fuss over everything we do.

HANOVER: I agree (*as do several others*).

THOMPSON: OK, then this list of major segments should be only those things you do in running your plant. OK?

SEVERAL: (*General agreement*)

THOMPSON: All right, then, what about number one?

ROTH: I've been listening through all this, and I don't think it should be on this list of major segments of our performance. I'm inclined to agree with Harry that it is a responsibility and not a major segment.

THOMPSON: Do you all agree?

GENERAL: (*Assent from all*)

THOMPSON: All right, for now then let's go along with that, and since no one really seems to want it on our new list, let's cross it off (*drawing a line through the first item on the posted list*), which means we have discussed it, we understand what it means, and we have agreed to leaving it off the new list we are making.

BUCKLEY: I still feel funny about ignoring it.

THOMPSON: You remember when we were talking about our management job a few weeks ago, we said that we needed to know what we *do*, that's what we are trying to find out today. We needed to know what our responsibilities and authorities were, and other things. I think I can promise you that we won't lose this item, because we will be discussing our responsibilities and authorities soon.

BUCKLEY: OK, I'll pass then for now.

THOMPSON: Now, we still do not have a first item on our new list. Old number one is out, number two is next (*he reads*): "Meet all production quotas." Is that something we all *do?*

ROTH: In view of what we have just said I would think we should cross off number two. It's a responsibility like number one.

LAMBARZI: I agreed before that that was right, but now I'm not so sure. I feel that this is something I do—I see to it that all production schedules are met.

ROTH: That's just it, you "see to it." But what do you do to "see to it?"

RICH: Yes, how do you "see to it?"

LAMBARZI: Well, for one thing I check on how my supervisors are doing.

BUCKLEY: Aha, that's number three—but that *is* something you do.

BECK: And I train my supervisors on new production routines.

HANOVER: And I see that they get raises when they've earned them.

THOMPSON: Hold up here a minute. Let's go back to number two again. Is this something you actually do?

LAMBARZI: Yes, I really believe I do that, but I'll go along with the idea that there are other things I do to accomplish it.

THOMPSON: What about this number two, "Meet all production quotas"?

ROTH: I think we should leave that off. It's just as Mannie [*Lambarzi*] said, there are other things we do to see that we meet the quotas.

THOMPSON: Anyone else want to get in his two cents' worth?

BUCKLEY: No, let's leave it off.

THOMPSON: OK? (*Walks over to posted list and crosses off the second item*) Now, what about number three? (*Reads*) "Evaluate performance of subordinates."

WHITE: Yes, that's something we all do, at least once a year for raises.

OTHERS: That's right. Yes. [Etc.]

THOMPSON: Fine. Then I'll put it up here as number one on the new list. (*He writes the item as on the old list and then goes over and crosses out the old number 3.*) Well, there is at least one thing we all agree that we do. And we'll all know more about it when we set a standard of performance as to how well we should make our evaluation of our subordinates.

HANOVER: What's this about standards? That's the second time you've used the term.

THOMPSON: It's like the other thing we mentioned, responsibilities and authorities. It's all part of doing our job better. And, now, what will be our new number two? (*Writes 2 under the first item on the new list. Reading the old number 4*) "Gives raises." How about that one?

WHITE: Sure, we all do that.

BUCKLEY: Would George's [*Roth's*] term be better? He said when that was listed that it should be salary administration.

WHITE: Maybe. And, anyway, that would cover *not* giving raises, too.

HANOVER: You're right. Of course, just giving raises or not isn't enough, it's important to know whether you should do either. I think it is important that we tie numbers one and two together, if this goes up here as two.

RICH: I don't think so. I think there is a lot more to evaluation of performance than just salary administration. It seems to me one would help the other, but performance improvement may be needed in some way, and you still may not be considering him for a raise—or a lack of one—for that matter, a reduction in rate maybe.

ROTH: That's right. I think we should put it up as number two and use salary administration.

SEVERAL: (*General assent*)

THOMPSON: Agreed? (*All indicate affirmatively*) OK. (*Writes "salary administration" after number 2.*) If you don't really agree, please say so, so we can talk it out.

ROTH: How can we disagree? We all do it, and that's what you want to list.

THOMPSON: Let's cross off the old number four. (*He does so.*) The next number is three (*writes the numeral 3 after the second item on the new list*). The next item on the list is (*reads*) "Planning." Is that a major segment?

ROTH: No, I don't think so. I think it is a tool of management.

WHITE: How is that? I thought we all have to plan and for that matter the next four items too.

ROTH: No, I still think these are all tools. Actually we use all of these tools, in varying degrees, for everything we really do.

RICH: That's probably right, though I'll admit that sometimes I do look as though I hadn't planned for it.

SEVERAL: Me too. [Etc.]

ROTH: Could be, but I don't think these five items have any place in this list of . . .

And here we stop the tape since a rather complete sample of steps 2 and 3 of the technique has been observed.

A SECOND EXAMPLE

For a continuation of the session of performance-description writing for the plant manager, Harry White, here follows another portion of the tape which illustrates steps 2 and 3 of the technique at a subordinate level.

Again, for ease of reading, the major segments of foremen's and fore-women's performance as worked out in the previous chapter are:

1. Handle complaints
2. Get work out
3. Enforce punctuality
4. Enforce production standards
5. Reduce scrap
6. Improve personal relationships
7. Fill out reports
8. Grant time off
9. Improve employee morale
10. Interview applicants
11. Evaluate performance
12. Train employees
13. Make pay adjustments
14. Recommend promotions
15. Control costs
16. Organization planning
17. Correct mistakes
18.

Now for the transcript:

HARRY WHITE: (*Beginning the next phase of his meeting by taking a fresh sheet of paper*) I would suggest that we start a new sheet now; head it as we did the first one. (*Writes as he talks*) Major segments of a first-line manager's performance are, colon, number one, period. Now let's look at these items one by one. As we discuss them and decide whether or not to include them in our new list, we will all perhaps get a better understanding of our job, and perhaps have additional segments to add to the list. I, for one, know that I'll benefit from this discussion.

The first thing on the list over there is "Handle complaints." How about that? Is that something we all do as we direct our people? Or is it something we should do? I know for a fact that we don't all see alike on this. What do you think?

BOB: I didn't contribute that item, and I'm not sure I know what it means.

HARRY WHITE: Anyone want to explain what it means?

TOM: Yes, I'll do it. To me it meant, and still does, trying to satisfy an employee who comes to me with a problem or situation which he is unhappy about. If it is something I can do anything about, then I do it; if not, I try to get help for him.

JOE: You mean we are to dabble in their personal affairs?

TOM: Of course not. That is, not unless their personal affairs affect their work on the job.

JOE: Well, I'll have no part of it. That's not my business.

HARRY WHITE: How do the rest of you feel?

MARY: Well, with my girls, we're always having a heart-to-heart talk about something—not all the time, really, but when they are bothered about something. I think I have helped a few of them over the years.

JOE: You're just talking about normal day-to-day supervision?

HARRY WHITE: Maybe so, but here today we are trying to list the things we *do* as we do our normal day-to-day supervision.

RALPH: I think that any discussion we have with our individual employees, whether it is over a complaint or just about the work, is normal. Even training them to do a job comes in the same category.

BILL: In that case, then, I think we should write it some other way than "Handle complaints." I think we should say, "Have contacts with employees."

RUTH: Yes, that's fine, provided we specify that it isn't a "training" contact. I think those are important enough to be listed separately just as we did in number twelve. "Train employees."

HARRY WHITE: Could we look at it this way? Here we are trying to list those things which you do in the direction of your people which I can observe in your performance. In other words, if I wanted to evaluate your performance in *this* activity (*pointing to one of the numbered statements*), I would be able to use some units of measurement for your satisfactory performance in it. We might go so far as to say that for any segment we list here, we should be able to set some standard as to how well you should do it. Is this in that category?

SEVERAL: Yes. It should be. Of course.

HARRY WHITE: Then, are we all in agreement that these normal (other than training, for now) contacts should be one of our major segments? (*Everyone agrees but Walt, who says nothing.*)

How about it, Walt? Do you feel we may be on the wrong foot on this?

WALT: No, I just had never thought of my job as having this as a measurable part of it. In fact, when you mention a standard of performance for it, I get a little concerned. I'm not certain that I've been doing a very good job with any of my contacts—what few I'm allowed.

HARRY WHITE: Do you feel that we should have contacts—more contacts, that is, than we have had? Or that I would be unfair if I expected you to do this—or, more than that, expected you to do this at a reasonably high level of performance?

WALT: Of course not. It's just that it is a new thought to me.

HARRY WHITE: Do all of you feel that I would be fair to you if I expected us to set a standard of performance for our contacts with employees?

BILL: No, I wouldn't feel that it would be unfair, but I just can't imagine how we would do it.

HARRY WHITE: Well, the actual setting of a standard we will postpone to another day. Today I'm interested in getting a list of the major segments of your performance which are common to all of us and for which we *can* set standards.

How about it, then? Will it be agreeable to put on the new list of major segments of your performance, as number one, "Contacts with employees"? (*All agree, so it is placed on the list.*)

That takes care of number one on the old list. Let's cross it off. (*He does so.*)

Now, let's look at the second item on our posted papers, "Get work out." Is that part of our job?

RUTH: Yes, it is, of course, but it seems to me that getting the work out is accomplished by doing all of the other things on the list, like training employees, getting new ones, correcting mistakes, and all the others.

VINCE: I agree that most of our production is accomplished by doing these other things, but we still have to do special things like scheduling, staffing, and chasing down slipups of other groups. But that is a subject of its own.

HARRY WHITE: How about that? What do the rest of you think?

JOE: I agree with Ruth. It's just the result of other things we do.

JIM: I don't. I think we should leave it on the new list, call it "Work production," and add another to the list called "Work scheduling."

BILL: Now, wait a minute; those last two are part of the same thing. Why split it up?

JIM: I can think of a lot of things about work production which have nothing to do with scheduling the work.

MARY: That's right. (*Several others agree.*)

HARRY WHITE: How about it? Will you allow me to put them both down now? We can change it later if we can't set standards for them. (*All agree verbally. He writes them both down on the new list.*)

That crosses number two "Get work out," off the old list. (*He does so.*)

BOB: Doesn't number four, "Enforce production standards," get included in our new number two, "Work production"?

HARRY WHITE: What do the rest of you think? (*There seems to be general agreement.*) I'm not certain myself but that number four on the old list, "Enforce production standards," won't stand on its own importance and perhaps should be listed separately. But I'll go along for now with the group and cross it off. (*He does so.*) We can always reinstate it if, when we set a standard for your performance in work production, it appears to be important enough to set one for that portion alone.

MARY: I think we should cross off number five, "Reduce scrap." It's part of work production.

HARRY WHITE: That's right, and here we are trying to make a list of what we do as managers. Some of these things are obviously things we do as we get work production. I would agree with Jim that we shouldn't have too many things under our new number two, "Work production."

BILL: In that case, then, where would you put number three on the old list? I think that is a silly one. It sounds like a schoolteacher habit.

MARY: I can't agree with you. If you are lax on punctuality, you are in trouble. Morale falls; so does production.

RUTH: That's right. If I didn't enforce punctuality and discourage tardiness, I'd be in trouble.

BILL: See what I mean?—tardiness, just like in school.

MARY: No, it's not, or rather yes, it is. Most of my girls are fresh out of school and need that kind of continued enforcement.

RUTH: Exactly! I think it should be there.

WALT: Well, I've let the ladies say it, but I must confess I agree with them. We all enforce punctuality in some way. Maybe we use different words, but still we see to it that it is accomplished. None of us can afford an employee who is continually late. Most of us do something about it. I think it should be on the list. (*General agreement sounded by all.*)

HARRY WHITE: OK, here it goes. (*Writes after number 4*) Enforce punctuality. Now we can cross it off the old one. There seemed to be agreement that the old number five, "Reduce scrap," should go on the new list. No objections? OK, then, on it goes, and we'll cross it off the old one.

Now for number six, "Improve personal relationships." What about that?

JIM: I've been thinking about that and about number nine, too, "Improve employee morale." I think they are the same thing.

VINCE: That's right, but they bother me.

RUTH: Well, they are *very* important, and I think they should be included.

HARRY WHITE: How do you improve employee morale, Ruth?

RUTH: Well, it's done in a lot of little ways: the way you treat the employees, for one; the way you enforce rules fairly—oh, a lot of things! (*Harry White makes mental note to add "Enforce rules" to old list.*)

TOM: It seems to me that this could be a little like the "work production" discussion we had, only maybe a little more so. I believe that employee morale is just as Ruth says, the product or result of a lot of other things we do.

HARRY WHITE: How do you mean?

TOM: Well, employees have a better attitude when they know they are being fairly dealt with.

JIM: That's right, they do; I've had that experience myself, too. I think actually that our own morale may improve through what we are doing here ourselves in this meeting. I've never heard from Harry before just what he expected me to be doing. Now I'm beginning to see, and, frankly, I like it. I think my own morale is improving as a result of it.

HARRY WHITE: In that case, then, if we all agree, these two items would not be included since they are definitely the result of other things. Right? (*All agree. He crosses numbers 6 and 9 off the old list.*) Now, the next item to discuss is number seven. How about . . . [and the discussion goes on until the list is completed.]

The new list as agreed to by the use of steps 2 and 3 as far as they had gone is as follows:

Major segments of a first-line manager's performance are:

1. Contacts with employees
2. Work production
3. Work scheduling
4. Enforce punctuality
5. Reduce scrap
6.
7.

It should be apparent at this stage of the meeting that all those taking part are learning new things about their job; but more important, they are learning without being told directly more about how their boss feels about what they should be doing. Also, it is becoming very clear to the boss that he has work to do with certain of his subordinates to get better performance from them. In short, this type of management meeting is management in action and is one of the best developmental tools available for accomplishing the task.

You will also note that some of the wording on both the first and even the second list may not seem as appropriate or literary as finished lists perhaps should be. It should be realized, however, that this list was worded by the people themselves and that they understood it, which is the important thing.

The three-step technique, while applied only to the preparation of performance descriptions in this part of the book, will be seen to be useful in the preparation of statements of responsibility and authority (Part Three) and managerial performance standards (Part Four).

CHAPTER NINE

Uses and Benefits of Performance Descriptions

HUNDREDS OF MANAGEMENT PEOPLE who have been through the three steps described in the previous chapters have told me that they had never before seriously discussed the managerial aspects of their subordinates' jobs with the subordinates themselves. And this was true in the face of the fact that some of them already had job descriptions for both their own jobs and those of their subordinates and were recommending raises or withholding the recommendations according to whether or not they believed their subordinates were performing as they should.

Many of them admitted that they had discussed the "what's" of the management job with their subordinates only when some unfortunate incident occurred or when results fell far short of what they expected. In other words, a subordinate learned what he really should be doing only after the boss discovered he had neglected to do it.

Frequently a boss feels a certain hesitation about employing the technique advocated here simply because he has never done it before, and if he has been in charge of a group for, say, five or ten years, he may worry that his subordinates will say (or, more likely, simply think): "Well, if this or that segment of the job is so important, how come it hasn't been stressed these many years?"

In this, the subordinates are right, but the fact that the boss has been somewhat derelict in his duty for a long time does not justify his continuing to be. He can admit frankly that he should have stressed certain segments of performance in the past, but make it plain that this state of affairs is not going to continue, that he is not going to let it continue.

There will not be immediate 100 percent acceptance of his change in attitude, but at least a start will have been made. If the boss really wants to help his subordinates to improve their performance, he must run the risk that his past omissions will be considered a weakness on his part. The benefits are worth it.

One of the most important of these benefits is that every one of the subordinates usually starts to improve his performance immediately—sometimes within minutes of leaving the meeting. From the original listing and the discussion of the items, each member of the group learns that there is something he should be doing which he has not been doing, or has not been doing often enough. For example:

A department head had just been through a meeting in which the group had agreed that it was important to plan ways of meeting manpower needs well in advance. As a result, he phoned his boss to say that he wondered whether the boss might not like to know that there had been two resignations in his department which would affect his requirements for the next year. Normally, he would have said nothing to his boss, merely put a request for replacements through at the end of the year. It developed that his boss knew of a projected cutback in another department that would cause a small excess of manpower, and it didn't take much effort on his part to steer the department head onto the idea of using two of the people who would be available. Had the department head neglected to inform the boss of the resignations, the company would have lost two good men, and it would have been necessary to expend extra supervisory time in training new employees.

Many other examples could be cited of the way people immediately start doing things that they have not been doing before, taking the kind of action that is an important and inherent part of their managerial jobs. Thus the mere preparation of a list of major segments of managerial performance—the "what's" of the managerial job—produces improvement, even before any standards of performance have been set.

THE MULTIPLIER EFFECT

Furthermore, each improvement is likely to have a "multiplier" effect. This can be illustrated by the chart on page 48, which shows four levels of management: Each of the first-line supervisors (the A's) reports to one of the B's, each of the B's reports to one of the C's, and the C's in turn report to D, who is the top man in the organizational unit.

It is immaterial whether this chart represents a whole company—in which case D would be the company president—or only a section of a company. D might be a division manager, or even a department head if the company is one in which there are fairly long chains of command. The point to remember is that the chart shows an organizational unit with four levels of management beginning with the first-line supervisors.

The way in which the multiplier effect works is this: When an A becomes a better manager, it is safe to assume that he will get an improvement in the performance of those under him, who are the people who are actually doing the work, rank-and-file clerical or production workers. Perhaps one may say that although some people (a few of them) *may* improve their performance in spite of their boss, a whole group seldom improves until the boss improves his performance. Improvement of the performance of a rank-and-file group is, of course, good in itself, and since the national average of ten subordinates varies little from year to year, we may say that ten people are performing better as a result of the meetings.

However, if a B improves his performance, the performance of ten A's who report to him will also improve, which means that a multiplier of ten is applied to the performance of the rank and file. When a second-line manager becomes a better performer, that is, 100 members of the rank and file show varying degrees of improvement.

The multiplying effect is even more important when an improvement occurs in the performance of a third-line supervisor—the C on the chart. Then improvement is achieved by $10 \times 10 \times 10$ people—1,000 in all. It should be needless to point out that the change can be evident throughout an entire organization when even higher levels of management improve their performance.

Electrical utilities have a term "line loss" to indicate that a certain amount of power is lost in transmission and cannot be billed to the customer. In all businesses there is a managerial "line loss" also, and the longer the chain of command, the greater it is likely to be unless there is good communication up and down the line. Even where there are only three or four levels, the line loss may be quite large, for as the top man's objectives and ideas are transmitted down through the chain, something is lost at each level. The middle levels of management, in fact, sometimes act as perfect insulators, so perfect that nothing at all gets through.

This insulating effect, which exists at every level to some extent, can be minimized only when each boss works with his own subordinates to ensure that they understand what they are supposed to do, and in addition, takes a very real interest in whether they do it or not. One of the benefits of the technique described here is that it cuts down the managerial line loss appreciably.

Still another benefit accrues, one that should go far to convince those who feel that they cannot waste their valuable time in meetings of this kind. That is, the technique eventually saves the boss much more time than he actually spends on it. In fact, a two-hour meeting devoted to the preparation of a list of the "what's" of his subordinate's job gives more value for the time spent than almost any other type of meeting. (It is seldom necessary for the meeting to last more than two hours.)

In addition to the fact that the subordinates gain a better knowledge of what is expected of them, the boss himself familiarizes himself with the content of their jobs. He acquires first-hand knowledge of what they should be doing and no longer needs to spend time referring to checklists or papers when he wants to determine whether a subordinate is doing everything he should be doing—he has discussed the matter so thoroughly that he has the knowledge in his head.

USES OF
PERFORMANCE DESCRIPTIONS

One of the principal uses of performance descriptions is, of course, in setting standards of performance, for it is necessary to know what a person is supposed to do in order to determine the level of performance he is expected to reach.

The performance descriptions are also useful to the manager in appraising his subordinates, for one cannot appraise performance without knowing what that performance should consist of. (And it is unfair to appraise performance on any segment of a job unless the boss has made it plain that the segment is definitely something the subordinate should be doing and that he and the boss understand it to mean the same thing.)

The descriptions may also be used in training new managers and in continuing training of those already on the job as they discuss various aspects of their work with their superior.

How do you acquaint a newly appointed manager with what he is supposed to do? Where there is an adequate induction procedure in use, there are no problems, for the performance description and the standards set for the various segments of the job are discussed with him, along with all the other facts he will need to know. And the procedure is adequate only if most of the discussion is with the immediate superior, not with a staff man. What the new manager wants to know, above all, is what his boss expects.

In many cases, however, there is no planned induction procedure, and the performance descriptions will be useful to the new manager only if the boss goes over them with him in detail. To hand him a typed list is of little value (although he should, of course, be given one to refer to later) for he has not taken part in the discussions and may not understand.

Only by man-boss discussion can a real understanding of them be attained. Without it, the performance description is of no more use to the new manager than a purchased job description—in other words, it is worthless.

Then, as the new manager works into his job, the boss can use the performance description to provide further training—referring to it as various problems arise.

In the case of the managers who took part in the original discussion, further training occurs as the major segments of the job are discussed for the purpose of setting standards for them, and again when the boss discusses the results of his appraisals with them.

PART THREE

Responsibilities and Authorities of the Manager

CHAPTER TEN

Introduction

THE AVERAGE JOB DESCRIPTION, whether drawn up within the company itself or borrowed from outside, generally purports to set forth the responsibilities (or duties) of the job and the extent of the authority delegated to the incumbent. Then why did so many of the management people to whom I posed the question: "What do you want to know about your jobs that you do not know now?" answer that they wanted more definite knowledge of the extent of their responsibilities and authority? Many of them came from companies that had a job description for everyone, from the president on down.

The answer is that most job descriptions are pretty indefinite, particularly in the area of authority. For example, the financial executive whose job description was given on pages 40 and 41 is "responsible" for the formulation of financial policies and "for seeing that they are carried out." But what does he do when some executive on his own level acts contrary to the policy? Can he call him to account? Or must he tell the president and have the latter handle the matter? The description does not say. Again, he is "responsible" for supervision of the controller and the treasurer, but what does "supervision" mean in this case—specifically, can he fire either man without higher authority? Can he give either one a raise without checking with the president?

Generally, too, a company has a set of written rules covering various aspects of behavior. It also has vacation policies, promotion policies, salary administration policies, and so on, often incorporated in manuals along with various interpretations and explanations.

But many managers are uncertain about how far they should go in enforcing the rules. Must they always insist on fifteen-minute coffee breaks? What about punctuality when the day starts? Is an occasional lateness the occasion for a serious talk with the offender? Or how often must a person be late before the offense is considered serious? Does the fact that the tardy subordinate has worked overtime the night before mitigate or excuse the tardiness in the morning, particularly if he is an exempt employee and does not get paid for overtime? When is it advisable to allow exceptions to policies governing leaves of absence? When the inspectors and the production foremen disagree about items to be rejected, whom should he support and on what basis? If no candidates appear for a job advertised at the regular rate, how does the manager fill it?

WHY MANAGERS ARE PUZZLED

There are several reasons why managers are puzzled about questions like these—and a great many others related to the extent of their authority and responsibility. One reason may be that there are so many rules, and so many different applications of them, that it is impossible to remember them all. It could also be that the rules are expressed in such stilted and legalistic language that they are not clear. Another reason why managers are often uncertain about their authority for enforcing rules is that their own superiors may be negligent in this respect—in fact, prefer to overlook certain infractions, or infractions by certain people—and if the subordinate manager attempts to go by the book he finds himself overruled.

The higher manager often has very valid reasons for disregarding some of the rules under certain circumstances, reasons that have nothing to do with favoritism or the whim of the moment. But every time he does so, the subordinate managers become more inclined to look the other way when the same rule is transgressed another time, or to duck action and let the superior make the decision himself.

Another reason why many managers have difficulty in this respect is that the rules are often written by staff people, who have never been in the position of having to enforce them. If line management is consulted at all, generally only the managers at the very top are given a chance to express opinions; sometimes only the very top man is consulted. The views of the first-line supervisor or the middle-management man who knows current conditions and understands what is feasible and what is not are seldom solicited. Also, little attention is given to overhauling the rules and weeding out those that may become obsolete; only in rare cases is a rule ever repealed once it has been instituted, even though no one ever enforces it.

It is significant that in certain industries, labor unions that find it inconvenient to strike can bring pressure on management simply by having their members "go by the book," that is, observe all the rules all the time. If going by the book produces an intolerable slowdown, one wonders why the book is never revised to reflect current conditions. Why doesn't it contain only the rules management wants enforced?

COSTS OF DISCREPANCIES

Possibly the discrepancies between the written rules and the rules the managers are willing to enforce arise because the managers have not participated in the formulation of the regulations. In addition, their superiors have never discussed the interpretation of the rules with them.

Labor specialists report that a great many grievances arise because different managers interpret the rules differently. When this occurs it is very easy to charge unfairness, discrimination, or partiality, and most unions can be counted on to do so. Complaint boards, grievance juries, and even arbitrators often find that they cannot uphold penalties for clear violation of the rules because so many precedents for the violation exist.

Moreover, the cost of inconsistent enforcement is large. An expensive work stoppage may be triggered by nothing more than a single instance of it. And even if the matter is settled peaceably, there is the cost of executive time spent in meetings as the case moves up through the various steps in the grievance procedure. Eventually there may be the cost of preparing a case for the arbitration proceedings and arguing it out.

There is also the incalculable cost of lost goodwill. If management backs up the supervisor even if he is wrong (and he may very well be if his boss has never discussed the rules with him), the aggrieved employee and his friends become convinced that the company itself is committed to unfairness whenever there is an advantage to be gained from it. If, on the other hand, the supervisor is overruled by a higher manager, *his* morale is damaged. From his point of view, he was trying to do his best for the company and instead of being rewarded he was punished by a loss of face.

The managers who said that they needed to know how far they were expected to go in enforcing the company's rules and regulations were waving a clear danger signal in the face of their complacent superiors.

There is no substitute for free, open man-boss discussion of these matters. The printed word alone is never enough. When the boss and his subordinates talk over the matter with frankness on both sides, the boss becomes much more aware of how far he can expect his subordinates to go in enforcing the rules. And when he and they have discussed the rule itself and the necessity for it, he knows that they understand it and will be more unbiased in enforcing it. However, unless the boss leads a discussion in which everyone has an opportunity to express his viewpoint, there will be little benefit. If he simply lays down the law, the subordinates will leave the meeting thinking: "It's all very well for him to talk, he isn't up against the things I'm up against," or words to that effect.

Any manager on the second level or higher can determine for himself whether or not his subordinates understand how far they are expected to go in enforcing the rules, simply by asking himself: "Have I ever discussed the matter with them?" If the answer is no, he can assume that they are uncertain.

Taking a subordinate to task when he has made a mistake in enforcing or not enforcing a rule does not count as "discussion." The subordinate does not, under these circumstances, gain any knowledge that will help him in the future. He has been put in the wrong despite his good intentions, which makes him feel that the best thing he can do is keep quiet and allow the storm to blow over. Thus he is unlikely to ask any questions that will clarify his understanding. He learns that he was wrong in the way he handled one special situation, but he cannot generalize from that situation to guidelines that will help him in the future.

An illustration may be drawn from municipal affairs. An incident occurred in which the police were prevented—either by their own superiors or by members of the civilian administration (where the orders originated is a matter of dispute)—from arresting people who were committing what the rules designated as crimes. This prompted a demand for "guidelines" from their association, for not only the rank and file of the police but many of their officers were completely confused by what had occurred.

In industry, first-line supervisors and managers at higher levels seldom have an organization to speak for them under circumstances like these; therefore their superiors cannot expect them to take the initiative and ask for guidelines. They are naturally afraid to speak up individually for fear of being considered critical of their boss and damaging their prospects for raises and promotions.

THE RESPONSIBILITY
OF THE BOSS

Thus the boss himself must take the initiative and ensure that his subordinates gain the understanding they need to manage effectively. If he doesn't, he is accepting his pay under false pretenses; he is being paid for doing a complete job and he is not doing one.

But suppose the boss himself is uncertain about how far he is expected to go—he is only a second- or third-line manager, and there are quite a few levels above him who may step in and overrule him. Perhaps when he first came on the job, he resolved to be a better manager than his predecessor and started to enforce the rules to the letter; then awrk-k!—just like that he caught it in the neck. It didn't take him long to realize that he would have callouses all around his neck if he continued on that collision course. What did he do? Like a good turtle, he pulled his head back into his shell, and now he only peeks out cautiously when he thinks it is safe.

If this is your situation, it is an unfortunate one; but if you are a manager, it does not excuse your putting your own subordinates in the same position. What they want to know is how far *you* expect them to go, and they can't get the information from anyone else—no one else knows. None of the written rules explains how far *you* expect them to go. They need to know which of the rules is important to you and what type of violation you will close your eyes to. They know from experience that you have closed your eyes to some infringements of the rules in the past, but unless you have made the exact extent of their authority clear to them, they still aren't happy about it, and they're still confused.

To repeat: *The knowledge they need must come from you. They can't get it from books, and they can't be expected to work it out for themselves.*

Further, you shouldn't put the discussion off. You may say to yourself: "No, I guess I haven't been doing what I should, and as soon as I get a chance, by George I'll really do something about it." But because the big pile of work on your desk never gets smaller, you revert to putting out fires and providing crisis supervision, much of which is needed simply because you haven't held the discussions. Once the managers under you really know how you expect them to operate, there will be far fewer crises for you to handle.

DEGREES OF AUTHORITY

No general rule can be laid down here about how much authority a manager at any given level *should* have, for the degree of authority and responsibility attached to any position varies widely among companies. But the *type* of information that should be available may be illustrated.

For example, a manager needs to know exactly how much time off he is empowered to grant without checking with higher authority—a half day, a whole day, a week, a month? An A in the chart in Chapter 6—that is, a first-line supervisor—may be given authority to grant time off for half a day, but if an employee wants more time it may be necessary for A to check with B, and if the time requested is as much as a week, B may have to get C's consent. This is the case in many companies, but in others even first-line supervisors have authority to grant time off for considerable periods. By the same token, one could examine company practice on almost any phase of the management job and find no general rule prevailing in industry.

These areas of authority may be merely implied in company manuals, or they may be spelled out exactly. Yet many managers still tend to use less authority than the written rules grant them because they are afraid that their bosses will disagree with their decisions in specific cases. Thus they tend to administer the rules either as rigidly as possible or as loosely as possible rather than discuss things with their boss. Because he has never sought their opinions, they are reluctant to approach him. They think he doesn't want to be bothered with these problems.

Again, a manager may have the authority to fire or discipline a subordinate for "gross insubordination," but how is he to know what his boss considers "gross insubordination"? It can consist of anything from a sneering look to knocking the supervisor's teeth in, and the lower manager's understanding of it will coincide with that of his boss only if they have discussed the matter face to face.

For management people who like a label for each bit of paper work they use, the document that is produced by free discussion of the rules by the superior and his subordinates may be called a "statement of responsibilities and authorities." It differs from the usual job description, which in many cases also lists responsibilities and authorities, in that it is not purchased from a consultant, filched from another company, or developed by staff personnel. It is hammered out by the line people who will operate under it and have discussed it freely with their superior, the man they have to please. To an outsider, it may seem not so well worded, or even not so clear as some of the descriptions prepared by consultants or staff men. But since the boss and his subordinates have produced it themselves, they have a common understanding of it, and that is what really matters.

The technique of preparing such a statement of responsibilities and authorities is the same as that used in preparing the performance descriptions, the three-step method described in Part Two of this book. Like the preparation of the performance descriptions, it requires only one or two 2-hour sessions, and the return for the time spent is greater than the return on almost any other type of management training.

In this type of activity, as in determining the "what's" of the job, the use of a coach is of immeasurable value to the person conducting the meetings for the preparation of statements of responsibilities and authorities. This coach can do much to make it easier for the leader. As mentioned earlier, the concept of the coaching role is discussed at greater length in Chapter Twenty-nine.

CHAPTER ELEVEN

Approaches

IN DETERMINING DEGREES of responsibility and authority, as in the case of preparation of the performance descriptions described in Part Two, either the individual or the group approach may be used, and the three-step technique is just as important in both cases as it is in developing the major segments of the job.

But here it is even more important to use the face-to-face boss-subordinate discussion than it is in preparing the performance descriptions, for there are many possible degrees of responsibility and authority, and hence much more possibility of confusion.

A boss who has become proficient in leading meetings concerned with the "what's" of the job will find this meeting fairly easy to conduct. However, here he will have to inject his own ideas to a greater extent, and state them in such a way that the subordinates will accept them and make them their own.

"Consultative supervision," as it is often practiced, has been criticized as "manipulation"—that is, it is said that what it amounts to is using psychological tricks to make subordinates accept what is really autocratic rule. But this criticism does not apply here. True, the boss does want to get subordinates to arrive at the same position regarding the rules he himself has taken, but he does so by frank explanations. Also, they *want* to find out what he himself thinks and why. They want to know what he is willing to delegate to them; regardless of what the rule book says, this is the point that is really important to them.

But again the boss does not simply lay down the law. He should be willing to modify his position if he finds that the extent of the authority he has accorded to them is insufficient for them to meet their responsibilities. If he encourages free discussion, he may learn a great deal about his own inconsistency in this respect.

Can the head of an organizational unit conduct such a meeting if he himself is uncertain just what the scope of his own authority is? He can, for at least he knows what *he* wants his subordinates to do. But, of course, the best results are achieved only when the practice begins at the top.

The multiplier effect often operates in reverse in this area. The top manager has never tried to think through just what rules and regulations there should be and how strictly they should be enforced. Consequently his treatment of his immediate subordinates is inconsistent, and they themselves are uncertain about what they should do and their uncertainty is reflected in the group under them, and so on down the line.

GROUP APPROACH

As in the case of the performance descriptions, the group approach is generally superior to the individual approach where there are several managers whose jobs are substantially the same. In the first place, there will be more minds brought to bear on the subject, which often means that more ideas are generated. Also, more specific cases in which clarification is needed will be brought up because everyone may not, at any given time, have experienced all the problems that can arise. In the second place, it is more important to ensure that all first-line supervisors in a plant, or all plant managers in a division, practice the same degree of enforcement than it is to ensure consistency between, say, the enforcement of rules in the controller's department and the enforcement in the research department. Because of the nature of the work, in fact, the rules may have to be different. But in each case there should be consistent enforcement.

INDIVIDUAL APPROACH

But just as the individual approach must be used in developing a performance description when the manager is the only one of his kind in the company or the division, it is necessary to use it for the unique jobs in discussions of authorities and responsibilities. There is only one research director, only one chief financial officer, and only one top marketing man. But each of these men is at least a third-line manager—and probably several levels above that if the company is at all large—and when he and his boss have arrived at a common understanding of his authority and responsibility, he can hold group meetings for those on the next level under him, who will in all probability be doing somewhat similar jobs.

In steps 2 and 3, the boss may be called upon to rule on the extent of the authority and responsibility his subordinates should possess because their conclusions go contrary to company policy. But, if his rulings are really commonsense rulings, he can get the group to agree to them by astute questioning rather than by fiat.

On the other hand, company policy may be contrary to common sense in some instances, and if the group can show that this is true, it would be a shortsighted boss who would not bring this fact to the attention of the proper person in higher management and recommend some modification.

How successful he will be in getting the policy modified will depend on the processes used in setting up the regulations in the first place. If the company uses the method described here, beginning with the top man and his immediate subordinates, it will be fairly easy to pass the recommendation up the line and obtain the modification. On the other hand, if the rules and regulations were drawn up by some staff group and then issued to the line by a top executive who believes that he can depend entirely on his "experts," getting a change will be more difficult. Each executive will have to decide what to do in this case, in the light of his own knowledge of the company.

It should be pointed out, however, that a rule should not necessarily be changed simply because a number of the people charged with responsibility for enforcing it do not like it. There may be very good administrative reasons for keeping it on the books, and if the boss knows these reasons or can find them out, he should pass on the explanation to his subordinates.

PHYSICAL REQUIREMENTS

The physical requirements for the meetings are the same as those required for the preparation of performance descriptions: a quiet room large enough to enable everyone to be reasonably comfortable, freedom from interruptions, the paperboard, and the space on the wall for posting the sheets of paper as they are filled.

The boss will probably do more talking himself in these sessions than he did in the performance-description sessions, and thus will spend more time on his feet. But he should not neglect to provide himself with the stool so that he can sit down when items are being discussed from the floor. Otherwise, he may get too tired and be tempted to cut short the discussion by saying, in effect, "This is the way it is going to be" before he has heard everyone's ideas.

Chapters Twelve and Thirteen describe the use of the three-step procedure in bringing about understanding of authorities and responsibilities.

CHAPTER TWELVE

Preparing Statements of Areas of Responsibility

PREPARATION OF STATEMENTS of responsibility and authority falls into two parts: (1) determination of the areas of managerial responsibility and (2) establishment of the degree of authority needed in each area.

In the latter case another important area needs to be clarified: the method used in exercising authority. It is especially important that members of the group learn what sanctions they can apply for infractions of the various rules and how far their boss is prepared to go in backing them up when they do apply the sanctions.

In this chapter, only the identification of the areas of responsibility will be considered. As in the determination of major segments of performance, the three-step method is used. In the first step, the boss writes down each item suggested by members of the group until an appropriate list has been developed. In steps 2 and 3, the group discusses each item in turn and arrives at agreement on the list.

STARTING THE MEETING

If the boss has not used the technique earlier for preparation of the performance descriptions or for development of standards of performance (which will be discussed in Part Four), he must start the meeting in the way that comes most naturally to him. He must word his opening remarks himself, and tell the group what he is really trying to do. As in other instances, the three-step technique will not work unless the boss himself believes in it and is convinced that it will help him to achieve better results.

Opening the Meeting

As an illustration, let's assume that the boss is a second-line manager who has called a meeting of the first-line supervisors under him to discuss their responsibilities and authorities. Then he might say something like this:

> This meeting has been called to discuss some of the things we talked about a few weeks ago when we were determining the major segments of performance of a supervisor's job. You may recall that responsibilities kept getting into the discussion. Today I would like to confine our investigation to just that phase of our job, our responsibilities and the authority we have to discharge them.
>
> I want you all to understand this meeting has been called so that each of us can benefit from the experience of the others. We're not going to criticize anyone; we just want to determine exactly what a first-line supervisor is responsible for and how much authority he has to carry out each responsibility.

It will probably be necessary also for the boss to explain just what he means by a "responsibility" and how it differs from a segment of performance. (As mentioned, the segments of performance are the things the manager does himself; on the other hand, he is *responsible* not only for these things but for the work he delegates to others.) This may take a bit of thinking on his part, for he may not be too certain of the distinction himself. He can perhaps illustrate it by examples, such as:

> Training new employees to perform a specific operation is something a supervisor *does,* a segment of performance. Ensuring that employees are properly trained is one of his *responsibilities.*
>
> Being aware of current pay practices is a responsibility, but actually going through the steps to determine whether or not to recommend a raise for an employee is a segment of performance.

Then he can say something like this, writing as he does so, "I'm going to start the paperboard with this heading: The supervisors are responsible for, colon, number one, period."

Despite the explanation of the difference between segments of performance and responsibilities, undoubtedly there will still be some confusion. But even if some of the items suggested are not responsibilities, the boss writes each one suggested, numbering them in sequence and posting each filled sheet on the wall where it will be visible to all.

The boss need have no hesitation about writing down items that he suspects cannot be classified as responsibilities, for the clarification will come later in the discussion that takes place in steps 2 and 3. This first list, like the first list of major segments of performance, is compiled merely to provide a basis for discussion. But it will probably (though not necessarily) be shorter than the list of segments, for several performance steps may be necessary in order to meet one of the responsibilities.

When the list seems long enough to furnish a good basis for discussion, the boss starts a new sheet and says that they will now use the same headings, but that this time they will read and discuss each item on the first list. Step 2, the discussion, leads naturally into step 3, getting understanding and agreement on the second, and more accurate, list.

The discussion continues until each item is either accepted and written on the new list, rejected entirely, or modified in some way, perhaps combined with one or more of the other items. The second list should produce a list of responsibilities that the entire group understands and accepts, one written by and for the group. Moreover, the understanding should include the exact degree of authority the managers have in each case.

A TYPICAL SESSION

To illustrate the use of step 1 of the technique, part of a tape recording of a session will be used. In this case, the production vice-president of an aircraft manufacturing company in the West was conducting a meeting for his department heads. The vice-president, who will be called Robert Allen, is a third-line manager, and his department heads, therefore, are second-line managers whose immediate subordinates are first-line supervisors.

> MR. ALLEN: I'm going to head this sheet (*he writes at the top of the sheet*) Department heads have responsibilities for, colon, number one, period. (*He places the numeral 1 under the heading. Turning back to the group he asks*) What are the things for which you are responsible as a manager?
>
> VAZQUEZ: I feel I'm responsible for a lot of things, everything that my

supervisors need to know. I want them to get all of their management information from me.

MR. ALLEN: Fine, that is probably a good attitude to have, but what specifically is one of the things you are responsible for?

VAZQUEZ: Well, umm—now look, I'm not sure I understand just what you mean.

MR. ALLEN: Let's look at it this way. What do I hold you responsible for?

VAZQUEZ: That's easy—getting all of the assigned work out of the department.

MR. ALLEN: (*Writing after the number 1*) Getting the work out.

VAZQUEZ: That's right, but I think there is a lot more to it than that.

MR. ALLEN: You could be right. Now, anyone, what else are you responsible for as a manager?

DUPREE: I think this business of getting the work out is too broad. I'd suggest something like "Maintain quality and quantity as assigned."

MR. ALLEN: (*Writing after the number 2*) Maintain quality and quantity. What other things are there?

VAZQUEZ: That's what I meant, but there is still more to it than that. I think . . .

MR. ALLEN: (*Interrupting*) Gentlemen, I'm merely trying to make a list of the things you fellows feel you are responsible for. The discussion of their scope, degree, and worth will come after we get a list to work with. Can we delay our comments on them until we have all had a chance to get our ideas into the kitty—so to speak?

SEVERAL: OK.

MR. ALLEN: What other responsibilities do you have? (*Places a 3 on the board.*)

WENTWORTH: I'm responsible for keeping my supervisors informed of personnel policies.

MR. ALLEN: (*Writes after number 3*) Keep subordinates informed of personnel policies.

WENTWORTH: Maybe I should have said "rules and regulations," too.

MR. ALLEN: (*Placing a 4 and writing*) Keep subordinates informed of rules and regulations. What else?

GAGLIANO: I feel strongly about my responsibility in the field of pay practices. I don't know just how to say it.

HARLAND: Why don't you say "Responsible for pay administration"?

MR. ALLEN: (*Writing number 5*) Pay administration. (*Turns back to the group*) What else?

GAGLIANO: Do you mean giving raises as part of that, or does it include telling them how they are doing?

DUPREE: I think interviewing them is something I am responsible for.

MR. ALLEN: (*Writing number 6*) Interviewing subordinates?

DUPREE: Yes.

MR. ALLEN: What else? (*He takes off the sheet and posts it on the wall.*)

DUPREE: I'm also responsible for appraising them.

MR. ALLEN: (*Writing number 7*) Appraising subordinates.

WHITE: I think we all have a responsibility for listening to subordinates' gripes.

MR. ALLEN: (*Writing number 8*) Listening to subordinates' gripes.

HARLAND: Gripes aren't as important as real worthwhile complaints—if they were unionized they'd have "grievances," and believe you me, we'd listen to them!

MR. ALLEN: OK. Let's put that down, too (*Writes number 9*) Listening to subordinates' complaints, and let's put "grievances" in parentheses.

WHITE: This is carrying things too far. I think those last two things, no, three things, are all one and the same. Numbers eight and nine.

MR. ALLEN: Well, as I said earlier, we can discuss the rightness of these items later, but for now we leave it, Ed? OK?

WHITE: OK. It just struck me funny that we seemed to be repeating ourselves.

MR. ALLEN: Fine (*Writes the number 10 next on the sheet*) What other responsibilities do you have? And since we are also interested in authorities you have, why not give me some of those?

EARLEY: I think we should put that we are responsible for training our employees.

MR. ALLEN: (*Writes after number 10*) Training our employees. What else?

EARLEY: Maybe we should break it down—the training, I mean.

MR. ALLEN: We can do that later.

BRANDON: What do you mean by authorities? Isn't that covered in our rule book? I can sign certain papers but not others, and I know what they are. We all know—(*muttering*)—if we can read.

MR. ALLEN: Authorities in management may be something we will have to talk over as we discuss the items on our list later. Do you have any other responsibilities to add? (*He writes the number 11 on the sheet.*)

BRANDON: Well, I'm not certain for sure about authority, but it seems to me that I have authority to discipline my subordinates, and for that matter, to approve the discipline exercised by my supervisors.

MR. ALLEN: (*Writes after number 11*) Authority for disciplining subordinates. (*Then he removes the sheet for posting and writes the number 12 on a new sheet.*)

WENTWORTH: I don't like the word "discipline." It smacks of school days—we are all responsible people who . . .

MR. ALLEN: (*Interrupting*) Will you hold it, Bill, so we can discuss that later? Do you have anything else to submit for our list?

WENTWORTH: Yes, I do. I feel I'm responsible for taking action when the rules are broken—or I could say I have the authority to take action when rules are broken.

MR. ALLEN: Let's put the responsibility first for number twelve. (*Writing as he talks*) Responsibility for taking action when rules are broken. (*Writes the number 13*)

GAGLIANO: But I don't see . . .

MR. ALLEN: Let's get the other part down first. (*Writes after number 13*) Authority to take action when rules are broken.

GAGLIANO: But aren't those last two the same as number eleven—in one sense at least?

The desire to discuss the items that is evident at this point can cause the boss to decide that the time has come to move on to step 2. Or, if he thinks the list is too incomplete at this point, he can keep on stifling discussion and ask for more items to add to the list. To continue the illustration, however, we will let the tape recording show what Mr. Allen actually did.

MR. ALLEN: Since we do seem to be getting some apparent duplication and some of us are concerned, let's stop making the list and get into the discussion. We can add more items as they come out in the discussion as we go along. I'm certain you all feel that there are more than just these thirteen items of responsibilities and authorities for you. (*He removes the third sheet and posts it next to the other two, immediately going back to the paperboard to write the heading at the top.*)

The first list, at this point, looks as follows:

1. Getting the work out
2. Maintain quality and quantity
3. Keep subordinates informed of personnel policies
4. Keep subordinates informed of rules and regulations
5. Pay administration
6. Interviewing subordinates
7. Appraising subordinates
8. Listening to subordinates' gripes

9. Listening to subordinates' complaints (grievances)
10. Training our employees
11. Authority for disciplining subordinates
12. Responsibility for taking action when rules are broken
13. Authority to take action when rules are broken

Item 14 was added later during the subsequent discussion:

14. Getting proper tools and equipment

MR. ALLEN: (*Continuing*) I wonder how you would feel if we rephrased the heading to read (*and he writes*): Department heads have the authority to discharge the following responsibilities, colon, number one, period. (*He places the numeral 1 immediately below and at left of heading.*)

BRANDON: There, that makes sense to me now. Why didn't you say it that way in the first place?

MR. ALLEN: Frankly, I wasn't certain about it myself—but I agree, this seems to be reasonable, as you say. How do the rest of you feel about it?

EARLEY: It makes sense to me, too—now.

GAGLIANO: Me, too. (*Others voice their agreement.*)

MR. ALLEN: OK, then. Now let's look at the first item, number one on the list we have posted here. You are responsible for (*reading*) "Getting the work out." Is that really true?

VAZQUEZ: Since I suggested it, I'd like to take a crack at your question. As I see it, I am responsible—and I think I have the authority to do it—for assigning all work which comes to me to be done. That's in addition, of course, to the work the various sections of my department are already doing, so I do assign each new job to the department best equipped to do it.

HARLAND: Yes, but when you assign it, as you say, you are *doing* something—then it becomes a major segment of performance. What is the difference?

MR. ALLEN: What *is* the difference?

GAGLIANO: Well, isn't it like getting proper equipment? That is what I'm responsible for, seeing to it that my groups have the right machines and tools to do their jobs, routine or new. If I get the tools, I *do* something. If I'm responsible for getting them, it is a responsibility, and within limits I have the authority to get them—order, check, and initiate their use.

HARLAND: Well, maybe, but it seems confusing. just where do you draw the line?

MR. ALLEN: Just a minute, please, before we lose something. Isn't this business of "getting proper equipment" something which should be added to our first list? We didn't mention it before. (*He walks over to the last posted sheet, writes the number 14 beneath the last item, and writes as he says*) Getting proper equipment.

HARLAND: Well, if you do that, I think I see what we are doing here.

BRANDON: Yes, and also I get the distinction between major segments and responsibilities and authorities.

MR. ALLEN: To go back to your point, Raoul, you feel that the assignment of work orders is your responsibility?

VAZQUEZ: Yes, I still think so.

MR. ALLEN: How do the rest of you feel about it?

GAGLIANO: I'd go along with it, though it seems to me it is very closely associated with the getting of equipment. Maybe they should be put together.

EARLEY: As far as that goes, our number two on the list is part and parcel of number one.

DUPREE: How do you mean—how do you maintain quality and quantity?

EARLEY: *How* we maintain it is what we *do*. Being *responsible* for maintaining it is part of our work production.

DUPREE: Yes, but being responsible for it presupposes we do things to accomplish it.

EARLEY: That's right, but what I think we are trying to do here is get a list of things we are responsible for and have authority to do.

DUPREE: In that case, then, it seems to me that number ten "Training our employees," comes in the same ball of wax—it's part of getting the work out.

GAGLIANO: And no one can deny but what we are responsible for training our supervisors.

MR. ALLEN: Is that what we mean in number ten when we say "Training our employees"? Are we really talking, in our case, about training our subordinate supervisors?

GAGLIANO: It must be that, because most of us don't have anyone else but supervisors reporting to us. Yes, that's it.

DUPREE: Then I think we should find some common area of responsibility—with, as you say, the authority to carry it out—which we can use, which will encompass the things which have to do with the same things.

WHITE: Yes, why don't we put all of these things under some heading like "Get the work out"?

BRANDON: I'd be more in favor of something general like "Work production." It seems to me that that would be more, oh—dignified isn't the word—maybe more managerial-sounding.

WHITE: That's OK by me. I like it better, too.

WENTWORTH: I'd go for that, too, and if we do use it we could put "Assigning work" under it.

BRANDON: Yes, and Joe's [*Gagliano's*] "Providing tools and machines" could go there.

WHITE: Sure, and training supervisors for new product manufacturing, too.

MR. ALLEN: Whoa—let's slow down until I can get some of these ideas written. Now first, some of you seem to feel that we should use a heading, sort of an umbrella heading, for all of those responsibilities we have which pertain specifically to getting the work out.

WENTWORTH: You know, when you come right down to it, everything we are responsible for has to do with work production in the last analysis.

WHITE: That's true, but we also could say we are just responsible for that, but when you come right down to it, it seems to me that what we are trying to do here is to break the different things we are responsible for—and have authority to do—into smaller bites, so we can see how we can do our job better. Right, fellows?

SEVERAL: That's right. Yes. Sure. [Etc.]

MR. ALLEN: Fine. Now then, how do the rest of you feel about this umbrella term, "Work production," which Harvey [*Brandon*] suggests?

SEVERAL: OK. Suits me. Fine with me. [Etc.]

MR. ALLEN: So, we will put "Work production" up here for the new number one. (*He does so; then, putting small "a," "b," "c," etc., in an indented row underneath "Work production," he turns back to the group.*) What will we put for these subheads?

WHITE: I'd suggest that for "a" we put "Assigns work."

MR. ALLEN: Any disagreement? (*There being none, he writes "Assigns work" after subhead "a."*) What else?

GAGLIANO: You can put my "obtaining proper tools and equipment" under "Work production," though I don't know whether it should be second or third or where.

MR. ALLEN: For now, if everyone agrees it should be there, let's put it after "b." OK?

(*General assent. Writes "Obtains proper tools and equipment" after "b."*) Where does "Improving our equipment" come in?

GAGLIANO: That's another thing that should be there. I think it could be "c."

MR. ALLEN: Shall I put that up there? (*Upon general assent he writes after "c" "Improving equipment."*)

WENTWORTH: Talking about improving equipment, what about improving methods?

WHITE: That's right. That should be in there.

MR. ALLEN: What do you think?

WHITE: I think it could be added to "c"—"Improving equipment *and* methods."

MR. ALLEN: Shall I add it to "c"? (*Upon agreement, he adds "and methods" to "c."*) Now what else?

HARLAND: I think number two from the first list should be included under the new number one.

VAZQUEZ: That's right—maybe it should be the next item right under "a."

MR. ALLEN: How do the rest of you feel? Should this be included here? (*General assent. Allen writes "Maintaining quality and quantity standards" after "d."*) We'll put it after "d" for now.

The paper work of the second list looks like this:

1. Work production
   a. Assigns work
   b. Obtains proper tools and equipment
   c. Improving equipment and methods
   d. Maintaining quality and quantity standards

By now the reader can see the type of meeting which often occurs when a boss works with his subordinates to help them determine their statements of responsibilities and authorities. True, only the first part has been worked out. An example of the entire statement, still only partial in respect to all possibilities, could be as follows. It must be realized that such a list as a model for others to use will not accomplish any improvement of managerial performance of lasting value. The only real value in improved performance will come when the boss discusses the subject with his subordinates.

1. Work production
   a. Assigns work
   b. Obtains proper work equipment and sees that it is maintained
   c. Makes improvements in equipment and methods
   d. Meets department standards of quality and quantity of production
   e. Trains employees
   f. Controls cost according to department standards
   g. Makes sure work practices are safe
   h. Schedules vacations
   i. Obtains good housekeeping

2. Authority
   a. Authority to act and inform supervisor afterward
   b. Authority to act without reporting to his supervisor
   c. Authority to recommend action to supervisor and take action after approval
3. Observance of rules
   a. Sees that rules and regulations are observed
   b. Takes appropriate disciplinary action when rules are broken
4. Pay (and related matters)
   a. Approves time reports
   b. Recommends pay changes
   c. Informs employees of pay changes
   d. Assists employees in securing company loans, leaves of absence, and other services when requested
5. Employee records and reports
   a. Supplies all information needed for keeping employee service and pay records up to date
   b. Maintains or has access to employee service and pay records
   c. Maintains records of employees' progress (or lack of it)
   d. Assists in preparation of job descriptions
   e. Prepares reports on accidents, injuries, and other matters as assigned

This list may look somewhat similar to the list of segments of performance given earlier, but this does not matter, for the members of the group understand that it embodies the areas for which they are responsible and the things for which they will be held accountable. Also, it affords an excellent basis for discussion of the exact degree of authority they possess in each instance, which is the subject of the next chapter.

CHAPTER THIRTEEN

Determining Degrees of Authority

GROUP MEMBERS, in the steps described in the last chapter, worked out a list of their responsibilities that they could all agree to and that they all understood. They and their boss arrived at a common understanding of the things they would be held responsible and accountable for.

In management theory, there is a principle that states: "Authority should be commensurate with responsibility," and many superiors believe —or act as though they believe—that the mere statement that a man is responsible for getting certain things done means that he has enough authority to get them done. But, as I have found by questioning several thousand managers at all levels, this is exactly the point on which managers are most uncertain. This chapter will illustrate one way in which a boss can help his subordinates determine how far *they* are expected to go in enforcing the company rules and regulations which apply to them and their subordinates.

The list that is developed in this chapter is merely the list agreed to by one particular group. In effect, it might be said to incorporate the methods of enforcement they and their boss believe they must use if they are to meet their responsibilities, and the methods the boss is willing to agree they must use. If the boss does not believe that he can back them up when they do use these methods, he must tell them so frankly and let them arrive at other conclusions. Another group with a different boss might find it necessary to develop an entirely different list.

Agreement on a list that the boss and the subordinates both understand in the same way can come only from open discussion of the varying experiences and past practices of the different members of the group. A manager may have the authority, theoretically, to discharge one of his subordinates or to discipline members of his group, but what he wants to know is: What penalty does his boss expect him to apply in given cases?

REALISTIC CONCLUSIONS NEEDED

Authority is, of course, never absolute, and for this reason it can never be exactly equal to responsibility. It could be argued that if a first-line foreman is to be responsible for "getting the work out," he needs absolute authority to hire and fire his subordinates, select the materials, decide on the sequence of the work, and so on. But it is impossible to give him so much authority, because the work of his department must mesh with that of other groups, and because there must be reasonable consistency in the enforcement of rules. Even the top man, in fact, never has authority exactly equal to his responsibility, for he must consider such things as public relations, union contract clauses, government regulations, and even the opinions of his subordinates before he decides that a given course of action is not only desirable but feasible.

What the boss is trying to get his subordinates to agree to in a session on the extent of their authority—their authority, say, to enforce a given rule or regulation—is a statement that is realistic in the light of what his own superiors want and what he wants. The discussion should also provide guidance in the wise use of the authority he is willing to delegate to them under the circumstances.

It should go without saying that if the boss wants them to use their authority wisely, he will have to lead the discussion eventually into the manner in which orders are best issued, ways of winning acceptance from subordinates, and related aspects of enforcing rules and regulations. Discussion of these points will come about naturally as members of the group begin to cite specific cases drawn from their own experience.

For example, consider the manager's responsibility for assigning work.

Certain work must be completed by certain dates, or even by certain times of the day; therefore, the manager does not have absolute authority to assign work in any way he sees fit. Most managers will accept these limitations if they understand the reasons for them. But beyond that, they are likely to encounter an employee who balks at an assignment because "that's not my job." What then? If union jurisdictional lines are strictly drawn, a manager has to observe them even if the observance hampers his efforts to get the work out, and sometimes it is unwise to force even a nonunionized employee to do work that he considers beneath him, for one may be sure that if the manager's attitude is: "Do it or else," the work will be done poorly and slowly. But in most cases, the results depend on the wording of the order, and more important, the extent to which an employee understands that it is necessary.

Here it should be pointed out that the list of responsibilities drawn up by a group and revised during the discussion should not be considered sacred. The fact that the group agreed upon it at the time does not necessarily make it so. The items that appear on the list are not the important thing; what is important is what is said in the discussion. The list serves merely as a basis for discussing the authority needed by the managers and realistic ways of using it. When the group begins to determine the degree of authority it possesses in each area of responsibility, a rearrangement or condensation of the list may be appropriate.

As the group begins to flounder through discussion of the items, it may seem as though more confusion than enlightenment is being engendered. When up to this point the managers have been forced to judge what is expected of them in the way of enforcing regulations merely by hints and by observing what others are doing, they *are* confused. Only as they begin to work out what is necessary and feasible in the circumstances and learn what their boss believes is necessary and feasible do they begin to understand what they should do and what they can do with the approval of their boss.

Perhaps the only way to show how this is accomplished is through another illustration, a portion of the taped session in which Robert Allen, the production vice-president, and his department managers discussed enforcing coffee-break regulations.

Coffee breaks may seem like a trivial matter, but enforcing the regulations regarding them is often one of the most difficult disciplinary problems managers have to face. Precisely because an extra five minutes on the coffee break seems on the face of it too trivial an infraction to notice, the violations have gotten out of hand in many companies. And if one affects not to notice the extra five minutes, it soon stretches to an extra ten minutes, then to fifteen more minutes than the rules allow. In the end, the coffee break may turn into a coffee hour, or very nearly that.

If the union proposes that an hour, or half an hour, be clipped from the working day without a reduction in pay, most managers are very conscious of the cost of such a concession. The overlong coffee breaks are equally expensive, perhaps more expensive, because they throw schedules out of kilter.

THE TYPICAL SESSION

Following is a portion of the tape recording of the session that Robert Allen conducted for his department heads to help them determine their authority to go with their responsibility.

MR. ALLEN: Today I would like to take at least one of the responsibilities we put on our list last week and see if together we can work out the authorities or degrees of authority needed to discharge the given responsibility. I have rather arbitrarily taken number three on our list to discuss first. My reason for this is that this applies to most of the already established rules and regulations under which we all have to operate.

DUPREE: Why not take the first one, "Work production"? We all have that responsibility, too.

MR. ALLEN: That's true, but since we are all caught under the same rules, I thought if we took this one first, we might find that what we agree to here under this number three might apply in a great degree to number one. So if you don't really disagree strongly, will you go alone with me on this?

SEVERAL: That's OK. Sure. Why not?

MR. ALLEN: Fine. Now let's put up on the paperboard the heading (*writes as he talks*) A department head's authority for the observation of rules is, colon, number one, period. (*He turns to the group.*) Just what authority do we have?

BRANDON: If you mean authority to *enforce* rules, I'd say it varies.

MR. ALLEN: How do you mean?

BRANDON: It varies with each rule. For some we have unlimited authority, like for being on the job. For others, not so much—like—oh, say, how far can we go in enforcing the fifteen minutes of the morning and afternoon coffee breaks.

EARLEY: I don't think that's right; we all have enough authority to see that all rules are enforced.

WENTWORTH: That's not really so, Bill; if we did have we wouldn't ignore some rules the way we do.

MR. ALLEN: I don't want to be facetious, but are you saying that we ignore some rules and enforce others? (*Laughter.*) Well, be that as it may, I'm not getting much up on this paper. Let's leave the discussion till later. Harley, you mentioned the coffee break. Let's put that up as a rule to be observed. (*Writes after number 1, "Coffee break."*) If we take this whole general item "Observation of rules," it becomes clear to me that you will probably have to work out the authorities for each one for a start at least.

VAZQUEZ: That's right. I couldn't see how we were going to do this on a general basis.

GAGLIANO: I'm not sure. I'll bet we could.

VAZQUEZ: Maybe, but I think we should prove to ourselves we can do it for one rule now, and then see what happens.

GAGLIANO: OK, but I'll still bet that there will be a lot of duplication.

MR. ALLEN: How do the rest of you feel about it? Should we try first for one rule? (*General assent.*) All right. Since we have the first rule heading up there, what authorities should we list?

WHITE: Well, I for one think we ought to list that part of the rule which says that only people on repetitive or so-called monotonous jobs should have a break. All of my people go, monotonous or not.

MR. ALLEN: Monotonous jobs only (*writes it after "a" under number 1*).

HARLAND: The fifteen minutes is too short for my department.

MR. ALLEN: (*Writing after "b"*) Fifteen-minute time limit.

HARLAND: And another thing. I think they should be staggered for each group.

MR. ALLEN: (*Writes after "c"*) Stagger participation.

WHITE: I agree.

MR. ALLEN: Fine, but let's get on. What else?

EARLEY: I think the telephone use is affected here.

MR. ALLEN: (*Writes after "d"*) Telephone use affected. What else?

GAGLIANO: Yes, but this is only listing the things we don't like about it. Where does our responsibility or, for that matter, our authority, enter into it?

MR. ALLEN: Well, let's look at this sheet. (*He takes it to the wall and posts it.*)

The paper work at this time shows:

A department head's authority for the observance of rules is:
1. For the coffee break
    a. Monotonous jobs only
    b. Fifteen-minute time limit
    c. Stagger participation
    d. Telephone use affected

MR. ALLEN: Let's start a new sheet. (*This time returning to paper-board, he writes*) A department head's authority in enforcing coffee-break rule is, colon, number one, period. (*Reading from the first list*) Number one "a" on the posted sheet is "Monotonous jobs only." What does this mean?

WHITE: Well, it seems to me that we need to know whether the order really means what it says. How can we tell one person his job isn't repetitious when another one goes because his *is* repetitious?

DUPREE: That's right. I just say nothing to any of them—they all go in my department, I think.

MR. ALLEN: You aren't sure?

DUPREE: No, I'm not, and I'll bet no one else here is certain about everyone in his own department.

WHITE: I for one think we are in trouble if we try to enforce the letter of the rule. Who is to say for sure a job isn't monotonous? Even I feel my own gets that way sometimes—and well, let's face it—I like my coffee break, too.

HARLAND: Oh, come now. If we can't keep interested enough in our own job to set a good example for, say, our supervisors, how can we expect them to enforce the rule?

WENTWORTH: Well, all I can say is I like my coffee, too, and I think I work better for it when I have it; besides, I usually have it with one or more of my supervisors and I know we always talk shop, so it is time well used.

HARLAND: You're all just dodging the issue. It seems to me that if we were really interested in our own job, we would be too busy to have to stop, by the clock, for coffee.

VAZQUEZ: I can't agree with you. I, too, go for coffee—not every day, but often.

MR. ALLEN: Well, folks, this is all very interesting, but where do we go on authority to enforce this phase of the rule?

EARLEY: I don't think we can enforce it as it stands.

BRANDON: I don't either, especially if we are the only section of the company trying to enforce it.

HARLAND: Mr. Allen, I think that we should go on record for having the rule changed to eliminate this inequality. If coffee breaks are so popular and important, and since most everyone looks on them as their right, why should we be disliked by trying to enforce the unenforceable?

WENTWORTH: Yes, it's going to be tough to start to enforce it after ignoring it so long.

MR. ALLEN: If as you say the coffee break is here to stay, do you feel that we should ignore that part of the rule?

GAGLIANO: Can't you get that part of the rule changed? Don't you have meetings with your boss like this? Couldn't you work on it?

MR. ALLEN: If you all feel that way, and I gather that you do, then I'll be glad to go into it with the personnel practices board.

GAGLIANO: In that case, can't we just ignore it for now? Since that's what we have been doing right along anyway?

MR. ALLEN: If that's what you want, I'll go along with you for the time being at least. (*He goes to the posted list and crosses off "a. Monotonous jobs only."*) What about "b"? (*He reads*) Fifteen-minute time limit. What about it?

DUPREE: That I can go for. I'd say we should agree on enforcing the fifteen-minute time limit.

HARLAND: Are you saying we should really hold them to fifteen minutes?

DUPREE: Yes, absolutely. Unless we start sometime, the coffee hour will be an hour.

HARLAND: I can't—that is, I don't think I can unless we all do it.

EARLEY: I, for one, don't want to be the "terrible-tempered Mr. Bangs" for the first time.

HARLAND: That's right—I'm in the same boat.

EARLEY: I feel we should approach this uniformly.

GAGLIANO: Yes, but that's what the original order was supposed to accomplish—uniformity.

EARLEY: But that's our fault.

HARLAND: We are just talking in circles. Boss, what do you want us to do?

MR. ALLEN: I think I'd go along with what you folks decide.

VAZQUEZ: Yes, but what are we to say to them?

HARLAND: I suggest that we all agree to ask all of our supervisors to direct their employees to be back on the job after the fifteen-minute break.

WHITE: Sounds easy—humph—I for one don't like it. I think we are getting along all right.

DUPREE: Well, there is a creeping thing going on—it's getting longer all the time, and that's more and more unworked but paid-for time.

MR. ALLEN: What, then, do you want me to put up here?

WENTWORTH: What's bothering me is, what if we can't get them to be back in fifteen minutes?

VAZQUEZ: Yes, where does our authority end—or begin—I don't know which.

MR. ALLEN: That's just what we are trying to decide.

HARLAND: Could we say that it is our responsibility to enforce the fifteen-minute rule?

MR. ALLEN: That's it, but with what authority?

BRANDON: Suppose, then, we say that we ask our supervisors to enforce the rule and give them authority to reprimand, say, by docking pay for infractions.

WENTWORTH: That's too tough.

WHITE: Yes, I think we should do it by talking rather than docking, sort of appeal to their reason.

WENTWORTH: What if it doesn't work?

BRANDON: That's why I say the ultimate authority is to dock them.

WENTWORTH: Perhaps you are right, but I'm not sure it will work.

BRANDON: It's worth a try.

MR. ALLEN: How will we word it?

DUPREE: Try "Enforce fifteen-minute limit, with docking as last resort."

WHITE: Yes, but docking how much?

DUPREE: The actual time in pay.

WHITE: Still seems bad to me. Almost childish.

DUPREE: I don't think so. It's just being realistic; maybe a little rough, but I for one bet we won't have to do it more than once in a department.

WHITE: Yes, and have a grievance right off the bat.

BRANDON: I don't think so. If we handle this thing properly, we will have talked to the union beforehand, pointing out the rule, and also the cost. Then we talk to our supervisors. We will explain our good reasons—and they are good, too—and, having set the stage, we will have something to go on which will work.

VAZQUEZ: That's probably so, but I think we ourselves, at least those of us who go for coffee, should also live up to the fifteen-minute time limit.

WHITE: That's true. I've overstayed the time, but I honestly didn't think about it. At least I didn't think about it as a pacesetter for the supervisors and employees.

VAZQUEZ: Right! I think I'll clean up my own backyard first, as the saying goes.

MR. ALLEN: OK?

SEVERAL: OK. Yes. Sure. [Etc.]

MR. ALLEN: (*Writing after number 1*) Enforce fifteen-minute limit, with docking as last resort.

BRANDON: Sounds too tough for me, but I'll go along with it if the rest do.

MR. ALLEN: (*Placing the number 2 next on the sheet*) What shall we do with (*reads from posted sheet*) "Stagger participation"? What about that?

GAGLIANO: There is nothing in the rule about that, but there should be. We end up with jammed halls of lines, telephones are tied up making appointments, and whole office forces and production forces gone at once.

SEVERAL: That's right. [Etc.]

GAGLIANO: That's another thing you should talk to the personnel practices board about.

BRANDON: Wait a minute. Can't we take care of that without writing it in the rule?

VAZQUEZ: Not if it isn't written.

WENTWORTH: I think we can—in fact, I did. Several years ago I told my supervisors that not more than 25 percent of any force could be at coffee at one time. It works, too.

EARLEY: I never thought of it.

WENTWORTH: You probably never tried to get an answer to a question when they were all out. It pays to check once in a while.

MR. ALLEN: Are you saying we can do this ourselves?

WENTWORTH: I am. If we all agree to that 25 percent figure it will keep continuity going.

DUPREE: I can't. I have to close down everything at once—at least I always have. Maybe I could talk to my supervisors and see if we couldn't do it the other way—maybe it's worth a try.

MR. ALLEN: How about it then? Can we say (*writing after the number 2*) "Stagger participation for 25 percent at a time?"

EARLEY: Where does our authority come in?

HARLAND: That's the authority. What we just said.

VAZQUEZ: Sure, if we all agree to this, we've . . .

Other parts of the discussion covered such things as the attitude the managers should take toward the various excuses employees offered for overstaying the time limit: "The coffee was too hot to drink in the time allowed," "The coffee lines were too long," "I had to wait for someone who was late in getting there." The attitude of the union was considered also, and the group came to the conclusion that "they'd never actually strike over the coffee break."

Other rules were discussed in the same way in this and subsequent meetings, and in each case the exact degree of authority to enforce the rule was explored and agreed on.

Later department heads met with the supervisors under them for similar discussions, using the same three-step method that Allen had used with them.

The following chapter will point out the ramifications of this last meeting and the benefits to be derived from the use of the three-step technique in determining areas of responsibility and the degree of authority managers possess in each case.

CHAPTER FOURTEEN

Benefits from Joint Determination of Responsibility and Authority

THE ADVANTAGES of using the three-step method of determining areas of responsibility and authority fall into three categories:

1. Those derived from the preparation of the statements
2. Those that are evident in the normal day-to-day conduct of the managers as they go about their regular work
3. Those that are realized through use of the statements in the induction of new members of the management group

**BENEFITS FROM
THE PREPARATION**

The preparation of the statements, like the preparation of the performance descriptions, helps to develop a new and better relationship between the boss and his immediate subordinates. This is not to say that the relationship may not, in many cases, be quite good—excellent in the case of some of the subordinates. But there is always room for improvement, and I venture to say that in the majority of cases the room for improvement is large.

The popularity of sensitivity training is an indication that most managers feel that there is not quite the understanding there should be.

Just as a company acquires an "image" in the minds of its customers, its employees, and the general public, so a boss builds up an image in the minds of his immediate subordinates, and new subordinates tend to inherit it from those already on the job. This image may be a good one generally—that is, by and large, the subordinates may consider the boss a good one and like him personally. But even so, they generally have a good many reservations. That the relationship usually leaves much to be desired is shown by the fact that so many managers say they do not really know what their bosses expect them to do, what they are held responsible for, and how much authority they have to enforce rules and regulations. If the relationship were as frank and open as the boss often believes it is, there would be no reason for the subordinates not to initiate discussions of these important points. Since they have not done so, it is obvious that they feel they would be considered stupid or "too dependent" if they were to ask questions about matters so basic to the management job.

When the boss himself initiates the discussions, these fears are minimized, especially when the discussions are carried on by a group of managers all on the same level. For one man to go to his superior and say: "Boss, people are spending too much time on coffee breaks. What shall I do about it?" would be embarrassing, and might well—since no one else had ever asked the same question—make him appear too uncertain and too dependent to be a manager. Certainly any manager who is mindful of the importance of the "image" the boss has of him would never do so.

But consider the situation when a group discussion of the subject is conducted. The boss knows, of course, about the coffee-break problem, and so does everyone else present. Further, everyone knows that all the other members of the group have the same problem. Thus it is the most natural thing in the world for the subordinates to express themselves frankly, once the boss has opened up the subject.

Sensitivity training is supposed to produce frank and open relationships between colleagues and between bosses and subordinates and make each man more aware of the effect he has on others. It may produce the second result, but I have very strong doubts about its capacity for bringing about the first one, for in an atmosphere in which insults and retaliation for insults are possible, relationships are likely to be disrupted rather than cemented.

The man-boss discussions of basic areas of responsibility and the authority attached to each one is a more painless method of bringing about the results aimed at in sensitivity training. When the boss learns how uncertain his subordinates are about how far they are expected to go in enforcing the rules, he is learning something about his effect on others, and when each man admits he has the same problem, colleagues are drawn together rather than forced apart. No one is criticized; there are no hurt feelings; the group and the boss simply solve a common problem together.

Of course there may be one or two people in the group who will endeavor to impress the boss by making themselves appear better than their colleagues. Harland's remark, "It seems to me that if we were really interested in our own jobs, we'd be too busy to have to stop for coffee," is an instance in point.

By not taking sides on this question, but simply calling for other viewpoints, the boss neither accorded Harland the recognition he was demanding nor criticized him for his somewhat holier-than-thou attitude. By the same token, he did not criticize or belittle those who expressed other ideas. Here Harland himself probably learned something about his effect on others from the way they took issue with him on this point. But it will be noted that no one felt it necessary to criticize him directly; the others merely stated their own opinions.

In addition to better understanding between boss and subordinates, the discussions of areas of responsibility and the authority vested in the managers produced other benefits: better knowledge of objectives, more understanding of the scope of the job, and a desire, on the part of both the boss and the subordinates, to meet higher standards of performance.

Further, the practical effects of one unrealistic rule were uncovered—the rule that only those with "monotonous jobs" were entitled to coffee breaks. As the discussion brought out, it is almost impossible to make a distinction between monotonous and nonmonotonous jobs, for what one person considers monotonous is challenging for another, and practically all jobs are monotonous at times.

If the boss cannot get this rule changed (and he should be able to if his superior has used the three-step method with him), the worst that can happen is that his subordinates will go on ignoring it as they have in the past. If he does get it changed, it will be easier to enforce the reasonable fifteen-minute limit on coffee breaks, for whenever any rule is transgressed with impunity over a long period, all rules tend to be regarded more lightly.

It may be noted in the tape recording of the session on areas of responsibility that members of the group were somewhat confused over the meaning of the term "responsibilities." This is probably due to the fact that for many years managers and writers on management have been using the word (erroneously, according to Webster) as interchangeable with such words as "objectives," "standards," and "authorities." Since the tape recording was condensed, the record of the typical session does not show more than a beginning of better understanding of what the word actually means, and even on the second list many of the items are too similar to those that appear on the list of major segments.

The boss can, however, clarify matters by the question method as they go along. For example, take the term "assigning work." Allen might, when this item came up for discussion later in the same session or in another session, have asked: "To whom do you assign work? Do you parcel out the work to production rank and file?" The answer would obviously be "no," for the second-line managers assign work only to the first-line supervisors under them, and the first-line supervisors, in turn, assign the work to the rank and file. Then Allen could ask: "But are you responsible for the way the supervisors assign the work?" and the answer would have to be "yes." The item might then be reworded to read: "Proper assignment of work throughout the department." Thus assigning work to the supervisors, insofar as their assignments are not dictated by normal standard practice, is something the second-line managers do, a major segment of their job, and assigning work to individuals within the department is a major segment of the first-line supervisors' job, but the department heads are still responsible for the proper assignment of work to the rank and file.

It is important for the leader to keep repeating the term "responsible for" in order to keep the group's eyes focused on the fact that he is endeavoring to call forth a list of responsibilities—that is, of the things he will hold the members accountable for rather than a list of the things they do.

In the example given, it will be noted, the boss did not find it necessary to inject his own views to any great extent, although he did exercise his prerogative by deciding that the discussion should not deal with the items in the order in which they appeared on the list. He was able to elicit most of the ideas he wanted by questions alone.

There may be cases, however, when he will be forced to put his own views plainly before the group. For example, if the group should agree that enforcing the coffee-break rule was impossible, and the boss did not agree, he might have to state that however difficult enforcement might be, it was necessary; and that the department managers were responsible for enforcement. He would be wise, however, not to do so until the subordinates had exhausted their own ideas on the subject.

ADVANTAGES ON THE JOB

When the subordinates have worked out a list of their responsibilities—the things the boss expects to hold them accountable for—they are more certain of their objectives and more disposed to seek improved ways of reaching them.

The discussion of the limits of their authority is of even more value on the job. If one department manager were to start cracking down on the coffee-break violations, he would be certain to have a number of grievances brought up against him on that account. And if his colleagues continued to ignore the violations, his record, comparatively speaking, would be somewhat damaged on that account. But if all follow the same system, no one will suffer from having more grievances than anyone else on the same level.

The personnel department, of course, may well be averse to having one section of the company start docking employees for overstaying their coffee breaks, and the difficulties this may cause should not be minimized.

The vice-president might handle the situation by asking that the matter be the subject of a meeting at a higher level, or he may take it up individually with his boss or with the personnel department.

If the coffee break is written into the union contract, undoubtedly the time limit is stated there also, and it would not be logical for an arbitrator to hold that the rule should not be enforced. Of course some arbitrators work on the theory that if unpunished violations have continued for a long period a tradition has been created and cannot be changed without a new agreement. But, even so, they generally decide in favor of the aggrieved employee only when it can be shown that one person was punished for infringements that others were allowed to get away with; that there was, in fact, discrimination against an individual.

As for the union itself, it should not be impossible to convince it that the cost of the overlong coffee breaks is unreasonable, and that if management makes a concession in this respect it will simply be unable to afford some other, more important, concession in future bargaining.

In any case, it has been said that some unions and industrial relations departments may make a practice of "trading off" grievances in final negotiations before the arbitrator is called in—that is, the union agrees to drop certain of the grievances on its list if management will settle others in favor of the aggrieved employees. And a grievance based on a supposed "right" to break a reasonable rule will be one of those the union will be most disposed to drop: first, because it will not gain much prestige with its members by winning such a case (the employees actually know they are wrong), and second, because it will have little chance of getting a favorable award if it takes the case to arbitration. And, once the initial batch of grievances on this point has been dropped, others of the same kind are unlikely to be brought up.

USE IN TRAINING NEW MANAGERS

The list of responsibilities and the exact degrees of authority should in all cases be used in orienting new managers to their jobs, and like the list of major segments it should be the subject of discussion between the boss and his new subordinate; simply handing the man a typed list will be of little value.

The conclusions reached as a result of the coffee-break discussion may be used as an illustration of the way in which the discussion will help the new manager. Suppose the new man is merely handed a list that tells him he is supposed to enforce the time limit on coffee breaks and dock those who transgress it. He may be hesitant about doing so if some long-service member of his group happens to overstay the time. The new manager's natural conclusion will be that it is the practice in the company to ignore the violations, and that he will start off on the wrong foot with his employees if he goes by the letter of the law as soon as he comes on the job. But if his line boss tells him that he is expected to do so and that others in jobs similar to his are doing so, he will have no hesitation.

Similarly, the boss can clarify the meaning of "responsibility" and of each of the responsibilities on the list. This should make the objectives of the job clearer, and also help the new manager to determine which of the things that he is responsible for he should delegate to someone else and which of them he should handle himself.

PART FOUR

Standards of Managerial Performance

CHAPTER FIFTEEN

Introduction

FROM TIME IMMEMORIAL standards of performance have existed for every job, whether they have been formulated in terms of quality and/or quantity of product, dollars (or any other monetary measure), services, or some other criterion. It is impossible to say whether a person is doing a good job or a poor job unless there is some standard to which his performance can be compared.

Standards may not be written down, but they exist nonetheless, although some people may not realize it. A seminar leader once told a group of executives that all their companies had standards, either written or implied, and encountered some skepticism.

"How can you know that?" one of the men asked. "There are nearly fifty companies represented here, and you can't have researched them all. I registered only a few minutes before this meeting started; you couldn't even know my company would be represented."

The leader's reply was: "The very fact that everyone here today is still on some company's payroll proves that everyone here has been doing well enough to satisfy someone—probably his boss. Anyone who hasn't been fired yet must be meeting some standard."

SOME STANDARDS ALWAYS EXIST

Everyone is, in fact, conscious—even if only vaguely—that there are certain standards of performance that he must meet if he hopes to stay on the payroll. But where the standards are merely implied rather than written, they tend to be fairly low, and they are likely to deteriorate. If many of the people in the group fail to meet them, the boss begins to believe that his expectations were too high in the first place, and that sloppy work is inevitable.

Of course, *some* standards still exist; otherwise the company would go out of business. The production department, for example, is still expected to fill orders with reasonably acceptable products; and the sales department is still expected to sell enough to make some profit possible. But the percentage of rejects in the production department may gradually grow, and the lead time it requires to fill orders may lengthen until it cuts seriously into sales.

When people fail to meet implied standards, their usual excuse is lack of time, and often they are able to make out a plausible case for this. Then the company hires more people to help them out, which is an expensive way of dealing with the problem.

Written standards are less subject to attrition, and when the boss and his subordinates agree on them after thorough discussion, they are likely to be observed. Further, subordinate managers become surer of their ground in dealing with their own people, for they have a better idea of the performance it is reasonable to expect from them.

The implied standards of performance, once they are brought out into the open through frank discussion by the boss and his subordinates, provide a springboard for the development of higher standards in the future. This Part Four presents a technique for using them in this way.

There are two kinds of standards: (1) those for quality and quantity results of routine efforts; and (2) standards for the managerial activities whose results are seemingly so intangible that many people feel they cannot be realistically measured. It is with the latter group of standards that this section of the book will be concerned.

The aim here is not to supply ready-made standards that a company can take over and apply to its operations, nor will this section present a survey of the field, what companies are doing. The illustrations, the tape recordings of sessions in which superiors and subordinates met to develop standards, are intended merely to make the technique clear, not to show the standards any given company should be attempting to install.

Further, it must be emphasized that the technique, like the techniques presented in Parts Two and Three, must be used by the line superior, the immediate boss of those who take part in the meeting. Unless the line boss believes that it will help him meet his own responsibilities, that it has a definite part in the man-boss relationship, use of the technique will be a colossal waste of time. The boss cannot use the technique successfully *unless he is willing to become personally involved.*

Some managers to whom I have shown the lists of major segments of the managerial job and the sample standards given in this book have commented they they seem too elementary. If the leadership of the meetings had been better, they have said, much more acceptable lists would have been developed.

However, the fact that a list of job segments or a set of standards of performance appears to be elementary is merely an indication of the stage of the group's thinking. If members of a group are to be expected to grow, they must start with elementary steps. Standards set later on are always more professional; in fact, the danger is that they may become cluttered with professional jargon and become less valuable on that account, for they will bear less relationship to the manager's day-to-day work. The professional jargon is likely to appeal more to staff people than to the line executives, and sometimes the staff people become so enthusiastic over the paper work that they reproduce the lists in quantity and make them available to anyone who is interested. The line managers, quite sensibly, refuse to take them seriously in that case.

Perhaps one of the reasons why so few companies have workable written standards may be that any impetus to produce them has come from the staff rather than from the line. In that case, they are generally filed and forgotten, and eventually thrown away.

THE CASE AGAINST
THE "NATURAL MANAGER"

Another reason for the neglect to provide written standards for managers has been the belief that if managers are chosen by some planned selection process, they will be "natural managers," people who can operate by instinct rather than by technique. In reality, the natural manager is a rarity; in fact, he may be a myth, for if a man is a good manager he will use most of the techniques of good management rather than attempt to operate by ear.

Many of the people in the management ranks who are considered "natural managers" are not really good managers at all. Often their reputation is built on the fact that they possess pleasant personalities and have more than average drive. Quite a few of them are so concerned with acting like managers when the boss's eye is on them that they neglect important parts of the managerial job, or at best handle them poorly. Their personalities enable them to keep things running with apparent smoothness, and they are ready with glib explanations when their practices are questioned.

Unbiased administration of company policies is usually not possible under these circumstances. Employees almost always know when they are not receiving equitable treatment, and their work suffers as a result, but often in ways that are not obvious and that are unlikely to come to the attention of higher management in the usual run of things.

Most management people can remember some direct contact with at least one such so-called natural manager, and will recall how difficult their work was when he was in charge of their group, also the amount of time and effort that had to be spent in covering up his mistakes. Eventually rough action is usually necessary to clear up the mess created by a natural manager. After he is fired, retires, or leaves of his own accord, the new manager who replaces him finds evidence in his files of the many things he has left undone, the mistakes he has made, the customers he has alienated, and so on. If he does not leave of his own accord before too much time has passed, he will be fired, for pressures of production and costs cannot be met by his methods. (If he is the top man, he may last longer, but no matter how persuasive he is, there comes a time when the board of directors can no longer ignore falling profits and a declining share of the market.)

The case for the natural manager is bad. He covers his mistakes by directing official attention elsewhere; he postpones dealing with his problems, hoping that they will eventually go away without any exertion on his part; he hides the skeletons of his human relations mishaps in dark closets and piles superficial successes in front of the door to cover the smell of the cadavers mouldering away inside.

The so-called natural manager cannot view managerial standards of performance as important, nor will he contribute intelligently to their preparation. He is afraid that participation in setting them up will reveal his own lack of knowledge and ability, and usually he is right in thinking so.

The real manager has no such fears. Rather, he sees higher standards as not only worthwhile, but challenging and interesting. He knows that no matter how good a manager is, improvement is always possible, and he wants to improve.

In this section of the book, therefore, managerial performance standards will be considered from the viewpoint that the most important gain from their development is that they help the manager *improve* his performance on his *present* job. Certainly there are side objectives, but this is the most important one. And improvement of managerial performance means that the manager is doing a better job of helping each of his own subordinates perform better. No thinking management person can disagree with such a goal, for if it is attained, the company and everyone who works with the manager in question will benefit.

In other words, the technique is based on a concept that is the direct opposite of the laissez faire philosophy of dependence on natural managers, who probably do not exist anyway.

In the next chapter, consideration will be given to how the term "standard of performance" should be defined if the standards are to serve as a basis for improvement.

CHAPTER SIXTEEN

Managerial Standards of Performance: What They Are

ON THE LOWER LEVELS of an organization, and for jobs that are almost completely routine, some standards are usually definite and easily understood; generally they are in writing. Thus a company may refuse to hire a stenographer who cannot type 30, 40, or perhaps 60 words a minute and take dictation at, say, 100 to 120 words a minute. This is about as simple a standard as can be set. Standards for production work exist in all plants and may be on somewhat the same quantitative basis, although they may include some qualitative units of measurement as well. Common also are standards for salesmen, which are often expressed in the form of quotas.

EARLY BEGINNINGS

All these standards are generally in writing, but this was not always the case. Before the days of Frederick Taylor, for example, production standards usually existed only in the boss's mind. Sometimes he had a record of the fastest time in which a job had ever been completed; more often he had an idea of the average time it had taken men to do the work in the past. And that average time, as Taylor proved, was a great deal longer than it might have been—two or three times longer in many cases.

It is not suggested that company presidents hold a stopwatch on their vice-presidents or that any of the features of the "Taylor system"—as the beginnings of industrial engineering were once called—be applied to management jobs. But it is suggested that companies follow Taylor to the extent of taking a fresh look at the managerial standards, written or implied, now in effect.

THE PACKAGE APPROACH

Management has been defined as "the direction of people, not the direction of things," but many managers who glibly quote this definition tend to spend less time on the direction of their people and devote less thought to it than they do to the more technical parts of their jobs. Only when a crisis situation develops do they devote full attention to this phase. Generally, then, their performance in this area is better than it has been, which provides clear evidence that "normally" they are not working in a way anywhere near their potential.

No one likes to admit that he dodges issues. The fact remains, however, that the average manager is looking for some easy-to-apply formula for supervising his subordinates. The proof of this is the number of managers who attend conferences that purport to provide concise, workable, neatly wrapped packages of routines and panaceas.

Many of these same seekers for packages of practices that they can install and then forget about are the very ones who claim that they haven't the time to discuss standards of performance with their subordinates and work out ways of raising the standards with them. Or else they say that this technique is not applicable to their industry, their company, or their particular job.

Another type of package is the type prepared by outside specialists, who often advertise that they will "tailor-make" standards for their clients, standards that take account of the characteristics of the company and the peculiar nature of each job. But investigation of many such sales shows that the prepared standards, if still around at all, are resting unused under the proper labels in an office file.

This seeking for predigested management techniques provides overwhelming evidence that many people are mentally sluggish regarding the direction of their subordinates. The consequence is that they, and their bosses, never realize how much better they could have done in this respect if they had been willing to devote enough time and attention to this part of their jobs.

THE BORROWED STANDARD

The packages that are presented at meetings have generally been developed by staff people who have not had to make them work, and who are often ignorant of the results, or rather the lack of results, they have produced.

But even if they are working well in one company, this is no proof that they will work well in another. Where borrowed ideas have been at all effective, a tremendous amount of modification and adaptation has usually taken place. It is quite possible that the effort required to make them work has been greater than the effort that would have been necessary had the managers worked out their own standards from scratch.

Borrowing standards of performance for managers is downright ridiculous, not only because they may be entirely inapplicable but because they may be lower than the implied standards already in force. Thus a standard that encourages improvement in one company may actually bring about a lower level of performance in another.

The extent to which a standard that serves one company well will be unacceptable, even if applicable, in another company is illustrated by the following case.

The chief auditor of one company came across a set of standards for works auditors that was being used by another company in the same industry, one that used much the same accounting methods that his company did. Accordingly, he had the imported standards duplicated, distributed copies to each of his subordinates, and asked them to comment in writing.

It is significant that his request brought only four replies from eleven subordinates, and only one of the four said he could accept the standards without change. A second one said that he didn't think the standards would be applicable to his operations, and a third straddled the fence by writing that he felt some of the standards would apply to his job but some of the others were irrelevant. The fourth man merely performed a monumental editing job, changing as much of the wording and the punctuation as he could, and then had the whole thing retyped.

At that, the chief auditor decided not to urge the rest to submit their comments. He realized immediately that his subordinates were unwilling to accept standards worked out for some other company. Later he developed a number of standards by the process described in the next few chapters, and it is interesting to note that they were almost identical with the borrowed standards, but because the members of the group realized that the chief auditor was interested enough to spend time on developing them, they felt that they were really applicable to their jobs. (Incidentally, not one of the works auditors recognized how closely these new standards tallied with the borrowed set.)

Packaged standards or borrowed standards do not work for the same reason that staff-developed job descriptions are inadequate: the managers do not report to the person who worked them out. They know that the boss merely thinks they might be a good thing to have, and that he will forget about them as soon as the momentary enthusiasm generated by a meeting or a consultant's sales talk has faded. Further, since they have had no part in setting the standards, they are unlikely to feel that the package that results is based on down-to-earth knowledge of their jobs and the problems they encounter.

IMPLIED STANDARDS

Where standards are merely implied, not written, they will, of course, include some that are related to company objectives in an important way. The production manager knows that he must see that a certain amount of output is obtained; the billing department head is aware that the bills must be mailed out eventually, even if not as soon after the first of the month as they should be, and so on. But often meeting even minimum standards of this nature requires far more people than ought to be necessary. Managers may devote much more effort to meeting sets of standards that would horrify their superiors if they realized that they existed. Such standards often include some or all of the following:

- Tell the boss only what you think he wants to hear.
- Be available when the boss calls for you.
- Don't get into any unpleasant arguments.
- Appear to be busy. Start new projects and tell the boss what you are doing and how well you are doing it. (This will convince him that you have initiative.)
- Dress inconspicuously but well. (Never outdo the boss in style.)
- When the boss suggests something new, never throw cold water on his idea even if you know it won't work out. (He'll probably forget about it later anyway.)

Needless to say, these are seldom the standards the boss really wants his subordinates to meet. But the boss is only human, and he may sometimes give the impression that they are the things he considers important if nothing is written down and the subordinates are forced to build their standards from hints and impressions gathered through isolated instances. For example, he may have become irritated by the man who is always arguing with his colleagues, the man who is never around when he is needed, or the man who opposes his new ideas. His subordinates are likely to draw incorrect inferences from his most casual remarks, or even from facial expression simply *because* he is the boss and the way they stand with him is so important to them.

THE CHIEF EXECUTIVE'S OBJECTIVE

Since each executive gains his ideas of what is wanted from his own boss, and so on up to the top, it is pertinent to inquire what the chief executive really wants. First of all, he wants the company to stay in business and to make as high a profit as possible commensurate with commonly accepted business principles—and not just this year but over the long term. Generally, also, he wants the company to grow, since a company that is standing still while its competitors are growing is actually shrinking. In pursuit of these ends, he is seriously concerned with the "good name" of the company, for to thrive and grow it will need to maintain a reputation for producing good products (or services if it is a service company), for dealing fairly with employees, suppliers, and customers, and for paying a good return to investors. Further, he generally recognizes that the company has a civic responsibility and must participate constructively in community affairs if it is to maintain its reputation. No company can maintain a good "image" by advertising and public relations alone. It must perform well in all these areas.

The chief executive must have a picture in his mind of the conditions that will exist when the company—which, in general, means all the managers in it—is making progress toward his objective. This picture is a composite of the conditions that will exist when each department, and each manager within each department, is doing well. His problem is to transfer the applicable parts of that picture into the mind of each of his subordinates, and the best way to do that is to provide written standards.

DEFINITION

The term "standards of performance" will be defined here as "*written statements of conditions that will exist when a job is being well done.*" One might, of course, use a lower common denominator and say that a standard of performance is a written statement of conditions that will exist if an "acceptable" job is being done. But this implies that the company is quite willing to settle for mediocrity. As a matter of fact, however, a company cannot even stay in business indefinitely if it does only a mediocre job. If a job can be done better, someone else will discover that fact, and the mediocre company will be unable to meet the competition.

One of the main reasons for having *written* standards is to help the managers improve their performance, and the phrase "the job is well done" indicates that something more than a merely "acceptable" job is wanted. Hence it encourages improvement, for it is natural for managers to conclude that as long as they stay on the payroll their work is at least "acceptable."

TOTAL COVERAGE

High-level executives often shy away from preparing written standards of performance with and for people in certain types of jobs, especially for those in line positions near the top and for those in staff positions at any level. Often they ask: "Aren't there some kinds of jobs for which you can't set standards of performance?"

The unequivocal answer is that a manager *ought to be able to determine how well he expects a person to do any job if he is willing to pay money to have it done.* If the boss doesn't know what he wants the man to do, he should abolish the job and save the money being paid out in salary. And if he knows what he wants the man to do, he had objectives in mind. So surely he should be able to judge whether or not the job is being well done. Even the duties of a staff position are not too nebulous to be reduced to specific areas of performance to which definite units of measurement can be applied. A staff man cannot expect to have his performance taken on faith any more than anyone else on the management team can.

CHAPTER SEVENTEEN

Approaches and Techniques

A STANDARD OF PERFORMANCE, in the last chapter, was defined as "a written statement of conditions that will exist when a job is well done." But there cannot be one standard for each management job, for—as the lists of major segments show—each job includes several major segments; that is, anyone who serves in a management capacity, even a minor one, must do several things if he is to meet his responsibilities properly.

There must, then, be a standard for each of the major segments of the job—both the technical facets and the purely managerial facets. The technical standards are generally easier to arrive at, for they cover aspects of the job to which quantitative measurements may be applied. But it is just as important, if not more important, to have standards for the segments that deal with the management of people.

In general, in fact, the extent to which technical standards are met or surpassed depends on the way in which the manager directs his people, for the technical performance is the product of the group effort: in the case of a sales manager, for example, the sales volume achieved depends on the work of the salesmen; the research director's achievement depends on the output of his department, and so on.

Most managers, it is true, do more than simply supervise a group. They have technical work of their own to do. The plant manager, for example, may have to work on new layouts; the sales manager may have to study markets and determine the potential of each, perhaps plan routes for his salesmen, and sometimes accompany them on their rounds and help them to close certain sales.

However, discussion of this type of standard will be reserved for a later chapter. In the present one, we will consider only the standards for the strictly managerial parts of the job, those having to do with the direction of people.

Many managers today are in the unhappy position of being dissatisfied with the performance of the people under them, but not dissatisfied enough to fire them, perhaps because they feel that "with the type of people you get nowadays" replacing even the worst ones will not do much good, and may even do harm. Therefore, they are reluctant to undertake the extra work that replacement will require: selection, orientation, training, and so on—in view of the fact that it may be useless in the end so far as improving their showing is concerned. Also, since firing people is a distasteful job, they avoid it when they can. Setting standards of performance is a major step toward the correction of a laissez faire situation of this kind.

PURPOSE OF STANDARDS

However, standards are not set primarily for the purpose of determining who should be fired and who should be kept. They may be used in that way occasionally, but their main value is that they produce improved performance on the part of those already on the job. Some people have more ability than others, of course, but all can improve if they learn how to use their abilities to the full. Often the improvement will be greater than the superior would have believed possible.

If the main purpose of the standards is to foster improvement, it follows that the standards must be higher than those most members of the group are currently meeting. But they must be realistic; they cannot be too much higher than the present standards, for it is unfair to expect people to reach levels of performance far beyond those they have ever attained. Telling them they should do so merely discourages them and makes them feel that the boss has absolutely no conception of the problems and difficulties they are encountering on the job.

The standards must be such that they are attainable within the near future, "attainable" in this case meaning attainable by the majority of the group. Further, members of the group must be able to accept them without mental reservations and feel that they are reasonable in the light of conditions on the job.

If even one standard is too high, what personnel managers call the "halo effect" is likely to occur; that is, people will believe all the others are too high and that the boss does not really expect any of them to be met. When a sizable number of the group feel that a standard is too high for all but a few exceptional people, they will lose interest in the whole matter.

How high is "attainable in the immediate future"? How much improvement can be expected when the standards first come into use? A good illustration of the answer is found in the often-used Figures 1 and 2. The horizontal line in Figure 1 indicates the average managerial performance of a group on a single "major segment" of the job, at the time standards were first set; the dots show the performance of each manager.

When realistic standards were set, all improved to some extent, and some improved more than others. And the average of the whole group should go up, even in so short a time as a month. Figure 2 indicates the type of change that occurred. Everyone improved somewhat, although relative positions remained the same. Two managers changed their position in relation to the "average" line, however—6 and 8, each of whom improved only a little—6 because he was already the top performer in the

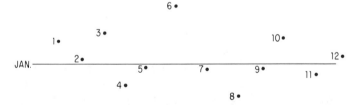

Figure 1

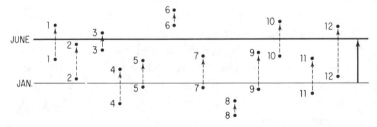

Figure 2

group and 8, who was the lowest before the standards were put into effect and may have been already working near the maximum of his potential for performance on the job in question. But it is significant that everyone, even 8, the poorest manager in the group, improved somewhat.

As time goes on and new and higher standards are set and performance improves still more, the average line will go up still further. Eventually, the poorer managers may fall so far below the average that action will have to be taken—more bluntly, it may be necessary to dismiss, demote, or transfer them, although the boss may, by working with them individually, be able to bring them up to a point at least near the average.

At no time, however, will the entire group reach the ultimate in performance. As new people are promoted into the group, as methods and products change, further room for improvement will always be discerned. Moreover, as people see that they can do better than they have been doing, they will want to do better still, and will accept higher standards.

TWO APPROACHES

In any case, the standards are set by discussion in which both the boss and his subordinates take part, and here again either the group or the individual approach may be used.

The group approach will be appropriate whenever it has been possible to use it in developing major segments of performance and a list of responsibilities with degrees of authority. In other words, it should be used whenever several management people who all report to the same boss have basically the same job of directing people, even though the technical parts of their jobs may differ somewhat.

For example, this would be true of a group of first-line supervisors who all report to the same production manager, even though each one may be directing a different type of operation. It would be true also of a group of craft foremen who all report to the same maintenance manager or plant engineer, even though the technical skills their subordinates possess are entirely different.

On a higher level, the group approach may be used for plant managers who all report to the same manufacturing manager or for a group of sales managers who all work under the same marketing manager.

In some of these cases it may be necessary to use the individual approach for the technical standards, but the standards for the direction of people are likely to be the same, although here again the manager is likely to encounter the feeling that "my job is different." As the group discusses the matter, however, its members are bound to recognize that the managerial parts of their jobs have many similarities, and they will be more ready to do so if the boss assures them that he will be available to consider any special aspects individually.

On still higher levels, of course, only the individual approach may be appropriate, for the manager's subordinates *will* be different, and perhaps will require different treatment.

TECHNIQUE

It goes without saying that the list of major segments of performance and responsibilities and degrees of authority must be developed before good standards can be set. There must be agreement on *what* the boss expects his subordinates to do and *what* he will hold them accountable for before they and he can decide *how well* they can be expected to do it.

The technique used is the same as that described in the two previous sections—the three-step method—and only the same simple equipment is needed: the quiet room, the paperboard, and so on. In step 1 each segment of performance and each responsibility is considered in turn, and the boss merely writes down everything suggested by members of the group, allowing no discussion until the list seems fairly complete. In steps 2 and 3 he leads the discussion, mainly by asking questions, and eventually the group arrives at agreement.

If the individual approach is used, the technique is similar, except that the suggestions are those of only one executive. But here also it is important to get a preliminary list before starting discussion.

Should the boss get a preliminary list of standards for each segment of performance before going on to step 2, or should he start the discussion of the first segment and get agreement on the standard for it before going on to the next segment? The second method is better, for more than one meeting may be necessary and it may seem as though nothing is being accomplished if a meeting is held without reaching agreement on anything.

It is up to the boss to decide which method to use when he sees how the meeting is going. And it must be stressed again that it is the boss who must conduct the meeting if he wants to get results in the way of improved performance. If he delegates the job to a staff man, the whole effort is wasted, for line managers are not interested in meeting the expectations of the staff; they want to do what their immediate boss expects them to do—meet the standards *he* will hold them accountable for meeting, the standards he will judge them by when it comes to deciding whether or not they remain on the payroll and are recommended for raises and promotions.

Moreover, the boss is responsible and accountable for the performance of his immediate subordinates. His own continued place on the payroll, his raises, and his promotions depend on how well they do their jobs, and it is to his own interest to see that the standards are standards that will help him make a better showing.

But, as in the case of the three-step method of determining segments of performance and a list of responsibilities with degrees of authority, the boss should not use the technique unless he himself believes in it. Unless he is convinced that it will help him make a better showing, he should stay away from it. The whole procedure will be an expensive waste of time if he uses it only because setting standards seems to be the fashionable thing to do, or if he delegates it to some staff department that is eager to enlarge its activities.

On the other hand, if the boss himself wants to work with his subordinates setting standards that both he and they can agree to, the activity costs nothing. Both he and his subordinate managers are already paid to manage, and the standards ensure that the time spent in managing will be better spent.

Of course, the boss can set standards unilaterally if he wants to, have them duplicated, and distribute copies to his subordinate managers. But the chances are that if he does so the standards will receive only grudging acceptance, if that, and the group as a whole will not meet them, which will mean that the boss will be in the same position he was before—dissatisfied with the performance of his subordinates, but feeling that he can do no better if he replaces them.

Perhaps the boss feels that the list of segments of performance developed by the group is inadequate or expressed in too-general terms. If so, the standard-setting session gives him a chance to see that it is improved. For example, if the group flounders in attempting to set a standard in such a way that the extent to which the members are meeting it can be judged in an objective way, he may suggest that the segment be rewritten.

It might seem that the list of major segments should be complete and accurate before standards are set, but in actual practice a more realistic "psyrological" approach may be necessary—"psyrology" being defined as a mixture of psychology and common sense. Rather than drag out the discussion of the content of the job unduly, it is preferable to start setting standards as soon as the second list is completed. If the list is too indefinite and too open to misunderstanding, this will become evident to the group members as soon as they try to suggest standards for the more questionable segments.

The final list of standards will consist of items that are susceptible to objective measurement, although the measurements cannot always be expressed in numbers. Quite often the preliminary list will be made up of "how to do it" steps rather than actual units of measurement, but this will become apparent to the group in the course of the discussion.

This point is illustrated in the next chapter by a transcript taken at a meeting in which a group of second-line managers were attempting to set a standard for their own performance in selecting first-line supervisors. It will be noted that practically all the items on the preliminary list are *steps* in the selection of supervisors, not units of measurement that can be used to determine whether or not the job was well done. A person may go through all the possible steps in selection—testing, interviews, and so on— and yet in the end choose, if not the worst of the candidates, one who is not the best. However, this group did, eventually, reach a list that is made up of true units of measurements.

One of the benefits of the standard-setting discussions, in fact, should be clarification of the difference between ends and means. Many lower and middle managers, and unfortunately even some of those on higher levels, feel that their main job is to follow certain prescribed procedures rather than to obtain results that contribute to company success.

CHAPTER EIGHTEEN

Setting
Standards
for Middle
Managers

THE BEST RESULTS are achieved if the standard-setting process starts at the
very top of the company, but any corporate officer who wants to improve
the performance of his second-line and first-line subordinates can initiate
the practice, provided he has already carried through the steps detailed in
Part Two of this book.

Since he is a member of the top group, his immediate subordinates will
be middle managers, and there will be at least one level of supervision
between them and the rank and file. In a very large company, the corporate officer's immediate subordinates are likely to be several levels
above the first-line supervisors, for some companies have as many as a
dozen levels of management, and there are even cases in which there are
twenty or more levels.

Generally, however, anyone who is the top man in an organizational
unit—a major department, a plant, or a division—is at least a third-line
manager and has at least two levels of supervision under him. Thus his
immediate subordinates may be termed middle managers.

Let us say that the middle managers are the plant managers, parts of whose discussions with their immediate boss, the vice-president for production, were given earlier, and that the plants are small enough to require only two levels of line supervision—that is, the plant managers' immediate subordinates are the first-line supervisors who direct the work of the rank and file.

These second-line managers and the production vice-president have already developed and agreed on the list of major segments and on their responsibilities and the degree of authority they possess in each area. There have also been two standard-setting sessions that have produced agreement on standards for one or two of the major segments.

Even if the plants are fairly close together, there will be some difficulty in getting all the plant managers together at one time. In this case, however, it had been the vice-president's practice to have regularly scheduled meetings for his plant managers monthly, and parts of these meetings were utilized for the standard setting.

If the plants were so widely separated that it would be prohibitively expensive to get all the managers together at one time, the boss could use regional meetings instead, or perhaps work individually with each of his subordinates on the standards. It might appear that under these circumstances the standard setting would take an abnormally long time. But the boss will begrudge the time he must spend only if he does not accept the fact that directing his immediate subordinates is the most important part of his job. If he does accept this concept, he will realize that to the extent that he can improve the performance of his subordinates, he will face fewer time-consuming crises in the future.

The major segment for which the plant managers and their boss, the production vice-president, were setting standards in the transcript that follows was "Selecting new foremen to fill vacancies." The company in this case had had a long-standing policy of allowing the plant managers to select the first-line foremen, although there were staff groups that commonly gave them advice on the selection and supplied them with records of the candidates gathered through application blanks, tests, and preliminary interviews.

In the past, some of the plant managers had been in the habit of having the personnel department handle not only the preliminary checks on the candidates but the final selection as well. When the major segments of their job were being discussed, some members of the group were not sure that they wanted to be responsible for deciding even between two candidates. They were convinced only when other plant managers pointed out that they, not the personnel department, were responsible for the work of the foremen, and that they could not be sure of getting the kind of performance they wanted unless they took an active part in the selection. One remark that may have gone a long way to change their attitude was: "The only reason why a plant manager would want to duck his responsibility, it seems to me, is that he is looking for an alibi if the man he chooses doesn't work out well. If he hasn't had anything to do with the selection, then he can blame the trouble on the personnel department."

STANDARDS FOR SELECTION: STEP 1

The portion of the meeting devoted to developing the preliminary list for discussion took more than half an hour; hence only a part of it will be transcribed here.

VP THOMPSON: Now that we've concluded the regular business of our monthly meeting, I'd like to have you start setting a performance standard for another segment of the job. Last month we got the standards for the first two items on our list down on paper; now let's see what we can do with "Selection of foremen." There was some disagreement at first over the inclusion of this item on the list, but I think we all agreed in the end that we'd be in a better position to meet our responsibilities if we selected the people we have to work with. First, however, let's get our heading up where everyone can see it. (*He turns to the paperboard and writes*) A plant manager has done a good job in selecting a foreman when, colon, number one, period. Now suppose I want to determine how good a job you have done in selecting a new foreman. How am I going to judge?

BECK: I'd say the plant manager has done a good job when the foreman turns out to be a *good* foreman.

HANOVER: That doesn't really tell us anything.

VP THOMPSON: We can fight over these items later. Let get the list as complete as possible first so we'll have something to discuss. (*He writes as the first item under the heading*) The foreman turns out to be a *good* foreman. What else?

HANOVER: When we're sure that each candidate has been given an appropriate battery of tests, for one thing.

VP THOMPSON: (*Writing as he talks*) Two. When we are sure that each candidate has been given an appropriate test battery.

RICH: I think we've got to be sure we check all references, too.

LAMBARZI: That's usually not necessary in my plant. We promote foremen from within.

RICH: Well, there are 300 production workers in my plant; so I can't know exactly how each one is doing and what kind of a foreman he'd make. I check all the records and also talk to his immediate supervisor, which amounts to getting a reference.

VP THOMPSON: I think we have two items there: getting records and checking references, which will be either references from past employers or references from the immediate supervisor if the man is already employed in the plant. (*He writes on the list*) Three. He has obtained records. Four. He has checked references.

WHITE: Isn't it the personnel department's job to get the references from past employers?

HANOVER: We can have personnel write for them, but we've got to go over them ourselves. I think we should also interview all the candidates.

WHITE: All the candidates? What about those who make lousy scores on the tests?

HANOVER: Yes, I think so. Some men who make very good foremen don't do well on the tests. There won't be so many candidates that it will take an enormous amount of time.

VP THOMPSON: Remember, no discussion until we've completed the first list. (*Writes*) Five. He has interviewed all candidates.

LAMBARZI: Where do we get the candidates from in the first place? Is recruitment part of our job?

WHITE: We can have personnel send us people.

HANOVER: But if we do, we have to draw up a list of qualifications. Also, I think we should post the job in the plant to ensure that we are really offering people a chance for promotion. Our union contract doesn't require it, but we do it anyway.

WHITE: I don't know. Everyone that wants more money will start applying and we will have to spend an awful lot of time interviewing candidates, unless we have personnel do some heavy screening first to knock out all but two or three of them.

VP THOMPSON: Remember, we're going to discuss each of these items later. Here we're only trying to get a list to form a basis for discussion. Now I think we've had two or three things suggested that I should get down on the paperboard. (*He writes*) Six. He has drawn up a list of qualifications. Do you do that only when you want personnel to bring in candidates from outside, or do you do it in any case?

HANOVER: I think we have to do it anyway. How can you make a good selection unless you know what you're looking for?

VP THOMPSON: Then we'll leave that as number six, and if anyone disagrees they can argue about it later. The same thing is true of posting the job. I'll make that number seven. (*He writes it down.*) Now what else?

RICH: I think we should put down that we get all the help we can from the personnel department even though we make the selection ourselves. After all, we don't administer tests ourselves.

VP THOMPSON: I'll put that down. (*He makes it number 8 on the list.*)

BECK: What about letters of application? I like to have each candidate write one. A foreman need not be a literary character; he may even be a good foreman if he speaks ungrammatically. But he has to be able to express himself in clear, logical language. Otherwise, he'll ball everybody up when he gives them directions.

VP THOMPSON: OK. (*He writes*) Nine. Has each candidate write a letter of application.

HANOVER: We're leaving out the most important thing—the proof of the pudding. No matter what means we use to select the foreman, the real measurement is how well the foreman performs on the job.

VP THOMPSON: I'll make that number ten. (*Writes*) Ten. The foreman performs well on the job. Is there anything else that we can use in this as a standard?

HANOVER: I think that's it.

RICH: So do I.

VP THOMPSON: Then we can start the discussion and determine whether all these items are valid and expressed in the proper way. In the meantime, if anyone thinks of anything else that should be added, I'll be glad to put it on the list. Just speak up, and I'll put it down as number eleven.

STANDARDS FOR SELECTION: STEPS 2 AND 3

At this point, three paperboard sheets have been filled and posted on the wall where everyone can see them, and the paperboard is blank and ready for the second list. The current list reads as follows:

A plant manager has done a good job in selecting a new foreman when:
1. The foreman turns out to be a *good* foreman.
2. He has ensured that each candidate has been given an appropriate battery of tests.
3. He has examined records of performance.
4. He has checked references for all candidates.
5. He has interviewed all candidates.
6. He has drawn up a list of qualifications.

7. The job has been posted.
8. He gets the help of the personnel department.
9. He has each candidate write a letter of application.
10. The foreman performs well on the job.

It will be noted that this list is far from a good list. Many of the items are simply steps to be taken in the selection process—they are not units of measurement. Others, like the first item, are too indefinite, and the last item is the same as the first one, although expressed in somewhat different language. This does not matter since the inadequacies of the list will become apparent to all members of the group in the course of the discussion.

> VP THOMPSON: Now we're ready to begin the discussion. But, first, I'll write the heading for the second list on the paperboard. (*He writes*) A plant manager's performance in the selection of a foreman is good when, colon, number one, period. Now should we include the first item?
>
> BECK: I think that's the same as number ten. A foreman is a good foreman when he turns in a good performance.
>
> WHITE: That's right.
>
> LAMBARZI: Yes, of course. There's no point in having both on the list.
>
> VP THOMPSON: Does anyone think there is any difference between the two? No one seems to; so we'll cross off one of the items. The question is which one. Which do you think we should use? Or should we phrase the idea differently?
>
> LAMBARZI: I like the way it's phrased in number ten.
>
> BECK: I think I do, too.
>
> HANOVER: So do I.
>
> VP THOMPSON: Anyone disagree? All right. I'll write it down that way. Now, are there any objective measurements that we can use to determine whether or not the foreman is turning in a good performance?
>
> HANOVER: Costs.
>
> BECK: Scrap.
>
> WHITE: Absenteeism and complaints in his department.
>
> LAMBARZI: Since we're setting standards in order to improve, I think we should be trying to get better performance from our foremen than we have heretofore. Therefore I think we should include something about improvement . . .

The discussion continued, and in the end the first item read:

The plant manager's performance in the selection of foremen is good when:

1. The foreman's performance is up to previously determined standards within an appropriate period.

Later on, most of the other items that were steps in the selection process rather than true units of measurement were combined under the second item, which read: "When there is evidence that a planned selection process has been used."

The group included the various steps in the selection under item 2 because it was felt that these could help the superior to evaluate the selection plan used. Members now understood, however, that these were merely steps, not standards.

Discussion brought out that these two steps would make it easier for the new foreman to win acceptance from the men under him. People who felt they were passed over without any opportunity to apply for the job, it was pointed out, would not be very cooperative with the man who did get it. It was also noted that if those who did not get the job heard the reasons why from the plant manager himself, they would be more reconciled to the fact that they were not appointed.

In addition, discussion brought out, some of those who applied from the plant itself might be good foreman material but lack sufficient experience, and it might be well for the plant manager to meet them in case he had further vacancies to fill. Moreover, many of the plant managers tried to know as many of the rank and file personally as they could; and interviewing all those who applied for the job would give them an opportunity to have talks with at least a few of them and learn how they felt about the plant in general, the rules and regulations, and the nature of their jobs.

The objections of those who felt that the interviewing would take too much time were met when those who were already posting the first-line foreman's jobs when vacancies occurred reported that, in general, there were only a few applicants in each case. As one man said: "If we make up a good list of qualifications, most people will realize that they couldn't handle the job. And by that I don't mean we should put in extra hurdles just to keep the number of applicants down. We don't need to. After all, the foreman has to have certain technical qualifications and experience in the work. He has to be able to answer his men's questions and help them when they get into difficulties. In other words, he should know more about the work than they do. That alone eliminates a good many people. In addition, there are many people who don't want to be foremen anyway. They don't want the responsibility, and they don't want to be on a different footing with their friends in the shop. Then there are others who realize that their past records are pretty mediocre and they wouldn't have a chance. So they simply don't bother to apply. Generally we get only four or five applications, at most, when we post a job, and I don't think it takes too much time to interview each of four or five men."

The complete standard for the selection of foremen, as agreed to by the plant managers and their boss, the vice-president for production, read as follows:

> The plant manager's performance in the selection of a new foreman is good when:
> 1. The foreman's performance is up to previously determined standards within an appropriate period.
> 2. There is evidence that a planned selection process has been used:
>   a. He has drawn up a realistic list of qualifications, which includes all those the foreman really needs and none designed simply to narrow down the field.
>   b. He has obtained the help and advice of staff departments where appropriate.
>   c. He has posted the job in order to obtain candidates from the shop and make it possible to promote from within whenever possible.
>   d. He has given due consideration to every candidate by:
>   i. Examining references, records, and test results (if he believes testing is appropriate).
>   ii. Interviewing all candidates.

Quite possibly this list could be improved on, and another group might have drawn up a somewhat different list. However, the list as it stands has the following merits:

First, it provides a set of objective standards. And since they are objective, they have "teeth" in them; that is, the superior can definitely ascertain whether or not the standards have been met.

Second, it ensures that the plant managers, in turn, set standards for their foremen, for they cannot possibly meet the first standard unless they have done so.

Third, it calls for somewhat better performance in this area than has been customary in the past.

It will be noted that the group not only arrived at objective standards for selecting new supervisors, but gained a clearer understanding of the major segment itself, or what they must actually do in selecting a new supervisor. Also, the objectives they should be working toward in performing the major segment of their job were clearer.

As one boss put it: "I have never been able to get clear through the standard-setting procedure without finding that it had produced a better understanding of the major segments of the job. The need for clarification always comes out in the discussion as members of the group display obviously different viewpoints."

If the boss suspects that his subordinates, even though they have agreed on a major segment, do not all understand it in the same way, he may be wise to ask them for their opinions on its meaning at the beginning of the standard-setting session.

Another part of the meeting devoted to setting a standard for "Induction of new supervisors" illustrates this. Here Vice-president Thompson felt that, even more than in the case of "Selecting new supervisors," there was likely to be some misunderstanding of the major segment. Therefore he began the standard setting by asking them exactly how they defined the term.

VP THOMPSON: Before we set a standard for inducting new supervisors, I'd like to get your opinion on what we actually mean by this major segment.

HANOVER: I think it means that we train them so that they can perform their new job well.

VP THOMPSON: (*Writes as he talks*) Fully train new supervisors so that they can perform their new job well. Any other definitions?

BECK: I think that statement is too broad. They already understand the technical side of the work if we've selected them properly, but they need a lot of information on the scope of their job, where it fits in with other jobs in the company, how to interpret the union contract—in fact, the new supervisor needs a whole lot of information if he isn't to make bad mistakes in the beginning.

RICH: We also listed "Training new supervisors" as another segment and we all agreed that it was a continuing job, not something that we could do once and for all. The question is: What part of the training must we conduct before we turn him loose on the job?

LAMBARZI: I think it's mainly a matter of giving him the information he needs to avoid getting off on the wrong foot.

VP THOMPSON: I'll write that down. (*Writes*) Giving him the information he needs to avoid getting off on the wrong foot. Now, what information does he need?

HANOVER: Company policies that apply to his job.

BECK: Objectives of his job.

LAMBARZI: His responsibilities and the extent of his authority.

RICH: We should inform him of the major segments of his job.

HANOVER: I think also that we can't just give him a list of either. We have to go over them with him carefully and explain what we understand by them. Further, we have to encourage him to come to us for further clarification if he gets confused. I think also that we must consider that the induction process is not only the explanations and training we give him before he starts actually supervising, but the training during the first three months on the job.

RICH: I'd rather say six months. After all, even six months is a pretty short time for a person to work well into a job. I know I felt pretty green until I'd been on the job for about a year—by that time I knew the sort of things I was likely to come up against and had a reasonable amount of confidence.

HANOVER: I'll go along with six months if you like. You're probably right.

VP THOMPSON: Can we say then that "induction" is the training the new supervisor receives (1) before he actually takes over the job, and (2) during the first six months on the job? Does anyone disagree? No? Then I'll write it down. (*Writes*) Induction is the training the new supervisor receives: (*a*) before he actually starts supervising and (*b*) during his first six months on the job. Now can we set a standard for each of these? How will I know when the plant manager has done a good job on the first one? (*Writes*) The plant manager has done a good job of inducting the new supervisor before he starts supervising when, colon, number one, period. I think some of the things you suggested should be done offer some clues to the standard.

HANOVER: When the plant manager has explained the company policies that will apply to his job and has informed him of the scope of the job.

VP THOMPSON: That's two. (*Writes*) One. When the supervisor has been fully informed of the company policies that apply to his job. Two. When he has been fully informed of the scope of his job.

HANOVER: I think we should add that informing him of the scope of his job includes a personal discussion of the major segments and responsibilities and degrees of authority that we and his colleagues have agreed upon.

LAMBARZI: Yes.

BECK: I agree.

RICH: So do I.

VP THOMPSON: But how will I know whether you have done a good job on these things?

HANOVER: When the supervisor doesn't pull any major boners.

RICH: He might anyway; you can't always tell what people are going to do.

BECK: Not if you've kept in close touch with him and encouraged him to come to you when he's in doubt. Unless, of course, you've made a very poor selection.

Eventually, the group arrived at a standard that—although expressed in part in negative terms—provided an objective measurement of how well the plant manager had performed the preliminary induction procedures:

A plant manager's job of preliminary induction (before the new supervisor actually takes over the job) is well done when:
1. The new supervisor has not transgressed company rules in any serious way.
2. He is performing all the major segments of his job.
3. He is neither exceeding his authority nor failing to exercise the authority he does possess.

For the second part of this major segment—the six months' induction period, the standard included:

1. All production schedules are met.
2. There are no slowdowns due to his failure or lack of knowledge.
3. Productivity of his group is at least up to the average.
4. He recognizes incipient trouble spots and takes steps to correct the difficulties before they become serious.
5. He has learned *all* pertinent company policies and practices and acts in accordance with them in every respect.

To see (or hear) another example of middle or second-line managers working out a standard for themselves with their boss, a chief accounting officer, let's investigate a portion of a meeting of an office group of accounting managers. Here the chief accounting officer, a vice-president, is in a meeting with his nine managers and they have started setting a standard for their performance in orientation and training of new supervisors.

The chief's name is Arnold Rayburn. His managers manage the following departments: internal auditing, payroll, cost accounting, plant records, engineering costs, customers' records, sales accounting, general bookkeeping, and final accounting records. The names of the managers will appear in the transcription.

The group is already into the first list where they have put up numbers 1 through 3 as follows:

A manager's performance in training a new supervisor will be satisfactory when:
1. The new supervisor has been given all the necessary books of routines for his job.
2. He has made his first round of evaluations of his employees.
3. He has accepted his new responsibilities.

We pick up the meeting at this point.

RAYBURN: What else will we add to this list?

ARCHER: I think that you can tell if we have done a good job of training if the new supervisor reaches a performance equal to the standard needed for the job.

RODEEN: How can we do that? We don't even have standards for our own job, let alone for our supervisors.

RAYBURN: You may be right, Bill, but who knows how it will come out when we discuss it later, so let's put it up here as number four now. (*He writes as he says*) The supervisor meets the standards of performance of the job.

ARCHER: Yes, but I think we should have a time limit in it, like, say one year.

RAYBURN: (*He writes*) Five. The supervisor meets standards in one year.

RODEEN: That won't work for all of us. I could never get a new supervisor so he does all he's supposed to do in a year. I'd suggest two years.

RAYBURN: Let's leave number five as it is for now and discuss the time in step two when we make our new list. Now what else should we use as units of measurements?

WRIGHT: I still think numbers four and five are parts of the same thing.

RAYBURN: You may be right, Wright (*laughter*) but let's leave it for now. Anything else after I put this sheet on the wall? (*He posts it.*)

WRIGHT: Well, I'd like to suggest something different from four and five. I'd say that our performance in training supervisors would be satisfactory if the routine parts of the work in his section are up to date at all times and he shows initiative in making improvements in those routines.

WILLIAMS: That's two things in one.

WRIGHT: Not necessarily—they can be combined into one.

RAYBURN: How will I put it up here then?

WRIGHT: I'd say "When the supervisor has all routine work up to date," no, "on schedule, and makes improvements in the routines."

RAYBURN: (*Writing as he talks*) Number six. The supervisor has all routine work up to date and . . .

WILLIAMS: I still think that is one unit of measurement and that the rest should be a separate one—number seven, maybe.

WRIGHT: OK, OK. I'll give in. Make number seven "When the supervisor starts improvements in the work routines."

RAYBURN: (*Writing*) Seven. The supervisor starts improvements in the work routines.

BELSON: I think that we should always . . .

The group continues giving their boss additional items to write.

Now we jump to steps 2 and 3 of the techniques—the discussion steps to get understanding and agreement.

RAYBURN: Now let's start a new list if we can agree on the items. Let's look at the number one item on the first list. (*He reads*) The new supervisor has been given all the necessary books of routines for his job. What about that?

BELSON: I don't think that is even pertinent.

WRIGHT: Nor I.

ARCHER: Neither do I.

THOMPSON: I do. I use that as one of the surest ways to know if I have the man all ready for his job. I give him the books on his first day.

SARLEY: I can't agree, Hen. I don't think just giving a person printed rules is any kind of training. How do you know he'll understand them or [slyly] that he can even read?

THOMPSON: Oh, come off it. That isn't even funny nor does it deserve any comment.

SARLEY: All right, I'm sorry. I didn't mean to upset you, but I still think that training a person is more than just giving him printed instructions.

JONES: That's right.

THOMPSON: I don't get it. I've always done it that way. How should I have trained them?

RODEEN: There is a lot more to it. You have to talk with them about the things you want them to do, and not just about routines.

ARCHER: Sure, and there is more than just talking to them, too. You have to repeat the important things and even ask them to explain things back to you. That's the only way you can be sure they really understand.

WILLIAMS: Yes, and after that you can give them the routines books for reference.

THOMPSON: Sounds pretty complicated to me. I don't know if I could do it the way you say.

RAYBURN: Now, what about this number one? Should we put it on this list? Is this something we should use as a unit of measurement for your performance?

RODEEN: No, I don't think so.

ARCHER: No.

SEVERAL: No.

THOMPSON: I don't know. I'm all mixed up, but since you all seem to feel that it isn't important I'll go along with you.

RAYBURN: OK. I'll cross it off the list. (*He does so.*) And now what about number two? (*Reading*) He has made his first round of evaluations of his employees. What about that? Should we use it as a unit of measurement of your performance?

WRIGHT: I don't think so.

RAYBURN: Why not?

WRIGHT: It isn't really important at the start. There are so many other things he has to learn to do before he gets to the annual evaluations.

SARLEY: I agree with Henry. I think that almost any of the other things on the list up there are more important.

JONES: That's right. I move we strike it.

RAYBURN: How do the rest of you feel?

All agree. Rayburn crosses it off the first list and reads number 3, continuing as before trying to get understanding of each item and agreement by all as to whether it is a valid unit of measurement for the performance of the members of the group.

There is really no purpose in listing their final standard of performance here, because it will serve no useful purpose. The benefit for anyone will be achieved only when his own group works out its own standards.

CHAPTER NINETEEN

Setting Standards for First-line Managers

First-line supervisors are quite as interested in doing a better job as anyone at a higher level, and often they are more willing to admit that they have a lot to learn. Generally, also, they show improvement in a shorter time. Thus working with them on standards may be one of the most rewarding of the standard-setting activities.

First-line supervisors are particularly likely to appreciate the technique, for, unfortunately, they are seldom consulted about much that has to do with their jobs. Methods departments may determine the order in which the work in their departments must be done; and other staff-developed procedures may be imposed on them from without until it seems that they have little leeway to manage. The technique of having them set standards in company with their boss, therefore, gives them more opportunity than they generally have to see themselves as managers, as people who make decisions and exert influence.

When the boss shows that he is sincerely desirous of getting their opinions, and that he will allow their opinions to influence him, he has taken a long step toward getting better results from them. Some research studies have indicated, in fact, that the influence a first-line supervisor has with his boss directly affects the results he gets. When supervisors who had little or no influence with their superiors used the same good supervisory practices that led to higher productivity in other groups, they were unable to effect much improvement.

**NOT A MATTER
OF WRITING SKILL**

Some companies are now hiring college graduates as first-line supervisors, a practice that may be either good or bad depending on the amount of technical knowledge the job requires. In that case, the boss may run into the same difficulty that is often encountered with higher managers, the tendency to quote textbooks rather than think through the real points at issue. (This is particularly characteristic of younger men who have studied management in college, for they tend to believe that they have learned all about the subject in their college courses, and it takes experience on the job to cure them of the idea.)

More commonly, however, the first-line supervisors will be men and women who have been promoted from the ranks, people who have not had much experience in expressing themselves in writing. But this is an advantage, for a standard should not be "literary" or expressed in the jargon of the textbooks, as it is likely to be if it is prepared by a staff department.

This is not to say that a standard should not be literate—the gist of it must be plain, and it must convey definite ideas about how improvement can be attained. As members of the group discuss the various standards with their immediate boss, they will clarify their own ideas and gain understanding of their jobs. And clear writing depends more on clear thinking than on literary skill.

Of course, the boss himself has often read a considerable amount of the so-called literature in the management field and is familiar with the jargon; he may even have a tendency to use it himself in talking with his colleagues and superiors. When it is used as a short of shorthand that everyone taking part in a discussion understands, it may be valuable. But even in the case of higher managers, the terms may degenerate into clichés that are used to disguise lack of understanding of important concepts.

But whether or not the boss employs the usual management terms in talking to his own superior and others on his level, he should stay away from textbook phraseology when he is talking to those who are not familiar with it. He will only confuse them if he starts using professional jargon.

At the same time, he should not "talk down" to them. If he does, he will alienate them and increase the gap between what he really wants from them and what they think he wants.

Adopting a style of discourse that avoids both errors may seem difficult, but it should not be. After all, the boss and his subordinates are both familiar with the work that is being done in the department and with many of the problems that are likely to arise; thus they have a good deal in common and should be able to find a common language for discussing it.

In addition, second-line, or B-level, managers usually do not set standards with and for the people under them until they have been through the same process with their own boss. At that point, then, they should have a better understanding of what their own superiors want from them. And once the superior has a clear idea of the standards his own boss expects him to meet, he is in a position to realize how important it is that those under him meet higher standards.

DEPARTMENT HEAD AND
SUBORDINATE SUPERVISORS

The transcript that follows is taken from a recording of a session held by the head of an accounting department (accounts receivable) with the first-line supervisors under him. He has already had a discussion with them on the major segments of their jobs and has taken part in standard-setting sessions conducted by his own boss.

DEPARTMENT HEAD: A couple of weeks ago, we had a meeting to develop a list of major segments of the first-line supervisor's job, or at least of the segments that were common to all supervisory jobs. I think we finally came up with a pretty good list. I think you all learned something from that discussion; at least, I know I learned a great deal from a similar session I had with Mr. Wallace and the other department heads.

Now we're going on to the next step—setting standards of performance. Many of us department heads felt in the beginning that it would be extremely difficult to set standards for some of the major segments of our jobs, but after we had discussed the matter, we changed our minds. After all, if it doesn't make any difference how well some parts of the job are being done, there wouldn't be any point in paying someone more than the minimum wage to do them. Certainly, you don't need a department head or a supervisor to handle them. And if there is some level of performance that must be reached, we should be able to determine what that level is.

Now all of you agreed that training employees is part of your jobs, and we all know that training can be done well or badly and that how well it is done makes a big difference in the performance of the group. How do we know when an employee has been well trained? (*No one speaks.*)

I know I have never given you any indication about this, and I think I have been remiss in not doing so. But I know you all have some idea of the difference between good training and bad.

HELENE: Do you think we've been doing a poor job of training? I know I try very hard to bring my girls up to standard in a reasonable amount of time.

DEPARTMENT HEAD: No, I think you've all been doing a pretty good job, all along the line. If any of you had been falling down in a serious way, I would have said something to you about it. But that's just the trouble. Instead of telling you what I expect, the objective you should be shooting at, I've left you to guess what I wanted. Now I want to correct that. Also, as you all know, we're continually having to raise salaries, which means that costs are going up all the time. If this company is going to make any profit at all in the years ahead, we've all got to be better managers. Maybe, if prosperity continues, our sales will continue to grow, and that should help. But the real factor in company success is management, which means you and me as well as all the people above us.

HENRY: But how can we set a standard for anything as intangible as training? Some people learn faster than others, and some have more skill to begin with.

WILBUR: But Helene spoke of "bringing new employees up to standard." She must have some idea of the standard she wants them to reach.

DEPARTMENT HEAD: That's exactly it. We do have standards, and we're just trying to get them down on paper, and perhaps raise them a little.

HELENE: Well, of course, I have some idea of what a capable girl can do. By "bringing new employees up to standard" I meant bringing them to the point where they can produce as much and be as accurate as the average girl who has been with us for some time.

HERBERT: But is the average good enough now?

HELENE: But I'm trying just as hard as I can now. I'm sure I'm not neglecting anything that I can do to help my girls improve.

DEPARTMENT HEAD: That's what I thought before I went through the standard-setting sessions with Mr. Wallace and the other department heads. I don't want to sound threatening; as you all know, this company is still making money and it's not about to go out of business this year, or next year for that matter. But the fact remains that competition is getting heavier, money for capital investment costs more than it did, and interest rates are going up all the time along with wages and salaries. We can't do much about those things; the only leeway we have is to manage better. And no matter how well we have been doing, there's always room for improvement. We can't all do twice as well as we have been doing just because we think it would be nice if we could. But we can give ourselves a somewhat higher mark to shoot at. One of the things that I can do to improve the results I get is to work more with you people on what I want and what you should expect from your own people. Does that make sense?

MARIAN: Yes, it does. We women supervisors always feel that we're kind of stepchildren around here. No one notices what we're doing and whether we are doing it well or badly. It gets kind of discouraging.

DEPARTMENT HEAD: Maybe that's because we felt you're so conscientious that we didn't need to. However, I think the men have probably felt the same way. Certainly, they haven't been treated any differently. But that's just the thing I'm trying to correct. I know you're trying hard; that's why I don't think it would do any good for me to tell you how much better you should be doing. But if you can agree on the standard, it will be reasonable in the light of the very real problems you have. Now (*reading*), "A supervisor's job of training is well done when . . ." What would you say is number one under that?

HELENE: When a new employee is up to standard in a reasonable length of time.

HENRY: What's a reasonable length of time?

DEPARTMENT HEAD: Just let me write it down. We can discuss it later when we get a good list of items.

WILBUR: But we have to keep training our employees. It isn't just new employees. All of them can improve, and it's up to us to help them.

DEPARTMENT HEAD: Yes. How will we know they are improving?

WILBUR: When there are fewer mistakes.

DEPARTMENT HEAD: Yes. (*Writes it down.*)

HENRY: When productivity per employee is going up.

MARIAN: When schedules are met.

The list developed by the group in this stage of the process read:
A first-line supervisor's performance in training employees is good when:

1. All new employees are up to standard in a reasonable length of time.
2. Productivity per employee is increasing.
3. Accuracy is improving.
4. All work is on schedule.

DEPARTMENT HEAD: Now, to consider the first item on the list. I think we all know what we mean by "up to standard." Of course, if we succeed in raising productivity, the standard will go up, but I think we can leave it at that. But "a reasonable length of time" is something else again. What is reasonable in the light of the type of job you people are supervising and the skills people have on the job?

WILBUR: I'd say a month.

HENRY: I think that's too long. All the people we have can either type a certain number of words per minute or operate a comptometer acceptably when we hire them. All we have to do is get them accustomed to the way we handle paper work. There isn't much to learn about the actual technique of the job.

WILBUR: Then let's say three weeks, or even two if you like. In fact, I have some people who've reached average productivity in less than a week.

HELENE: I think we can say two weeks. A week might be feasible later, but we don't want to set the standard too high at first. Some of the girls I get have the typing skills but they have no business experience and everything about a big office is new and confusing to them. They have to keep stopping work to ask me how to handle things. Everything seems like a special case to them.

HENRY: I'll go along with that.

MARIAN: So will I. It will mean some improvement on my part in some cases. As Wilbur says, some people learn in a couple of days, but those are the people who have had some business experience.

The group went along with the two-week provision, and this definite measurement was set as a standard.

DEPARTMENT HEAD: Now we are in agreement that a new employee should be up to standard in two weeks—or should we clarify that by saying that he or she should be up to the average in both productivity and accuracy? (*The group assents.*) Now let's consider meeting our schedules as an indication that the training job, of both new and old employees, is being well done.

WILBUR: I don't know. Some of my beginning jobs have no effect on the schedules.

HENRY: That's right. Very few of my jobs will affect the schedules the rest of you have to follow.

HELENE: I had to wait two hours for those record cards from your group last Tuesday. My girls had nothing to do for two hours, and then they had to work overtime to get them out.

HENRY: Well, that was an unusual case. I had a new girl on it and she got behind.

HELENE: That's just it. The new girl wasn't meeting her schedule; so our schedule was disrupted.

HENRY: I guess you're right.

DEPARTMENT HEAD: That's why a discussion like this is valuable; it brings out points like that. Henry, when did you discover the work was late?

HENRY: I'd put her on the job at noon, and I'd taught her how to do it myself. Then I got tied up and couldn't get back to her as soon as I had intended to. It wasn't until Helene called about the cards that I found out that the girl had coded the last two or three hundred wrong, and we had to do them over again. If Helene had called sooner . . .

HELENE: I kept expecting them any minute. How was I to know . . .

DEPARTMENT HEAD: Wait a minute. We're not trying to blame anyone for anything that happened in the past. We can't do anything about it now, but we can minimize the likelihood of similar occurrences in the future. I think this merely emphasizes that what every employee does may affect the schedule. Now, one other thing about this scheduling business. We are saying that the training job is well done when all our present schedules are met. As you are all well aware, our complete billing cycle covers eighteen days. Can that be shortened?

HENRY: I don't see how. We are all solidly scheduled now.

MARIAN: That's right.

WILBUR: I think we could make a real contribution if we could shorten it. Let's say fifteen days.

HELENE: That's too much, at least for now. But I'm willing to try for seventeen days.

WILBUR: Let's split the difference and say sixteen.

DEPARTMENT HEAD: We have to keep in mind that standards must be realistic and attainable. I'd rather have you make them just a little higher now, then shoot for a still higher mark later if necessary. If most of the group doesn't think the standard is attainable, it's not going to have any influence. Now how shall we phrase that one?

WILBUR: Let's say that our performance will be good if we meet present work schedules and by, say, six months, we, as a group, have shortened the present schedule to seventeen days.

MARIAN: I think six months is too short a time. The last schedule change we made took two years.

WILBUR: That was because the "specialists" did it. After they'd spent a year on it, it took almost another year for us to convince them of how it really ought to be. They didn't understand our problems.

DEPARTMENT HEAD: That's a good point. Then do you think you can be reasonably sure of effecting the change within six months? Perhaps you can even do it sooner, but it's going to put an extra burden on all of you. For one thing, getting your employees to be able to do it is one thing, and getting them willing to do it is another. It will call for more intensive instruction, perhaps a change in teaching tactics.

MARIAN: I don't think we should rush into this schedule change, or announce it yet. We don't want to announce it, and then fall on our faces.

DEPARTMENT HEAD: We won't have to worry on that score. These standards are just for us. You'll each have a copy and so will I, but no one else will.

MARIAN: That's all right then. I'm willing to try.

DEPARTMENT HEAD: Since we all understand what we mean by it, can we word it this way: "When the cycle schedule is working on a seventeen-day basis and there are no delays that affect it adversely"? (*There is general agreement.*)

At this point the standards for "training new employees" read:

A first-line supervisor's performance in training employees is good when:
1. New employees reach average productivity and accuracy within two weeks.
2. Productivity per employee is improving.
3. Accuracy is improving.
4. The cycle schedule is on a seventeen-day basis, and there are no delays which affect it adversely.

DEPARTMENT HEAD: The second item on the ... (*And the group continued to determine units of measurement for their own jobs.*)

You will note at this point that no specifics were mentioned beyond the time element. That, in itself, however, is an excellent specific. Next to the dollar value, which in this case is still not measurable, it is the strongest specific which can be used. Further, it can be seen that since that unit was in the area outside of pure production or volume figures, the supervisors were latching on to the most pertinent aspect possible.

It should be pointed out that the written standards, as finally agreed to by this group, will serve no purpose for anyone else; hence they are not given here. There is no question, however, that this meeting is only the forerunner of many future meetings by the entire group and by smaller subdivisions of it. Actual production meetings usually follow a standards-setting session.

This session represents a case where the boss had to start from scratch, as it were. He found it necessary to explain his objectives, the company need for such a managerial sharpening process, and how he was going to proceed, as well as answer very real questions about motive and urgency. Yet he found it advisable to plunge into setting standards. A critical person may feel that the subordinates were too pat, too amenable, too easy to convince; that their language and manners shout "fake." But observation of many different standard-setting meetings has shown that this example is a typical one. Perhaps it is due to the fact that the average management person really wants to do the best he can, really wants to improve. If that is so, it merely points up the fact that in this area of setting management performance standards there is an untapped source of know-how waiting to be put to work.

This example happens to be for a clerical department. A shop or manufacturing unit would probably use different language to get the same points across. In the matter of rephrasing the words of the supervisors, you will note that the department head did a *minimum* of such changing. Wherever possible he used the exact words of the supervisors in the initial listing, shortening or condensing only when it was really necessary.

It should be noted, also, that in the original listing of units of measurement these first-line supervisors are very direct and to the point. Their statements are uncluttered with personnel jargon. They know what they mean, and they state it simply. It was their boss who perhaps did too much talking. Nonetheless, he made his points. If a criticism were to be made of this example, it would be to point out that the boss perhaps overdid his own role at the beginning. He might, by less talk on his own part and more stimulation, have brought out the same points from his subordinates.

CHAPTER TWENTY

Further Examples of Standards

THE EXAMPLES of standard-setting sessions given so far have dealt mainly with production groups: plant managers and first-line foremen in a factory. The single exception is the session in which the head of the accounts receivable department worked on standards in company with his first-line supervisors. It may be of value, therefore, to show examples of standards that have been set for other types of managers.

It should be emphasized, however, that these standards are *not* model standards that can be used by other companies. They are included here merely as illustrations that may encourage superiors to use the technique by indicating that it is possible to have written standards for all important segments of every managerial job.

STANDARDS FOR SALES MANAGERS

The sales managers in this case were regional sales managers in charge of groups selling nontechnical products, office supplies, to industry and business. Before the standard-setting procedure went into effect, the company had had quotas, but no other standards. The regional sales managers' superior, the general sales manager, judged the performance of the regional managers mainly by whether or not they met or exceeded their quotas, but even though most of them were up to standard in this respect, he felt that they tended to neglect some parts of their jobs. Sales were rising, it was true, but the market for the products appeared to be widening; and it did not seem to him that sales were increasing as fast as they should. Thus competitors must have been gaining an increased share of the larger market.

As an example of a few of the many possible standards of performance for a given manager, the following excerpts will show standards for a high-level field supervisor who operates away from the home office.

In this example you will note that the standards are for those items of general and obvious nature, encompassing such things as work performance, communications, personnel administration, safety, and public relations. In this case, the less obvious items are written into the standards as individual units of measurement. Which method is best must be left up to the boss when he is conducting standard-setting sessions.

Standards of Performance for Regional Sales Manager

PERFORMANCE IS SATISFACTORY WHEN:

Work Performance
1. Sales slips written by each salesman per month are over eighty-five.
2. Sales-slip errors are less than ½ percent of slips written.
3. Loss of samples is less than 1 percent per month.
4. Total loss of product is less than $\frac{1}{10}$ percent of total sales.
5. Cost of supplying supplies is less than $480 per year per salesman.
6. Salesmen are required to see twenty customers per day.
7. Operating overtime hours are less than 1.5 percent of hours scheduled to be worked.

Communication
1. Regional staff meetings are held at least every month.
2. The boss visits each district at least once each month.
3. Employee meetings are scheduled at least two weeks in advance.
4. Training review sessions are held for each class of salesmen at least once each month.
5. Written memos are worked out so there is no kickback.

Personnel Administration
1. Vacations are scheduled so that they affect a minimum of less than 10 percent of customer coverage per month.
2. Hours paid for but not worked (except for vacations) are less than 10 per 1,200 man-hours.
3. Overtime hours worked are less than 3 percent of scheduled hours (except in extreme situations).
4. Holidays are observed by all employees except for rare customer need.

Safety
1. Car accidents are of noninjury status and minor equipment damage (less than 5 percent of depreciated book value of equipment).
2. Frequency of vehicle accidents is less than 0.25 per 100,000 miles.
3. Frequency of lost-time injuries is less than 8.0 per million man-hours.
4. Frequency of serious injuries is less than 5.0 per million man-hours.

Public Relations
1. At least one visit every two years is made to city and county officials in the area. (This needs to be to but one meeting.)
2. At least one visit per year is made to competitors in the region.
3. One or more presentations are made to local schools when applicable.
4. Newspaper coverage is favorable in local newspapers when there is news.

Another abbreviated example, and perhaps a more workable one from a basic standpoint, is for a firm with a number of sales managers who are in charge of somewhat smaller areas. You will note that in this case the major segments of the managers' job cover entire functions as well as individual responsibilities. This set of standards was sent to me by the president of the company.

STANDARDS OF PERFORMANCE

A. *The Sales Function*
Performance is satisfactory when:
1. Regular attention is given to market research (actual and potential share, to all possible outlets).
2. Advertising and promotion are planned and controlled.

3. There is evidence that the sales program has been planned and is well administered and controlled.

4. Constant study is given to product suitability (new and modified products, uses, colors, proper stocks, number of items carried, variety, obsolescence, and packing).

B. *The Service Function*

Performance is satisfactory when:

1. Customers' credit ability has been investigated, shipments are in accordance with credit policies, collections are handled in an orderly manner, and funds and petty cash are properly managed.

2. All equipment is sufficient, of the right type, and well maintained.

3. Expense reports and budget comparisons show evidence of economical administration.

4. There is evidence that methods and procedures have been well planned and rigidly controlled.

C. *Organizational Planning*

Performance is satisfactory when:

1. Position descriptions and standards of performance exist for all positions and are thoroughly understood and accepted by both job holder and his superior.

2. Adequate control procedures exist and there is evidence that they are in active use.

3. The organization chart is up to date, publicized, and understood by all concerned.

4. Organization review is conducted at least once every two years.

D. *Personnel Administration*

Performance is satisfactory when:

1. Salary and wage policies in general are understood by all, and in particular all conditions affecting a particular job.

2. There exist proper procedures for selecting new employees.

3. Induction plans are worked out for all new employees.

4. New employees are guided and counseled on new jobs.

5. There is evidence that insurance, hospitalization, and retirement plans, and miscellaneous services are thoroughly understood.

6. There is evidence that safety standards, inspections, and education receive consistent and continual attention.

7. Working conditions are maintained at required levels, particularly in respect to housekeeping, sanitation, rest periods and lunch rooms, and ventilation and lighting.

E. *Work Supervision*
Performance is satisfactory when:
1. There is participation in the development of the human resources of the company.
2. Evidence exists that the work of all subordinates is periodically inspected.
3. There is coordination of effort among all executive personnel reporting to the divisional manager.

F. *Work Delegation*
Performance is satisfactory when:
1. There is evidence of planning for the appropriate delegation of responsibility.
2. There are indications that subordinates are being given additional responsibilities and authority to meet their individual requirements.
3. Subordinates are informed of and understand their responsibilities and authority.
4. Subordinates retain full information on department matters without burdening themselves with the performance of unnecessary detail.
5. Subordinates are permitted to exercise fully the delegated authority and are adequately accepting and performing their responsibilities.
6. Each department operates at high efficiency both with the boss and in his absence.

This set of standards was accompanied by a well-thought-out set of words explaining what was really meant by each major segment. Oftentimes these are incorporated into the actual written standards. Many of these have been used by a great number of companies. Some of them appear in standard reference works. All of them can be worked out in appropriate words by a boss and his subordinates. They follow here:

1. *Sales Function:* Planning, promotion, and coordination of sales and merchandising policies to ensure the progress of the division; focusing attention on the greatest opportunities and special weaknesses

2. *Service Function:* Planning and reviewing the operation of the ancillary services, warehouse, office, shipping, and so forth

3. *Organizational Planning:* The process of defining and grouping the activities of the division so that they may be logically assigned and effectively executed

4. *Personnel Administration:* The creation of a feeling of understanding

between the company and the men and women in the organization; and the development of plans and practices toward these ends

5. *Supervision:* The direction of subordinates

6. *Assigning Work:* The process of assigning responsibility with commensurate authority so that work and personnel functions will be performed most effectively

SOME STAFF FUNCTIONS

Another approach to the written standard of performance is shown in the next example.

The performance of the production staff function is satisfactory when the following conditions are present:

1. *Procedures and Policies*
   a. Research is done which serves as a basis for the preparation of policies on production-cost improvement, new-product development, and quality control of production.
   b. Competitors' policies are reviewed periodically to provide for revision of our policies.
   c. Manufacturing decisions are in line with present policies.
   d. All production policies are communicated to all manufacturing departments.

2. *Production Planning*
   a. Proposed manufacturing plans are submitted by each September 1.
   b. All production plans submitted are reviewed by the production staff.
   c. Cost data studies are adequate for preparation of cost estimates for new products.
   d. Production staff services supply background information and general instructions in advance of the planning period.
   e. Timely staff studies are made on new developments in related areas.
   f. Budgets are explained so that action can be taken.

3. *Product Quality*
   a. Effective procedures are followed for testing the product to meet established design specifications.
   b. There is a continuous effort to improve the company's products.

    c. There is an established procedure for quality control of all raw materials, packaging material, and finished goods.

    d. There are established procedures for the control of product quality.

    e. The checks used to control quality are evaluated semi-annually for effectiveness.

There are certainly other important areas for this standard, but the above serves to show how this type of standard could be worked out.

The marketing field poses still another challenge for preparing technical standards of performance. The next example combines a research function with the marketing function. This, too, uses the same kind of "conditions which will exist" for its structure. Again, only a short portion will be shown.

STANDARDS OF PERFORMANCE
FOR MARKETING RESEARCH MANAGER

The technical performance of a marketing research manager will be satisfactory when the following conditions are met:

1. There is a departmental organization chart in existence, positions are filled, and job descriptions and standards for each position are prepared.
2. There is a planned schedule of projects with adequate progress reports in evidence.
3. All supervisory or top staff positions are filled by professionally trained personnel.
4. All pertinent data are available to all interested personnel.
5. Up-to-date data of all previous projects are on file.
6. Effective audits of all research projects, both used and unused, as well as in progress, are made by appropriate personnel.
7.

AVOIDING "EMBROIDERY"

I constantly hear of personnel directors who have mistakenly been given "responsibility" for getting standards of performance prepared for the major sections of companies and who attempt to embroider or change the terminology in order to do what they call "making it more acceptable" to the line people.

Such word-mollycoddling is juvenile. Most people in management ranks can understand and accept for their own worth words which, upon dictionary definitions, mean simple things in the business vernacular.

One company's attempt to "ease" the problem comes to mind. This company coach advocated the use of "a good job is done when . . ." rather than "performance is good when . . . ." He said "To make the finished product more acceptable, it is preferable to hold to the informal 'a good job is done when . . . .'" To this I can only say "pish and a healthy tush." What difference can it possibly make which type of sentence is used? One is as good as the other as long as the people concerned understand the terms. Such picayunish thinking usually serves only to make the personnel staff man feel more important.

Another type of embroidery work on the standard-setting process is one which states that, and I quote from a company's directions to its line management people, "the main segments of the _____'s job should then be arranged according to importance and agreed on by the group." What earthly advantage is gained by this time-taking embroidery work? If there is one type of activity that will jeopardize a worthwhile management activity it is the interjection of time-taking exercises just because they seem to be nice.

It might also be added here that any term to be used or type of activity to be included will almost always be susceptible to lax observance if it comes from a staff person. On the other hand, any term or activity used by a boss in discussion with his subordinates will stand up as useful and understandable, and will not have to be interpreted or made more palatable by a staff man. I personally feel that the time has come to treat management people as adult, intelligent, normal, and reasonable people. The term "budget" seems to be understood and acceptable, as does the term "production" or any of the other standard ones in almost universal use. Why then should we be so delicate in approaching the managerial functions? It is probably true that these are perhaps more important than some of the other types, and that is all the more reason to be realistic rather than namby-pamby with their use.

A CORPORATE OFFICER

One of the commonest and perhaps easiest standards to prepare is one for a corporate officer, especially for the technical aspects of the job of treasurer, secretary, or counsel. A sample of a corporate secretary's job has been sent to me, of which I will quote only two major segments of his technical job. These two are probably the most obvious activities the corporate secretary performs. They are "corporate meetings" and "corporate records." An example follows.

The corporate secretary's performance in connection with corporate meetings is satisfactory when:

1. All timely notices, statements, and proxies are submitted for counsel approval (if necessary), prepared, and distributed the proper number of days in advance of any corporate meetings of shareholders, board of directors or executive committee.
2. Meetings of the board of directors, the executive committee, and the shareholders are attended by the corporate secretary or an assistant secretary.
3. All minutes for board of directors, executive committee, and shareholders' meetings are prepared in legal and proper form.
4. Agenda for all corporate meetings are approved by the chief executive office and supplied interested personnel in adequate time for suggestions to be made.
5. Adequate physical arrangements for all corporate meetings have been made prior to such meetings.

The corporate secretary's performance in connection with corporate records is satisfactory when:

1. The proper number of approved minutes of the corporate meeting have been prepared and filed in all designated places.
2. Adequate provision is made for binding corporate records and storing in appropriate places for legal, corporate, branch office, and shareholders' use.
3. Microfilming has been done as needed.

OTHER TECHNICAL STANDARDS

The preparation of some technical standards of performance is apt to degenerate into a blank-filling exercise. This is often the result of an uncoached boss (see Chapter Twenty-nine) who is figure-minded in his thinking. This column-type standard is effective but could be much more effective if the blanks could be worked out in a descriptive-sentence type of standard, so that the persons involved will understand the meaning of the figures. One advantage of the "blank filling" process is that it allows different people on the same type of job but with different working conditions or situations to agree with their boss on their own peculiar figures to put in the blank spaces.

In the area of customer service for a manager of production, words and blanks as follows show this method:

Ship product to meet _____ percent of all of our promises to customers per given year

To measure: max. _____ percent performance = 100 percent
accomplishment
min. _____ percent performance =   0 percent
accomplishment

It can be seen that an objective is woven into such a type, and of necessity, this is not a pure standard of performance.

Another example, which, in essence, smacks of goals or objectives, might be illustrated by:

General maintenance costs per unit not to exceed $_____ for whole year 19_____. Tool maintenance cost per unit goals for year 19_____.
_____ $_____ per unit
_____ $_____ per unit
_____ $_____ per unit

The trend, fortunately in only a few companies, to attempt to incorporate objectives with standards leaves much to be desired.

Objectives, by popular and dictionary definitions, are one thing. Standards of performance are another. True, they are related to each other—standards are not much help without a goal to shoot for. But when the attempt is made to make them both into one document, too often the resulting mixed verbiage nullifies any real worth of a standard.

Combined with the standard and objective is sometimes a set of steps of "how to." Thus, the still more mixed-up document defeats it own three purposes.

It is better to determine goals, set standards, and work out routines separately.

A preferable approach to combinations is the common and often-used form in which major segments are listed alongside the standards of performance for each segment. This makes for an overall use of the two related lists and actually produces a worthwhile combination.

A very small portion of a performance description and standards of performance will serve as an example of this type of "written work."

Major Segments	Conditions which will exist when the job is well done
A. Supervises sales for area	1. All quotations are accurate.
	2. All records, reports, correspondence, etc. are accurate and current or completed as scheduled.
	3. All quotations are on schedule.
	4. Telephone requests are handled efficiently and courteously .

B. Supervises warehouse

1. Inventories meet sales requirements and provide a _____ percent turnover every six months.
2. All warehouse shipments are made on time.

C. Trains sales forces

1. Salesmen regularly meet established standards of performance.
2. Salesmen meet sales quotas and sales coverage.
3. Performance appraisals are conducted every eighteen months.

CHAPTER TWENTY-ONE

Variations

THE INDIVIDUAL APPROACH to setting standards is another way to handle the matter when it is not possible to use the group approach illustrated so often in the preceding chapters.

THE INDIVIDUAL APPROACH: TECHNICAL STANDARDS

Up to this point, the examples have covered the setting of standards by the group approach only. Without question, where the use of the group approach is possible the results are most fruitful. However, in some cases such an approach is impossible. This could be because the manager reporting to a specific boss is only one of a kind, as, say, a personnel director who reports to a given superior along with several other executives of like level in their own specialized fields. It is not practical (it won't even work) to have the personnel director prepare his technical standards in conjunction with others having different technical jobs. (It should not be overlooked, however, that this same personnel director in company with the others of his level who report to the same boss can and should use the group approach for setting those standards which apply to their common duties, the direction of people.)

To cite an example of the individual approach in setting a technical standard of performance, let's look at a session in which the president of a small manufacturing company in the Southwest helps set a technical standard of performance for and with his personnel director. In this case the standard has to do with the contract-negotiating segment of his performance. With certain changes to camouflage the situation, an illustrative portion of the session follows.

President John Gormley and Personnel Director Hildreth Nelson are seated before a paperboard placed on an easel in Mr. Gormley's office. They are starting to state the units of measurement for the first list, the step 1 of the technique.

PRES. GORMLEY: Hildy, we've made good progress on setting standards for several of the technical duties of your job. I've held off on the one I've chosen for today until we both have had some experience in the process. Today I'd like us to set a standard for your performance in contract negotiating. This is a very important one, and I have a few ideas on it myself and, I might add, I'm afraid I feel rather strongly about them.

NELSON: Fine by me, and I'm sure I have a few questions on that subject, too.

PRES. GORMLEY: Let's see, then. I'll put the heading up first. (*Writes*) A personnel director's performance in contract negotiating is satisfactory when, colon, number one, period. What units of measurement shall we use?

NELSON: When there is no strike at deadline.

PRES. GORMLEY: (*Writing after number 1*) There is no strike at deadline. (*He puts down the number 2.*)

NELSON: When the settlement is reached within the preset guidelines.

PRES. GORMLEY: (*Writing after 2*) The settlement is reached within the preset guidelines. What else? (*He writes 3.*)

NELSON: When a minimum time-taking is used for negotiating.

PRES. GORMLEY: (*Writes after 3*) A minimum time-taking is used for negotiating. (*Writes 4.*)

NELSON: When the terms of the contract follow a middle road, neither too detailed nor too general.

PRES. GORMLEY: (*Writes after 4*) The terms of the contract follow a middle road. (*Writes 5.*)

NELSON: When there is evidence that the company has gained something for the concessions it has given, like more freedom to make assignments, for instance.

PRES. GORMLEY: (*Writes after 5*) There is evidence that the company has gained something for concessions given. (*Writes 6.*)

NELSON: When the union can't bring up any point which the company hasn't already thought of. This might be in the nature of a surprise, or asking for something in the benefit line and we haven't already checked the cost.

PRES. GORMLEY: (*Writes after 6*) The union can't bring up any point which the company hasn't already thought of. (*Writes number 7.*)

NELSON: When the term of the contract is extended over the current term.

PRES. GORMLEY: (*Writes after 7*) The term of the contract is extended past present contract. (*Writes 8.*)

NELSON: When a minimum use of line people is needed for fact-finding or proof.

PRES. GORMLEY: (*Writes after 8.*) A minimum . . .

This continues for several more sheets of units of measurements.

Now we jump to the use of the discussion in steps 2 and 3 to get agreement and understanding.

PRES. GORMLEY:· (*Heading a clean sheet as before*) A personnel director's performance in contract negotiating is satisfactory when, colon, number one, period. The first item is (*he reads from posted sheet*) There is no strike at deadline. How do you mean that?

NELSON: Well, I think it is obvious that it means just what it says.

PRES. GORMLEY: Are you saying that this unit of measurement should always apply on each negotiation?

NELSON: Sure, otherwise it will cost us a lot more, or—well, maybe not. (*Pause*) Do you mean that we should let a strike occur if it is wise?

PRES. GORMLEY: I don't know. What do you think?

NELSON: Well, if their demands were outrageous, then I wouldn't think we should give in, but I still think that the statement is right—usually, that is.

PRES. GORMLEY: How would you change it then?

NELSON: You could say, "There is no strike at deadline if the guidelines were followed."

PRES. GORMLEY: You are combining numbers one and two. Do you want that?

NELSON: No, not really, but I guess we'd have to have some guidelines.

PRES. GORMLEY: Where would you get them?

NELSON: By consultation with others, yourself included.

PRES. GORMLEY: What would they be like?

NELSON: Well—they certainly would have to be financial or economic as well as personnel-policy-wise.

PRES. GORMLEY: Then you are saying that you *should* combine numbers one and two.

NELSON: No, I don't really think so. I guess what I'm trying to say is that a realistic approach to the demands must be made from an over-all viewpoint.

PRES. GORMLEY: How will we state number one if you want to use it, then?

NELSON: Conditions being reasonable, there is no strike at deadline.

PRES. GORMLEY: Fine, but what do you mean by "conditions being reasonable"?

NELSON: That would depend on conditions in any given negotiation year. They would vary. I think we'd have to set those conditions at the time for each period of contract ending.

PRES. GORMLEY: You mean then that we, you and I, should have to agree on the "conditions" for each contract? Would that be satisfactory to you?

NELSON: Yes, it would; in fact, I'd like it that way. That would clear me on the "no strike" problem if we had agreed to take a strike under certain conditions.

PRES. GORMLEY: OK. Let's leave it up there, knowing that between the two of us we will agree on "conditions" when necessary.

NELSON: That's fine, and I feel that the same arrangement could be made for number two, too.

PRES. GORMLEY: Now then, number two reads (*reading from posted list*), "The settlement is reached within the preset guidelines." Now how would you word that, then, if you think it should be a variable factor?

NELSON: That should be easy. We could say, "The settlement is reached according to variable conditions agreed to with top management."

PRES. GORMLEY: (*Starting to write—then*) But how is that really any different from number one?

NELSON: Well, I guess it really isn't when you think about it. Maybe number one does cover it.

PRES. GORMLEY: Well, let's skip it for now. We'll come back to it before we finish, just to see if we still feel the same.

NELSON: OK.

PRES. GORMLEY: Let's go to number three. (*Reads from posted list*) "A minimum time-taking is used for negotiating." What about that one?

NELSON: It seems to me that that isn't so hot now, either. Too many different possibilities. Maybe we should go "variable" on that, too.

PRES. GORMLEY: Wait a minute. Let's not get carried away with variables. It's true things change every year, but let's be sure first.

NELSON: That's so, but offhand I'd say that the minimum time angle isn't too important unless it is a routine negotiation.

PRES. GORMLEY: You show me a routine negotiation period and I'll show you how the company got the short end of the deal.

NELSON: Could be, but I still think we could eliminate number three.

PRES. GORMLEY: That's OK for now, then, but we may come back to it. Let's look at number four. (*Reading from posted list*) "The terms of the contract follow a middle road." What about that one?

NELSON: Well, let's see—I think that I'd stand by that one as is. I really feel that we have to keep the contract terms sort of "down the middle."

PRES. GORMLEY: Why?

NELSON: It gives us all leeway during the life of the contract.

PRES. GORMLEY: Is that necessary? I thought a contract is a contract.

NELSON: It is, but a certain amount of leeway is always needed.

PRES. GORMLEY: I don't follow you. It seems to me that when we spend so much time in negotiating we ought to be able to live with the resulting contract without any leeway. Anyway, maybe I'm naïve, but wouldn't these things which call for leeway properly be negotiable for the next contract-negotiating session?

NELSON: Yes, I guess that's right, but it has always seemed to me to be more advantageous to keep the contract "on center" so we could take care of any special needs as they come up.

PRES. GORMLEY: What do you mean, "take care of any special needs"? How can there be if both sides have agreed to the negotiated contract?

NELSON: Well, I suppose there shouldn't be, but there always are situations coming up which the contract hasn't covered.

PRES. GORMLEY: You know, Hildy, I get a funny feeling to hear you talk this way. Is there really this laxness in living under the contract? Just how does it work, this what you call "adjustment"?

NELSON: It's really very simple, though I must say I think it is going to be hard to justify it in words. As a matter of practice it has always seemed to work well, but right now it seems hard to talk about.

PRES. GORMLEY: How do you mean?

NELSON: Wel-l-l, I'm beginning in my own mind to question the legitimacy of it now.

PRES. GORMLEY: Explain it, please.

NELSON: It has always worked this way: Whenever a steward received a grievance he would bring it to me. Together we would talk it out to see if we could resolve it. Many were settled at that talk stage. But if the contract didn't have a provision covering the problem, we, the steward and me, that is, would write a memorandum of agreement covering the specific grievance—just for this one person, not all future ones—to solve the situation.

PRES. GORMLEY: What did you do with these memos?

NELSON: I filed them with the copy of the contract, and the individual steward got a copy.

PRES. GORMLEY: Were they used for a new contract negotiation then?

NELSON: No, usually not, though once in a while we did. You see, we really didn't want to clutter up the contract with incidentals.

PRES. GORMLEY: This surprises me. Do you feel, honestly, that this is a good way to operate?

NELSON: I always have or I wouldn't have done it, but I get the feeling that you don't think much of it.

PRES. GORMLEY: That is truly the understatement of the year. I not only don't like it; I am convinced that the company welfare, costwise and qualitywise, is distinctly jeopardized by such a practice. I feel we should get our counsel in on it at once and see how far astray we have gone—legally, that is—especially as regards where the NLRB is concerned.

NELSON: I never really thought of that.

PRES. GROMLEY: Do you have any of these memos you can show me?

NELSON: I can get some, it'll only take a minute. (*He leaves the room, returning in a very short while.*) Here they are.

PRES. GORMLEY: (*Leafing through them*) Hm-m-m. I see what you've done. Most of these appear to be reasonably unimportant, but they could be very disrupting to the company under certain conditions. (*The two men discussed several of the memos, then later went back to the standard.*) In view of this discussion, how do you want to word this fourth item as number two on the new list?

NELSON: Well, I think we should change that to read—mmm . . .

You can see the freedom of technique and participation which can occur by using the individual approach for technical standards, especially when the participants are high level.

The president learned a good deal about things he apparently did not know. It is clear, though, that the boss, the president, injected himself and his own ideas into the discussion.

Further, the personnel director has a new insight into this part of his own job and probably will be more apt to discuss things with his boss.

GROUP VERSUS INDIVIDUAL APPROACH

To point out further the advantages of the group method, where it can be used, the group tends to set a higher standard than many of the people in it would do individually, and some members of the group learn that there is more *what* in their job than they had realized. Also, the group method fosters uniformity where uniformity is needed.

The individual approach has some advantages, too. It can lead to a discussion of problems previously kept under cover and to solutions of them. The boss may gain a new understanding of the situation in which the subordinate finds himself, and he can take action that would not be practical or appropriate in a group. Individual standard setting allows him to do some personal work with his subordinate under the most favorable conditions possible.

A franker discussion can be held, specific examples of performance can be used, and specific goals can be set. There is no dilution of the standard by consideration of what the slower performer will find possible. However, any pushing up of the new standard over present performance rates will depend on the skill of the superior in leading the discussion—discussion which must be acceptable to both parties if improvement is to occur. No amount of browbeating, even if tempered with pleasant platitudes, will stimulate improved performance.

In the individual approach, however, the leader usually participates more fully in the development of ideas rather than acting largely as a catalyst for the group. And he may find it more difficult to keep the discussion to the point at issue—the establishment of standards—since there will be a greater tendency to digress. If the leader permits too much digression, he may find that the session has been important from a training standpoint but that no standards have been developed.

If the leader does his job well, an individual session can probably be completed in less time than is required for a group session, for the simple reason that it is generally easier for two people to agree than for a group of five or ten to do so. Usually, sessions for top-level officers can proceed with a good deal of speed because these men start out with a fairly clear idea of what their objectives should be and because they work closely with the top man. Individual sessions with middle and first-line managers may take a little longer. There are, however, exceptions to this generalization, and the boss should be prepared to spend as much time as necessary with each man.

Variations can also be observed at the middle management level, and even at the first-line level, since technical assignments of many first-line supervisors differ. Though the differences in job content tend to be less the lower down the organization chart we go, it is often a good idea at least to take a look at segments of performance that are peculiar to each individual and attempt to set standards for them. Again, this will be done by the individual method, and the technique will not differ from that used at the corporate level.

This technique is practically the same as that used in the group method, except that only two people, the man and his immediate boss, are present. It is still appropriate to use the paperboard method and post the sheets on the wall. While it might seem that with only two people present it would be easier to use a standard-size piece of writing paper and have the boss and his subordinate work on it together at a desk or a table, experience has shown that the paperboard technique works better even under these circumstances. With all suggestions on the wall where they are readily seen, it is much easier to combine, condense, or add to the statements as the discussion proceeds. There is no passing of paper back and forth, craning of necks, or hunting among several pages for a statement suggested earlier in the meeting.

One company president who tried the method with a small sheet of paper remarked, "One of us was always reading upside down or twisting his neck out of joint trying to see what was written. Further, the original list took up more than one sheet, and we began forgetting what we had already put down and started repeating ourselves. I think, too, putting the list on the wall gives a greater sense of urgency to the meeting. Memoranda on ordinary paper are so common in business that a list on a standard-size sheet seems of no special importance."

AN INDIVIDUAL STANDARD-SETTING SESSION

A partial transcript of another individual standard-setting session is given below. This taped meeting, between the president of the company and his vice-president of marketing, took place in the president's office. The paperboard and a crayon were used for the list. No secretaries were present to take notes. The president did all his own paper work. We will call the president John Olsen and his vice-president Fred Sheridan.

In this case the sales of the company were good, and Mr. Olsen did not originally think that any radical change was needed or would occur as the result of this meeting. After the meeting he said, "I had no idea we would find so many changes we could make for the better. It certainly pointed up my own lack of interested direction where the sales department was concerned."

For purposes of brevity, we will start the transcript at the point where discussion of the actual standard for "market coverage" began. Earlier in the meeting Mr. Olsen had explained what he wanted to do and convinced Fred Sheridan that he was not being critical, that he merely wanted to do his own job better, and that together they would try to work out something that would help Mr. Sheridan to do a better job too. This preliminary discussion took some thirty minutes, and the time spent in working out the list of major segments of performance for Mr. Sheridan totaled several hours, since the duties on the initial list numbered in the forties. By the time the two men had discussed all of them, it was clear that there were several areas in which it was realistic to expect improvement.

Realization of this fact was of terrific import to both men. As Mr. Sheridan told his boss, "This puts a whole new slant on my job. I'd felt that I'd about had it here and was thinking about looking around for a new job. Now I see that I've really only started."

STEP 1: THE LISTING PROCESS

In the transcript below the two are making the initial list of items to be considered in the standard.

PRES. OLSEN: OK, then, Fred, now let's put down the things you feel are important in this area of your performance, dealing with market coverage where our products are concerned. (*He writes at top of paperboard*) "Your performance in market coverage is good when:" Now, what are the things we'll use here?

SHERIDAN: Well, one of the most important ones would be scope of products. (*Mr. Olsen writes as stated.*) Another thing would be our ratio to our competitors' sales. (*He continues to write as Fred makes additions.*) Then there would be divisional figures by sections—what we do in one division compared with other divisions. And you could add the same thing applies to sections and cities within sections. Market analysis by divisions and products has to be considered. Consumer surveys and product analysis count here, too.

PRES. OLSEN: How about obsolete products?

SHERIDAN: Yes, they are important. Just last month we found that we were selling only 8 percent of our manufacturing capacity on our brand 332. It's been going under 20 percent for the last three years. It just never occurred to us to check that.

PRES. OLSEN: Well, obviously we can't make a profit that way. I'm glad you caught it when you did. Now, is there anything else?

SHERIDAN: Yes, this whole area of product salability by test areas should be looked into. We have never needed to do that yet, but I think we should.

The listing goes on for some twenty minutes more before the president calls for a discussion of clear-cut standards.

PRES. OLSEN: Now, Fred, we've got a good start on a list of measuring units up here. Let's set some standards. Take that first one, "scope of product." How can we use that item as a unit of measurement? (*He writes at the top of a new page*) "Your performance in market coverage is good when:"

SHERIDAN: Well, what I had in mind there was the completeness of our line. When one of our salesmen goes into a customer's office, he needs to be able to handle all of his painting needs—not only the paints and varnishes, but the related needs. I think we could amplify our related lines more.

PRES. OLSEN: Yes, I'd agree to that, but when does *your* performance come into it?

SHERIDAN: Our salesmen know what is needed. It would merely be a case of my getting the information back from them through the divisional and regional managers, so I could assemble the data and discuss it with you.

PRES. OLSEN: How often should this happen?

SHERIDAN: Offhand, I'd say on an annual basis. After all, this isn't a fast-moving thing, and it will have to be approached carefully. Maybe a lot of this won't be feasible.

PRES. OLSEN: That's right, but it also will open up new revenue sources for us, too. One thing I want to caution you on now, though, and that is that our discussion isn't designed to make you do a lot more work. It's just to help you do the agreed job better by using your specialized talents to a higher degree.

SHERIDAN: I understand that, and this will be new. But I think it's something I should be doing, so I'll not worry.

PRES. OLSEN: I know, and I'm glad. But, Fred, you've got to remember that in making the list of the major segments of your job, most of the items had to do with the new way you were going to supervise the regional managers and, in turn, get them to do a better job of supervising the district managers.

SHERIDAN: That's right, and I've not forgotten it either. But the more I think of it here, the clearer it is to me that if I get these regional managers to do some of these things, I will be doing a better job myself and so will they.

PRES. OLSEN: OK, then. Now, how will we word this portion of the standard?

SHERIDAN: Well, we could say that my performance in scope of the market determination will be satisfactory when I supply you with annual data for recommended additions to the line and there is evidence that the data has been supplied by the salesmen through their divisional and regional managers.

PRES. OLSEN: Could I word it (*he writes*) "Data for recommended additions to the line is presented at least annually"?

SHERIDAN: That's good as far as it goes. I really think we should add that "there is evidence that the data has been supplied from the whole country."

PRES. OLSEN: OK. Suppose I add (*and he writes*) "and there is evidence that the data has been supplied from the sales force through its own line organization channels"?

SHERIDAN: That's good! Umhuh, I like that.

PRES. OLSEN: OK again, but how much weight should be given to the recommendations?

SHERIDAN: I'd say that when we receive the same recommendations from 75 percent of the salesmen. That's without our suggesting anything to them. These must be their own figures and recommendations.

PRES. OLSEN: Seventy-five percent might be enough to convince you, but I'm sure the board would want a higher percentage before they would authorize capital expenditures for new products.

SHERIDAN: Maybe we should split it then and say 75 percent for those items that would require capitalization of under $5,000, or maybe $3,000, and say 90 percent for anything over.

PRES. OLSEN: That's more like it. If I know our salesmen, these things will have a tendency to build up as they chat with each other at their meetings.

SHERIDAN: Sure, and if they get new lines which they ask for, it stands to reason they'll work hard to sell them, too.

PRES. OLSEN: Probably, but let's see how we are coming with this standard. We said (*and he writes again*) that performance is satisfactory when you supply annual data from the field for recommended additions to the line as evidenced by (*a*) recommendations from 75 percent of salesmen for items under $5,000 cost to start manufacturing, and (*b*) 85 percent for items costing more.

SHERIDAN: I'd prefer 90 percent on that. I think we'd be on safer ground if we used a higher figure, say 90 percent and $3,000 for the break level.

PRES. OLSEN: OK by me. (*He makes the changes on the paperboard.*)

SHERIDAN: That's better. I think that's a lot more realistic.

PRES. OLSEN: I do, too. Now, the second item on the other list is our ratio of sales to our competitors'. How about that?

SHERIDAN: For a starter, how about something like this? My performance is satisfactory in connection with our share of the market when we have gained 33 percent of the available sales. (*President writes as dictated.*) That is a bit over what the surveys show we now have. Last year we had 27.8 percent of the market. That gives me something to shoot at.

PRES. OLSEN: (*As he writes*) That's a good aim, but it may be a little high. Why not shoot for 30 percent this year? OK?

SHERIDAN: OK, if you say so. You won't mind if we go over.

PRES. OLSEN: Of course not, but we want to be realistic. You are going to have a lot of other new things to do, and we can't make huge strides on all fronts. Let's let it stand at 30 percent for now.

SHERIDAN: That's fine with me.

PRES. OLSEN: Now, the third item had to do with the division ratios . . .

The discussion continued until each item was either pinned down with specific measurements or was eliminated or combined with another.

As this standard-setting session goes on, it is clearly evident that there is no hint of overdirecting, oversimplification, or overelaboration. There is no tinge of face-saving or overconfidence, nor is there any attempt at whitewash. Rather, the discussion soon becomes very worthwhile, pertinent, and useful, one which may bring about change in the future emphasis of the sales effort. More significant, a good executive who was ready to change jobs has been given a new enthusiasm for his present work.

Standards set for the vice-president of sales, it can be seen, are largely technical ones, in the sense that they are standards that will apply only to the sales function. To meet these standards, however, the top sales executive must improve his direction of people. Obviously, he cannot hope to improve the share of the market unless he improves the performance of his regional sales managers, they in turn improve the performance of the district managers, and so on down the line. He has agreed, even volunteered, that it is possible to meet the standards with the present force and without extra aid in the way of more advertising.

This is true of nearly all technical standards for managers, which will include such things as:

- Units of production produced per given period of time
- Number of research efforts (failures and successes) for a given period of time
- Total sales, sales breakdowns by types, specific items sold, and similar sales-reporting devices
- Number of bills collected by due dates

- Value of suggested changes in manufacturing processes
- Specific quantity of product designs
- Dollar savings in purchase of insurance
- Medical proof of improved employee attendance

A DIRECTOR OF MANUFACTURING

A further illustration is the following example, which is a *performance description*, not a job description, with the accompanying standards for a director of manufacturing.

A. Major Segments of Responsibility of Director of Manufacturing:
1. Maintain quality through adequate product control.
2. Continuously work toward improving operating efficiency with the objective of achieving cost reduction in manufacturing, material handling, maintenance, and other factory departments.
3. Schedule manufacturing in such a manner that the shipping schedules and inventory levels agreed upon are maintained.
4. Provide a long-range manufacturing program so that seasonal fluctuations in orders do not result in excessive layoffs during slack season or excessive overtime in peak season.
5. Provide a preventive maintenance program to ensure minimum breakdown and idleness of machinery and maintain machinery to prescribed standards of appearance and serviceability.
6. Provide a maintenance program for buildings and equipment to avoid excessive deterioration and to maintain appearance.
7. Develop improved machinery for manufacturing processes and maintain awareness of improved machinery offered on the market.
8. Provide an adequate fire-prevention program, including alarm systems, plant fire brigade, fire-extinguishing equipment, etc.
9. Provide and maintain a mechanic shop.
10. Maintain the highest degree of labor relations and conduct collective bargaining in such a manner as to reach equitable agreements.

B. Satisfactory Performance on the Part of the Director of Manufacturing Is Achieved in Respect to:
1. *Maintaining quality through adequate product control:* When there is evidence that adequate facilities, personnel, and procedures have been provided to ensure that products manufactured continually meet established standards.

2. *Continuously working toward improving operating efficiency with the objective of achieving cost reduction in manufacturing, material handling, maintenance, and other factory departments:* When there exists a continuous program of cost improvement which is understood and accepted by departmental units; when the results show improvement over accepted standards; and when there has been full participation with other departments in cost-reduction programs where such cooperation is desirable.

3. *Scheduling manufacturing in such a manner that the shipping schedules and inventory levels agreed upon are maintained:* When agreed-upon shipping schedules are continuously met and agreed-upon inventory levels are maintained.

4. *Providing a long-range manufacturing program so that seasonal fluctuations in orders do not result in excessive layoffs during slack seasons or excessive overtime in peak seasons:* When there is evidence that there has been long-range production planning and production scheduling to reduce the effect of seasonal fluctuations in order volume upon manpower requirements to the end that excessive layoffs during periods of low-volume sales and excessive overtime in periods of peak-volume sales are eliminated.

5. *Providing a preventive maintenance program to ensure minimum breakdown and idleness of machinery and maintain machinery to prescribed standards of appearance and serviceability:* When there is evidence that there has been regular and effective inspection and servicing of machinery and there is no excessive breakdown or enforced idleness.

6. *Providing a maintenance program for buildings and equipment to avoid excessive deterioration and to maintain appearance:* When there is evidence that there has been regular and effective inspection and maintenance of buildings and equipment and there is no excessive deterioration; and when appearance is maintained at agreed-upon standards.

7. *Developing improved machinery for manufacturing processes and maintaining awareness of improved machinery offered on the market:* When there is evidence that there has been periodic evaluation of production equipment in each department; when there is evidence that there has been improvement and/or replacement of obsolete, inefficient, or worn-out equipment; and when new equipment available on the market has been considered.

8. *Providing an adequate fire-prevention program, including alarm systems, plant fire brigade, fire-extinguishing equip-*

ment, etc.: When there is evidence that an adequate fire-alarm system exists; that a plant fire brigade has been organized and trained and regular drills have been held; when adequate fire-extinguishing equipment has been provided; and when the advice of local fire-prevention officials has been sought and considered.

9. *Providing and maintaining a mechanic shop:* When a machine shop and tools and trained personnel have been provided which are adequate for making repairs upon and building machines, equipment, etc., on our own premises and by our own personnel, for which expensive or specialized equipment or specially skilled personnel are not required.

10. *Maintaining the highest degree of labor relations and conducting collective bargaining in such a manner as to reach equitable agreements:* When the records of unresolved grievances and labor turnover are not in excess of agreed-upon standards; and when equitable agreements are regularly reached with the employees' association.

A PURCHASING AGENT'S STANDARD

A simple standard of performance, worked out by a group of buyers with their boss, the purchasing agent, gives us still another example of the standard for a specialized job.

Buyer: Performance is satisfactory when he:
1. Readily recalls names and faces
2. Communicates, both orally and in writing, clearly and logically
3. Quickly summarizes facts and arrives at accurate decisions
4. Makes comparisons of available materials and makes recommendations to requesting parties
5. Seeks direction as needed, but on the whole operates effectively without supervision
6. Undertakes work on a priority basis
7. Accepts constructive criticism and adjusts practices accordingly
8. Establishes and maintains harmonious relations with workers
9. Before placing an order, checks to see if a company standard has already been established
10. Actively participates in standardizing activities
11. Punctually keeps appointments
12. Summarizes all completed transactions
13. Secures maximum competition commensurate with price, quality, and service

Evaluation of Managerial Performance

CHAPTER TWENTY-TWO

Introduction

IN THE FIRST CHAPTER of this book, I pointed out that managers generally are often in doubt about:

1. *What* they are supposed to do. (Part Two.)

2. How *far* they are expected to go in doing it—that is, the degree of authority they possess in each area for which they are responsible. (Part Three.)

3. How *well* they should perform their jobs. (Part Four.)

4. How well they *are* doing them. (Part Five.)

The earlier sections of this book have covered techniques which the line boss can use to ensure that he and his subordinates have a common understanding of the first three. This section will deal with a technique that will enable the boss to determine a realistic answer to the fourth one and to discuss performance with his subordinates in such a way that they will be given not only impetus to improve, but definite ideas about the kind of improvement the boss wants and how they can go about achieving it.

I am speaking, of course, of a technique of management performance evaluation and of the counseling which the results of the evaluation should make possible, counseling that should result in management performance improvement that will really benefit both the company and the person himself.

Most large companies have "management development programs" of one kind or another; many, perhaps even most, have some kind of evaluation plan. Yet few of these programs seem to be producing the results expected of them.

Why do so many managers say that they are not being told how well they are doing their jobs even though many of them work for companies that have evaluation plans? And why do so many companies that have management development programs find it necessary to go outside when they need top-level managers despite the fact that they prefer to promote from within? (The great growth and prosperity of the firms engaged in executive recruitment is proof that many of them do.)

The answer to both questions may be that the evaluation programs and the management development programs are just that—"programs" in the sense that I defined a program earlier: "any activity that is superimposed on the normal operation of the business," something that seldom has any lasting effect on the normal operation of the business. It is because the evaluation programs, and in most cases the management development programs, are simply activities superimposed on the normal activity of the business that the managers do not take them seriously.

It is a well-known fact that managers do not like to make formal appraisals of their subordinates and many of them dread the appraisal interviews. And this is understandable. Usually they have been given a form developed by some staff department and are supposed to fill it out in detail whether or not they feel the questions it asks have any real bearing on what they want done. Naturally, then, it is embarrassing for the boss to talk to a subordinate about some shortcoming that the boss has never really bothered about on the job. And if the boss hasn't bothered about it in his day-to-day management, the subordinate is likely to feel that it is unimportant anyway and to believe (rightly) that the boss will forget all about it as soon as he completes the unpleasant chore of the appraisal interview.

PEOPLE DO
WHAT THE BOSS INSPECTS

It might be stated as an axiom (or a principle of management) that "people do what their boss inspects." Lawrence A. Appley, of the American Management Association, was perhaps the first to point this out—or rather to sharpen the common management saying, "people do what the boss expects," in this way.

The two sentences really mean the same thing, for people identify what the boss expects by what he inspects, by what he comments on, by what he seems pleased about, and by what makes him angry or, perhaps, merely cast a cold and fishy eye on a subordinate when he finds him doing it. If what the boss talks about in the appraisal interview differs from what he talks about on the job, or communicates by facial expression or tone of voice, subordinates are not going to pay much attention to what he says in that interview, especially when they know that conducting it is something imposed on the boss from without and that he doesn't really believe in the program himself.

The appraisal technique advocated in this section is designed to ensure agreement between what the boss really wants and what he appraises his subordinates on. But it will be of no more value than any other technique of appraisal unless the boss himself really wants to use it.

It may be introduced by the top man in any organizational unit: the company president, the division manager, or even a department head who is a second-line manager. But he must not introduce it simply because other companies are doing it or because he feels that it might be a good thing. He must be convinced that it is really something that will help his company, division, or department get better results in the way of lower costs, higher profit, better service, or smoother operation. He must regard the appraisals as he regards reports of financial variances and other reports he examines regularly.

Of course if the company president, the division manager, or some other high-echelon boss adopts a technique and requires his subordinates to use it in appraising the people under them, it is, in effect, being imposed on them from without. But there is a big difference between this situation and the one in which he merely permits a system to be introduced because some staff department has told him that it is a good thing to have, and gives it his blessing because he thinks it *might* do some good.

When the top boss in the organizational unit regards the appraisals as an essential part of the management job—not just something superimposed on the normal conduct of the business—the appraisals and the results become something he inspects—something, therefore, that his subordinates will not try to escape doing or do perfunctorily. They will regard use of the technique as they do meeting production or sales quotas or anything else they regard as a normal part of their jobs.

An appraisal of how well a subordinate is doing the things that his own line boss considers are a normal part of his job offers clues to the type of management training he needs—training that will enable him to improve in ways that will help the organizational unit meet its objectives.

Like many appraisal systems, many of the management development programs introduced in the past have been "programs" superimposed on the normal operations of the business, and as such they have not had much, if any, effect on the normal conduct of the managers.

For example, take the courses in human relations that have been so popular and have often been conducted by staff departments which have suggested them to top management and gained consent to go ahead, top management being convinced only that since most companies were giving them they were "probably" good to have. In many cases, they were given to people who did not need them (which meant a waste of money) and because those who did need them realized that the courses were only "programs" that superiors would shortly forget about in the normal course of business, they had little effect on performance. One manufacturing vice-president tells this story:

> Our personnel director suggested a course in human relations for the plant managers, and I told him to go ahead, develop the course, and have one of his men give it. I never attended any of the sessions until the final one—the graduation program, so to speak—at which I presented certificates to those who had completed it.
>
> We held the session at one of our plants, and of course, since I and several others in the top group were there, the plant manager had tried to make sure that the plant was a model of good housekeeping in case the higher-ups decided to inspect the production floor. We did.
>
> Everything was in order except in one corner where a man had a lot of tools and grease around, and was sitting down apparently doing nothing, merely contemplating a machine. The plant manager didn't stop to "get all the facts" as he had been instructed to do in the course; he didn't even ask the foreman what the trouble was. In practically one bound, he was all the way across the room and bawling out the man at the top of his lungs with liberal use of profanity. And all the while he still had his diploma in human relations clutched in his hand.

Why this happened is quite obvious. The plant manager did not believe that his superior considered the practices he had been told about in the human relations course as important as good plant housekeeping. No matter how hot his temper he would have controlled himself if he had, for executives are generally able to control themselves if they think a display of temper will jeopardize their jobs or their chances of raises or promotions. (An executive seldom unleashes his temper on the boss himself, no matter what the provocation, unless he is prepared to climax his tirade by resigning his job.)

It is possibly because of the failure of the human relations courses introduced as "programs" extraneous to normal business activities that sensitivity training was developed. Since teaching people to give the right answers appeared to have little effect on their conduct on the job, it was felt that the only way to change their attitudes would be to shock them into taking a fresh look at themselves. But, although the problem is a very real one, sensitivity training is not necessarily the answer, for like all "programs" it is regarded as something extraneous to the job itself, and, as mentioned earlier, it can have harmful effects.

Is there no value, then, in courses in human relations in which managers are advised to "get all the facts" before bawling out a subordinate and are given related pointers on handling their subordinates? On the contrary, they may be very valuable if the line boss has found, after appraising a subordinate, that such a course is what the subordinate needs and has frankly told him so, and further, is prepared to follow up and to see that the subordinate knows that he will follow up to ascertain whether the subordinate is using the knowledge on the job. But when there is a blanket prescription, when everyone on the same level takes the course regardless of what he has been doing or not doing in the past, it becomes "just one of those things" that people feel must be lived through and forgotten as soon as it is over.

How can the boss know that a plant manager is inclined to blow up when he finds a subordinate apparently idle? He can know if he wants to know—if he regards directing the people immediately under him as the most important part of his job. He will make it his business to know and to appraise the people under him at intervals on all phases of the work that he believes are important. He won't have to wait until there are wildcat strikes or an excessive number of grievances to find out whether or not a subordinate manager is handling human relations well or badly. And he will be particularly sure to make it his business to know if his own line superior is going to question him on these points during his own appraisal.

Despite the fact that an executive is unlikely to tell his bosses that he doesn't believe in, say, the things that are taught in the usual human relations class ("You can't get out production that way"), the alert boss can easily ascertain his attitude on the matter. And he doesn't have to go on snooping expeditions, either, or transgress protocol by questioning the people who report to his subordinate. If he has frequent contacts with his subordinate, and really pays attention to him, he will be quite aware of his attitude toward the various phases of his job *if* he is really interested enough. There are innumerable clues to what a person really believes is important in even the most casual conversation.

Many of the courses offered in management development programs present valuable information that will be of use on the job, and managers will apply it to their work when they are convinced that their line bosses really want them to. But they can never be convinced of that fact if their bosses do not show, by both word and deed, that they want them to. Each man must know that the courses he takes will give him knowledge that his line superior wants him, personally, to take to heart and not something that is routinely prescribed for everyone in his position.

PURPOSE OF APPRAISALS

Appraisals are, of course, valuable in deciding on promotions and raises, and even on occasion for deciding who will be kept on the payroll and who will be dismissed. But they are not conducted primarily for any of these reasons. The primary purpose is to help each man handle his current job better.

This is a point that should be emphasized in any announcement of an appraisal plan and in the talks each boss holds with each of his subordinates on either the plan itself or on the results of an appraisal. If the promotion aspect is prominently featured, false hopes may be aroused, for higher jobs may not be available or likely to be available in the near future. Continuing improvement as shown by successive appraisals will in many cases mean that a man should have a raise, but it is not always possible to grant one at any specific time; therefore, it should be understood that the boss is not making any promises of more money even if any given appraisal shows that the man is doing an excellent job.

And, of course, the boss should endeavor to avoid any tinge of a threatening attitude in his conduct of the appraisal interview. If he does not, his group will become nervous as appraisal time approaches and the work will suffer.

CHAPTER TWENTY-THREE

Why Many Evaluation Plans Fail

MANY EVALUATION PLANS fail because, as stated in the last chapter, line management regards making the appraisals as something extraneous to the real work—an extra chore that interferes with work toward their real objectives and a simple waste of time. In many cases, the line managers are quite right in thinking so because of the nature of the forms they are compelled to fill in. These forms often call for information that has no pertinence to the jobs and for judgments that are difficult or impossible to make, and even more difficult to discuss with the subordinates once they have been made.

TRAIT RATING

Perhaps the worst offenders in this respect have been the trait-rating forms, which, although they are less common than they once were, are still in use in some companies. When appraisal systems first became common, shortly after World War II, trait rating seemed quite logical to most people, for everyone is accustomed, mentally at least, to judging his associates in terms of traits. Jones, we say to ourselves, is intelligent, but a little harsh; Brown is kind hearted, but too easygoing; Talcott is not very logical, and so on. These judgments are quite natural; people can scarcely avoid making them, even though they may not always be accurate and not everyone ascribes the same traits to the same person. It also seemed quite logical to suppose that the more of the traits usually considered desirable a person possessed, the better the performance he would turn in.

For these reasons, common practice was to have a staff department draw up a list of desirable traits, duplicate it, distribute it to the line managers, and ask them to rate each of their subordinates on each trait, frequently on a numerical scale. In some cases, each trait is weighted in accordance with its supposed importance—thus a good score on "intelligence" or "ability to get along with others" may count more toward the final rating than a good score on "accuracy." In the end, each man's personality could be summed up by a number, and those with the higher scores were considered better than those with lower scores.

The trouble with this plan is that in many cases high scores do not have much relation to performance. There are, for example, many people who are rated highly intelligent by everyone who knows them, but who are so sadly lacking in common sense that they do everything wrong, or don't do anything at all, and this is true even when the judgment of their associates is confirmed by supposedly scientific tests. Then there are people who are so "cooperative" that they spend their time appeasing others rather than getting things done.

It has never been shown, in fact, that successful performance depends on possession of any particular trait to any given degree.

For example, some years ago many studies were conducted in an attempt to determine the traits that differentiate "leaders" from those who lack "leadership ability." They came to nothing because there did not seem to be any clear-cut traits that successful leaders in various activities had in common. The same is true of successful managers.

Numerical scoring was abandoned fairly early, for it was soon found that it was impossible to handle it accurately. Anyone can differentiate a boor from a person with a reasonable amount of tact or courtesy. But who can determine whether executive A rates 10 points for "tact" whereas executive B should get only 8 or 9 points?

But abandonment of numerical scores did not mean that trait rating itself was discarded. Instead, a graduated scale was used on which the boss was asked to rate each subordinate on each trait as, say, "outstanding," "good," "average," "below average," or "poor." Or, as a further refinement there might be blocks of statements, and the boss would be told to check the block most applicable to his subordinate, but to cross out any phrases that did not apply and underline phrases in other blocks that did apply.

A blank of this type may be easier for the boss to fill out than those which call for numerical scores on the various traits, but it is still difficult to complete because the boss is not really interested in whether or not the subordinate possesses all the traits the personnel department, or some psychologist, believes are good traits for a manager to have. He is interested in what the man accomplishes; that is what the boss observes. Thus when he comes to make the rating he has no idea of how to rate the man on many of the traits, especially since some of them may be very nebulous: "vision" for instance, or "personality," or even "acceptability." I have actually seen one form that included no less than 516 traits, and the unfortunate line bosses were expected to rate each of their immediate subordinates on each one—an impossible task.

THE FORCED-CHOICE METHOD

Another type of rating is the "forced-choice" method which some companies have borrowed from the Army. This has a number of blocks of statements, perhaps as many as thirty, and the boss must check the statement that is most applicable to the man being rated and the one that is least applicable in each block. For example:

BLOCK I
1. Has great technical knowledge
2. Is often late to work
3. Very accurate
4. Does not delegate

BLOCK II
1. His subordinates like him
2. Is very decisive
3. Not immediately promotable
4. Works very hard

Now a man might have great technical knowledge, be late to work, be very accurate, and be unwilling or unable to delegate, or none of these statements might apply to him. The same is true of the second block, and will be true of all blocks included on the form. But the rater is forced to indicate a most applicable and a least applicable statement in each case.

In developing its own forced-choice, the Army had some 13,000 officers rated as "outstanding," "average," or "poor" by people who knew them well, and then tried out the statements on 9,000 on whom the judgments were unanimous: 3,000 whom everyone considered outstanding, another 3,000 whom everyone considered average, and a third group of the same size composed of those whom everyone considered poor officers. Only items on which all the outstanding officers received high scores, the average officers were rated "average," and the poor officers made poor scores were included in the final blank.

This sounds as though the blank might be used with confidence—for Army officers. But even those who favor the plan do not believe that the Army blank will be useful in industry. Each company is supposed to develop its own. And few companies have enough executives to ensure that any studies they conduct of "poor," "average," and "outstanding" executives will be statistically valid. Further, it may be true that the Army blank is applicable to all officers, whatever their ranks or assignments (although even this is debatable), but industry's case is different. Different jobs require different qualifications, depending on the work to be done and the level in the organization.

Another difficulty with all these forms is that they make the appraisal interview extraordinarily difficult for the boss, and painful and unenlightening for the man being rated. Because most people think of traits as a permanent part of the personality, a man who is told he lacks certain supposedly necessary traits is likely to be completely discouraged. Further, the nebulous terms used confuse both him and the boss. A man has been found, let us say, only average on "vision" or "acceptability." What can he do to improve, and how can the boss counsel him?

In the case of the forced-choice method, the difficulty is as great or greater when it comes to the counseling interview, for even the boss himself doesn't know whether he has given the man a good score or a poor one. Some of the items that appear favorable will count against the man since the developers of the blank have felt that other items in the same block are more important and would have been checked instead if the man were not falling down in some particular, and some of the items that would appear to reduce the score do not count at all.

The mysterious method of scoring, which is known only to the staff department that developed the form, is thought to be advantageous in that it makes it impossible for the line boss to overrate his favorites or underrate people to whom he has taken an unaccountable dislike. But it also makes it impossible for him to express his real opinions or to discuss the results intelligently. Many bosses have found that the summary scores presented to them by the staff department entirely misrepresented their views of most of their subordinates.

Another type of evaluation form calls for an essay rather than a numerical rating. The boss simply writes a little essay on the man listing his strong points and his weak points with notes on ways in which he can improve. Then he grades him as "immediately promotable," "eventually promotable," or "not promotable."

Many bosses don't like this one too well either. They know in a general way whether they consider the man a good performer, a bad one, or just average, but they find it difficult to determine just why. If they are helped by job-oriented questions, such as, "Does he meet all schedules on time?" and "Does he meet or surpass his production (or sales) quota?" things become a little easier for them, but they still feel at a loss for words when they try to pin down a complete picture of the man they are rating. On the other hand, some bosses can use such a form to give a very clear and succinct picture of the man *as they see him.* But they do not know, unless there have been complaints or compliments from other executives in other departments, how what he does is affecting groups outside his own. A sales manager, for example, may be causing difficulties for production or for the credit department and his boss may never hear of it, for people are not likely to complain unless the man's performance is causing them very serious trouble. Also, it is unfortunately true that many busy managers are apt to forget to transmit their favorable opinions of people in other departments. They will probably thank the man himself when he is helpful to them, but they won't realize that his boss would like to hear about the compliment, too.

Perhaps the most serious difficulty with the essay-type forms is that each boss fills them out in isolation, and higher management never checks on whether he has done so, and more important, how well he has done so. He is never called upon to justify what he has written except that the forms are examined in an effort to find out who is promotable to a given job that has just opened up.

Until that point is reached, all the forms are simply filed away, and when the search for a candidate begins the essays written by highly articulate men and by those whose brains become practically paralyzed when they are confronted with writing jobs are given equal weight. The reports are simply not comparable, if they exist at all, and often it is found that after the first few times the practice of making them has been quietly dropped.

**THE GROUP
SUMMARY APPRAISAL**

The method advocated in this book, the group summary appraisal with higher management control, is designed to minimize the difficulties that have developed with other types of evaluation, and to ensure that managers consider making the appraisals and the subsequent interviews with the men appraised a definite part of their regular jobs.

CHAPTER TWENTY-FOUR

Conducting a Group Summary Appraisal

THE REASONS WHY many evaluation plans tend to fall into the discard should be clear from the last chapter. Superiors dislike them for one or more of the following reasons:

1. They require the superior to make judgments that he knows he is not capable of making—for example, to determine on a graduated scale how much or how little of each of a large number of traits each of his subordinates possesses. Although the form that listed 516 traits was exceptional, probably unique, many forms list more traits than the superior has an opportunity to see evidence of, one way or the other.

2. They are not job-oriented. The superior is interested in performance; yet many of the traits listed on the forms have no bearing on performance.

3. They make it difficult or embarrassing for the superior to justify his views in the evaluation interview. This is true of trait-rating forms and also of the forced-choice forms. When the superior talks over his trait judgments with his subordinate, he is, in effect, compelled to tell him: "You, as a person, are lacking in certain innate qualities," and no matter how tactful the superior is, the interview takes on the character of a per-

sonal attack. In the case of the forced-choice forms, the superior is likely to be at a loss because he does not know, until some staff department tells him, whether he has given the subordinate a good score or a bad one.

4. They require the superior to write an essay, something many superiors find difficult to do.

In addition, many forms are less helpful in planning management improvement measures than they might be because:

1. If they deal entirely with results (for example, with meeting production or sales quotas), they do not deal with the methods used to produce those results. Yet the methods used may actually be damaging to the company in the long run.

2. They do not show how the work of a given department has affected the work of other departments. The superior is not likely to know this except by chance.

It may seem as though it would be impossible to design a system that would not suffer from at least one of these faults. Yet the way out is simple. The group summary appraisal is in fact the simplest of all the systems to use—it requires no carefully designed forms, no graduated scales. The only tools that are actually necessary are a few sheets of blank paper and a pen or a pencil. The superior does not have to compose an essay or to make fine judgments on qualifications he has had no opportunity to observe; he merely talks out the appraisal with a few other people on his own level who may be able to fill gaps in his own knowledge and help him to avoid any bias, favorable or unfavorable. Only the statements with which everyone agrees form a part of the written appraisal.

The appraisal group generally consists of three or four people, including, of course, the immediate superior of the man who is being appraised. Four is perhaps the best number, large enough in most cases to ensure that all those who are in a position to know much about a man's work are included, yet small enough to make for free discussion. In some instances, it may be necessary to have as many as five in the group, but if the number is any larger than that, the process may become unwieldy.

THE VALUE OF A GROUP

The immediate superior has, of course, a more intimate knowledge of what the man does and how well he is doing it than anyone else. But he cannot always remember everything, and more important, he does not know how the man's methods of working affect other departments, and since every business is interested in overall results rather than in results in one department or section, this is an extremely important point. In addition, as in sessions described earlier in this book, a group is often able to generate more ideas about steps that can be taken to help the subordinate than a single person can.

Sometimes a department head will feel that he knows everything that it is important to know about his subordinates, and will object to the group appraisal method for that reason. But once he has had experience with it, he is usually convinced that it will be helpful to him.

One department head smugly informed his superior, a corporate officer, that he knew "all about" his own people. "Getting other people in on this," he said, "simply doesn't make any sense to me at all." Yet the very first round of appraisals brought out two important facts about one of his subordinates that he had been ignorant of: (1) For years, the subordinate had acted as a semiprofessional adviser to a group of employees interested in one of the arts. (2) The subordinate had not been getting along very well with people not under his direct supervision. These two facts suggested one approach the superior could use in his appraisal interview: "Why not," he decided to say, "use the same approach in dealing with other departments that you have used so successfully with the extracurricular group?"

Many companies that use special appraisal forms find it necessary to give appraisers training in their use. The terms used must be explained in advance, and superiors must be cautioned against what personnel men call the "halo effect," the temptation to believe that a man who is obviously good (or bad or average) on one or more of the factors listed should get the same score on all the others.

In contrast, participation in a group appraisal requires no special experience or training. Members of the group make only the kinds of judgments they make mentally every day about the people with whom they come in contact and sometimes express informally to others on their own level. There can be no "halo effect" because they are not compelled to put anything into the appraisal on which they do not already have an opinion.

SELECTION OF APPRAISERS

As mentioned, an appraisal group always includes the immediate superior and others whose own work is likely to be affected by the conduct of the man being appraised. But there is another important point to observe in selecting appraisers: They must be managers on a higher level than the man they are to appraise.

Some people believe that men on the same level should take part in the appraisal, on the theory that people are likely to be more intimately acquainted with the work of their colleagues than superiors can be. But this is unrealistic. If men on the same level are personal friends, they are not likely to say anything against each other. If they are rivals, they may see the appraisal as an opportunity to cut down someone whom they consider a threat to their own advancement. Or, if neither of these things occurs, there may be tacit, or open, agreement among the group that all appraisals will be entirely favorable.

It has even been suggested that superiors should be evaluated by their own subordinates. This is useless, or worse still, actually harmful to the man-boss relationships. In the first place, subordinates may be afraid of reprisals if they evaluate their bosses realistically, even when their remarks are supposed to be entirely confidential. Superiors sometimes want to know. "Who said that?" And often they have ways of finding out. In the second place, superiors might be tempted to curry favor with subordinates whose opinions carried weight. And, in the third place, subordinates are really not competent to judge their superiors except in a few areas. It is all to the good if a superior is popular with his subordinates, but he may be so only because he is extra permissive and lax in enforcing rules or maintaining standards; therefore his subordinates' opinions of him are no indication of his performance.

But the most important objection to evaluation by either equals or subordinates is this: People are not hired to judge their colleagues or their superiors; doing so is no part of their jobs. They do not know what the boss's superior expects of him.

Should staff people be members of an appraisal group that is dealing with the work of a line manager? Occasionally they may be, particularly in cases where plants or offices are widely scattered. Thus a plant manager may have no one on his own level to work with him on the appraisal of his immediate subordinates and may find that he has to use staff people from headquarters in order to make up a group. For example, he might use men from the headquarters production engineering group or from the industrial engineering staff at headquarters in appraising his production manager. Where possible, however, it is best to have a group made up of higher line managers with whom the man comes in frequent contact. Thus an accountant might be appraised not only by his superior, but by two or three department heads to whom he furnishes reports.

Who should select the appraisers? The immediate superior may do so, but it is sometimes wise to have the man who is to be appraised suggest the names, the only restriction being that they must be people on a higher level than he is and people who have had a chance to observe some part of his work.

One advantage of the latter plan is that the man who is allowed to select his own appraisers will have positive evidence that the process is not designed to put him on the spot or "get something on him," that the primary aim is to help him, not to find fault with him. There need be no fear that this will result in appraisals that are unduly favorable. Any man who is considered outstanding by three or four people on a higher level who are familiar with his work is probably really outstanding. Since all the points that go into the finished appraisal must be agreed to by everyone in the group, one biased appraiser cannot have much effect on the results.

If the superior selects the appraisers the first time around, he may find that a subordinate who has been appraised in somewhat unfavorable terms suspects that some one member of the group is prejudiced against him. In that case, the superior can eliminate suspicion by letting the man recommend appraisers the next time.

In one instance in which the superior followed this course, the second appraisal—for which the man had recommended the appraisers—turned out to be little different from the first, a concrete demonstration that there had been no prejudice the first time. The third time around, the man voluntarily suggested that the man he had suspected of bias be included in the appraisal group.

Although the appraisers need no special experience or training in the process since they will be required to do only what they have been doing informally all along, they do need two qualifications aside from some familiarity with the work of the man who is to be appraised. These qualifications, however, are a matter of attitude rather than skill.

First, they must believe in the value of the appraisals, not regard them as something extraneous to the company's real work. If they look upon them as a "frill," they will not make much attempt to get down to cases. Their attitude will be: "I'll go along with anything the rest of you say," in which case there is no point in having them there.

Second, they must understand that the main reason for the appraisal is to help the man improve his performance on the job, not to determine whether he gets a raise or gets fired. The possibility of promotion will enter the discussion only at the end of the appraisal, and will not hinge on whether there is a higher job available.

It should not be too difficult to get a group of executives on a given level to believe in the pertinence of the appraisal to their own jobs if they are people with whom the man "does business." Nor should it be very hard to persuade them it is worth their while to help him improve if the way he handles his job affects their own showing.

THE ROLE OF THE CHAIRMAN

Any group discussion requires a leader or a chairman if the talk is not to wander down byways that have nothing to do with the subject at hand. The immediate superior, as the man who is most interested in getting results, always acts as the chairman.

There should always be a secretary also, someone to makes notes of what is said so that the group can eventually summarize what they have agreed on and come to firm conclusions. The chairman may act as his own secretary (usually he does, in fact,) or he may ask one of the group to undertake the role. Since the chairman has to conduct the appraisal interview, he will find it better if he has notes he has written himself.

The first rule of conduct for the secretary is that he must write down everything that is said—not, naturally, word for word since he is unlikely to be a shorthand expert. What he should get down on paper is merely the gist of the comments—which he may record in single words or phrases if these are sufficient to refresh his memory when someone asks about a comment that has been made earlier. He can use any blank sheet of paper for his note taking, although he may find it convenient to group the comments under three headings that can be printed on an appraisal form: results, methods, and personal qualifications. If the final appraisal appears under these headings, the chairman will find it easier to present the results to his own superiors later on when the higher management review takes place.

The chairman takes part in the appraisal as well as making notes, and records his own comments as well as those of his colleagues. He must be alert to everything that is said, and generally it is better for him to record each comment as it is made rather than wait until agreement is reached. When there is consensus he can check or underline the points that all the participants agree on. These points will make up the notes that he will read back later to the other members of the group, but if he has noted down the opinions expressed only by one member of the group, he will be able to read these back as well if the group would like to discuss them further at the end of the session.

Can the chairman take adequate notes and still take part in the appraisal himself? It is true that he may not be able to do much talking during the early part of the session, although undoubtedly he can throw in an occasional remark. Then, when he decides that all the important points have been given sufficient consideration, he can read back his notes and at the same time can express his own opinions if he has anything to add to what has been said. Then the group analyzes what has been said and completes the appraisal. The chairman, of course, makes further notes on the final discussion to ensure that all the points the group has agreed on are clearly indicated.

Experience has shown that the chairman seldom finds that the note taking prevents him from participating in the discussion, for his notes need only be in the nature of reminders that will enable him to read back the gist of what has been said. And, of course, if he has missed anything, the other members of the group can remind him of the points he has omitted when he reads back the notes.

Later he writes up the appraisal and sends it to each member of the group for approval and signature. This provides a further check, for if anyone feels that the summary misrepresents what has been said, he can offer corrections before the appraisal is considered final.

His role as chairman is more exacting, for the success of the meeting depends largely on the way he conducts it. He must start the meeting, encourage each member of the group to participate, and determine when there has been enough discussion of each point brought out.

The chairman cannot simply begin by saying: "What do you fellows think of so-and-so?" If he does, he will find that everyone is practically tongue-tied. The only comment such an approach is likely to elicit is: "Why, I guess he's all right."

Particularly in the case of a first appraisal, the chairman may begin by stressing the confidential nature of the appraisal and the fact that only unanimous opinions will get into the final summary. This will eliminate fear that the man being appraised will later be able to determine who said what. Even though all those taking part are on a higher level than the man who is being appraised, none of them will want to be identified as the meanie who made the unfavorable comments.

The chairman should also read the man's job description or perhaps make copies of all documents bearing on the nature of his job available to the appraisers. If he has used the techniques described earlier in this book, he might also make available a list of the "what's" of the job, and the findings of the group or individual discussions in which there has been agreement on the degree of responsibility and authority it carries.

This is important, for all the appraisers must know what the man is supposed to be doing and how far he is permitted to go in various areas in order to judge how well he is performing. Frequently, those from other departments may not have too clear an understanding of these points even though they have had a considerable amount of contact with the man.

Once the chairman has made his brief opening remarks, he must endeavor to provide positive leadership without dominating the meeting. If he imposes his own opinions on the group, he might as well make the appraisal without their help.

If he is accustomed to dealing mainly with subordinates, it may be difficult for him to avoid unconscious domination, and he may find the others only too ready to go along with him. This will be particularly true if he is on a higher level than the other members of the group. And even if they are men on his own level, as they should be if possible, the other members of the group may be inclined to defer to him because he is the man's boss, and, particularly if it is their first experience with the group appraisal, they may feel that if they volunteer opinions contrary to his, or do not agree with some of the things he says, they will be trespassing on another man's territory.

There will be, of course, a number of aspects of the man's work that only the boss knows much about, and he will have to include his own opinions on these points in the final appraisal if no one is able to offer any evidence that induces him to change his mind. But at the beginning of the session, he should encourage the others by asking questions rather than by immediately putting forth opinions of his own. Experience has shown that this technique produces the best results.

The chairman may not be too successful at keeping his own opinions to himself when he first starts using the technique, for he can comment by means of facial expression as well as in words. But the staff coach, who should be present at the meeting, can help him to improve if he is willing to accept criticism later, as he should be if he is really serious about using the technique.

Again, the chairman may find that although some members of the group are quite willing to talk freely—even eager to get their opinions into the record, especially if they believe that the man being appraised has been hampering their own work in some way—others may be inclined to hold back. Then he will have to do some prodding to get them to speak up. Thus he will have to put specific questions directly to them: "Hank thinks Al is too impatient when he tries to get data from other departments. Do you find him so?" Or, "George has found that Stu always gives him his budget variance reports on time. Does he always meet the dead-line for the reports he prepares for you?"

Properly prompted, members of the group soon find themselves talking freely even if they have mental or vocal objections to expressing opinions about someone in another department. In one case, when a company had just started using the technique, one of the men in the group announced that he was there simply as a favor, but he didn't propose to criticize any-one. In order to emphasize his detachment, he sat down without removing his hat and coat.

The chairman wisely did not attempt to argue with him. He merely asked the man to listen to what the others had to say. It took only eleven minutes for the man to become interested in the discussion and begin contributing to the appraisal.

In an instance like this, the chairman may feel an impulse to say: "You see, you were interested after all." But this is a privilege he must deny himself as the chairman did in this case. When the meeting was over, he said only: "Well, thanks for helping us. You gave us several good points to consider. I hope you'll help us out another time." If the man realized that he had changed his attitude completely, he gave no indication of that fact, and he may even have been unaware of his right-about-face.

One way of helping to persuade those who are reluctant to take part is for the chairman to keep emphasizing that the purpose of the appraisal is to help the man improve, and to bring out his good points as well as his bad ones, if any. The chairman should stress this whenever there is a new appraiser in the group, and certainly during the initial round when every-one is new to the process. Many people retain a residue from their school days in the form of a feeling that criticizing someone to his boss is "tattling" and as such something to be despised.

Another of the chairman's duties is to keep the discussion on the track. When there is disagreement on a point, talking it over may lead to a con-sensus or it may lead to an impasse, and the chairman will have to deter-mine which is likely to happen each time there is strong disagreement and two or more of the appraisers seem inclined to continue arguing indefinitely.

If he feels that the arguers will never come to agreement, he will not want any of this part of the discussion included in the final appraisal. Then he may suggest that the subject be dropped or he may simply ask them to table discussion of it for the moment until some of the other points have been agreed upon. He has to be careful here not to interrupt too abruptly, even if the discussion has degenerated into a mere repetition of opposite viewpoints. Otherwise, the dogmatic arguers may be offended and make a point of contributing nothing during the rest of the meeting.

Keeping the discussion moving is, of course, one of the duties of the chairman, and he may find that some people will continue belaboring a point even after there has been substantial agreement. Some of those who have used the technique say that there cannot be too much discussion, that more and more evidence comes out as the talk proceeds, and that the appraisers voice their real opinions only after the discussion of a point has gone on for some time. This is often true when agreement is reached too soon. Therefore the chairman should determine whether the accord is merely perfunctory, or whether it represents general and spontaneous agreement that reflects the evidence as the appraisers have seen it. If the former, he might say something like this: "Well, we're all agreed that George is very accurate? Does he never make a mistake? Or would you say that he is generally accurate, and that the mistakes he does make are unimportant? Can anyone cite any specific examples one way or the other?"

On the other hand, when people are simply repeating themselves and bringing up the same evidence again and again, it is time to move on to the next point, and the chairman should suggest that the group do so, although again he should not be abrupt about it. Certainly he should not interrupt anyone in the middle of a sentence in order to bring the discussion back on the track, even if the man who is talking is merely repeating himself.

It is to be expected that some members of the group will bring up points that are merely gossip. Gossip is a natural part of any discussion, and appraisal meetings are not likely to be an exception. To what extent should the chairman rule it out? He should not stifle it completely, because a little of it may remind the appraisers of one or more points for which objective evidence is available. However, the chairman must keep the gossip within reasonable bounds or the meeting will take too much time and little will be accomplished.

When agreement has been reached on all the points that have been discussed and no one seems inclined to bring up any new ones, the chairman, as the secretary, should read off the items that have been agreed upon, then ask the group whether these should be included in the written appraisal that he will use for the appraisal interview. Sometimes members of the group may feel that some of the items should be omitted because there is not enough evidence to support them. If so, the chairman may decide to have a little further discussion on these matters, but if no objective evidence is brought out, they may be crossed off.

Items that are finally agreed upon as pertinent and supported by the evidence do not, however, necessarily go into the final summary in the form that they have been phrased. All members of the group must agree on the wording of the statements, for inaccurate or slipshod phraseology can create an impression quite different from what the appraisers intended. Everyone does not have to concur positively with all the statements, for some of them may not know enough about the man under discussion to feel strongly one way or another about a given item. No statement should go into the record if there is any opposition to it, but if a member of the group is asked whether he can offer any evidence that it is untrue and is unable to do so, this can be considered agreement from a practical standpoint. It is not to be expected that each member of the group will know all about the man's performance in every respect; rather the very purpose of having a group is to obtain data on different aspects of performance that no one person has had an opportunity to observe.

The chairman notes down the statements that have been agreed upon by the group, using the exact phraseology on which the agreement has been reached. These will constitute the written appraisal that will be sent to each of them for signature.

Then the chairman closes the meeting, and in doing so he should stress the confidential nature of the discussion. Some executives feel that this is no longer necessary once the first few meetings have been held. Once the procedure has been established, they say, no one will be likely to forget this point. Nevertheless, a rule that is no longer emphasized will eventually fall into the discard, and it is better for the chairman to repeat the reminder at each meeting.

If the private nature of the discussion is not maintained, opposition to the whole procedure could develop. The man should learn of the results only from his immediate boss, the man he has to please and to whom he looks for guidance. Hints from anyone else—even if they indicate a very favorable appraisal—are likely to make him uneasy. And if the results, or portions of them, are made known to anyone else, he is likely to be angry and feel that his boss has let him down.

It can be seen that the rules for conducting the sessions are few and simple. But a successful session does not depend merely on the observance of the rules. It depends on the skill of the chairman and on the ability of the appraisers to marshall their thoughts and express them clearly. The abilities of both will increase with experience. Both will learn by doing, and the chairman can get an objective view of his own performance as a leader of the meeting from the comments of his coach. In this way, the meetings become of more and more value as time goes on.

Some variation in the procedure outlined is permissible when the man who is being appraised is high in the organization and the appraisers must be the operating heads of the company or the corporate officers. In that case, a high-level staff man can act as secretary, if necessary, and the top people may agree to let him phrase the conclusions later. Such a man should be able to reflect the flavor of the discussion accurately. But even in these cases, the draft should be submitted to each of the appraisers for possible corrections before the appraisal is considered final. Generally very few changes in his draft are necessary.

This may appear to be a violation of the rule stated earlier: that the appraisers should work out the phraseology themselves. Experience has shown, however, that those who are very high up in the organization are likely to express their opinions with precision, and it is often necessary to save their time by having someone else do all the actual writing.

CHAPTER TWENTY-FIVE

What an Appraisal Covers

THE PURPOSE of the group summary appraisal is to answer just two questions:

1. How well is the man handling his present work?
2. How can he be helped to do his present job better?

Once these two have been answered, his potential for promotion and steps to help him reach his full potential can be discussed.

Thus it is essentially a job-centered method. Personality characteristics, stressed so heavily in many appraisal systems, enter into it only to the extent that they facilitate or hamper the man in his present job or are likely to help or hinder him on a higher level. Further, they are not considered from the viewpoint that they are necessarily an inherent part of his personality that cannot be changed or can be changed only if his boss practically treats him to a deep psychoanalysis during the appraisal interview. The appraisers deal only with what the man does on the job, and it may be assumed that anyone who is reasonably stable is capable of changing his behavior if it is giving an unfortunate impression of his personality.

The review of the man's performance on his present job is designed to determine two things: What results has he achieved? What methods has he used to achieve these results?

Results are measured by such things as the quality and quantity of the work turned out by his department or section, the improvements he has instituted, the extent to which he has facilitated the work of other departments or groups, the human relations atmosphere in his department, the special problems he has solved or failed to solve. In addition, the number and the value of the new ideas he has suggested are considered, for his value to the company depends not only on his administrative ability but on his ability to further company progress through innovation.

The methods used to obtain results are evaluated because short-term results can be achieved at the expense of trouble later. There have been cases in which it has been found that an executive who appeared to be achieving excellent results was sweeping innumerable problems under the rug, problems that were bound to emerge later in more serious form. Sometimes the true situation is discovered only when he leaves and his successor must repair the damage, for such men are often adept at getting another job just before they are shown up. Chances of this sort of thing are greatly reduced when there is definite and searching consideration of methods in the appraisal. Clues to what is happening are always present if those on a higher level will take the trouble to look for them.

Conversely, examination of methods often leads to evidence that failure to achieve any very outstanding results in the current period under review may be due not to inadequacies but to building for the future. For example, a sales manager who has his men doing spadework on new accounts that will be very profitable later may not be reaching as high a volume as one who is contenting himself with seeing that they make the easy sales. Yet the former may be far more valuable to the company than the latter. Or a production manager's record may show higher costs during a period when he is instituting changes in layouts, processes, or machinery that will produce very large savings later.

Discussion of methods also makes it easier to uncover the reasons why a man is succeeding or failing in various aspects of his job. Thus it can help the superior to discover both his development needs and his potential.

Brief excerpts from a few case examples will show the type of subject matter that is discussed in an appraisal session. These are not presented as models of style or leadership, although each of the chairmen did a fairly good job. Rather, they are partial transcriptions of real appraisals.

AN EDP MANAGER'S APPRAISAL

In the first case, Mac, the man who is being appraised, is the manager of an electronic data processing department which includes 40 people—systems analysts, clerical help, and so on, and four first-line supervisors. The chairman of the session is the administrative vice-president, to whom the EDP department head reports, and others in the group are the secretary-treasurer of the company, the controller (who is also a vice-president), and the head of the research and engineering department.

ADMINISTRATIVE VP: As you know, the purpose of this meeting is to appraise Mac's performance as head of EDP. Each of you gets some service from that department; so each of you may have seen some evidence of what he is doing, both good and bad. As you know, we hired him from outside when Al left. Al started the department at a time when it was under Bill [the controller], and it was placed under me when we began to extend the applications to other areas of the business besides finance. The control applications, handling the billing and the payroll and so on, still take up a good deal of time, but we made time available to the other departments as the applications were developed. Mac came to us from MBB, which is, of course, a much larger company than ours. He has a Ph.D. in math, and he was in charge of an OR group there that did a lot of experimental work on new applications. That was one reason why we hired him; we felt we were spending so much on computers and auxiliary equipment that we ought to get more good out of them. Bill, how is he doing so far as the accounting functions are concerned? Is he getting out the reports you need and getting them on time?

CONTROLLER: Well, so far as payroll and the other routine matters are concerned, I have no complaints. Everything that was being done when EDP was strictly an accounting function is being done now and being done on time. But he seems to be asking for more and more new equipment. I know the equipment we had before he came paid for itself in a comparatively short time; in fact, we might not have been able to get the work done at all—what with the shortage of clerical labor and the prices you have to pay to get clerks—if we hadn't had a computer. But I'm disturbed at the way expenses are mounting in the department, for both salaries and equipment. After all, we're in business to make a buck or two, and we have to keep costs down.

ADMINISTRATIVE VP: Do you think we've spent too much? That what we have now isn't paying for itself?

CONTROLLER: I wouldn't say that. But I would say that it's too much if one considers only the accounting applications. Whether it actually is or not depends on what the rest of you are getting out of it.

SECRETARY-TREASURER: Well, Mac suggested to me that I use a program he had to evaluate possible investments. There's a regular program developed by the supplier for that sort of thing, but Mac had some new twists that he thought up himself. I'm not sure it would work. Perhaps I'm too conservative, but it seems to me you can't do these things entirely by machinery. There are too many intangibles. Of course the information supplied by a computer can help you in a lot of cases, but I don't think a computer can make the type of decisions a man in my position has to make. There are too many intangibles.

ADMINISTRATIVE VP: Can you think, offhand, of any examples?

SECRETARY-TREASURER: Well, the fact that an investment has always proved worthwhile in the past doesn't necessarily prove it's the one to make in the future. Suppose you're buying stocks, for instance. You have to look not only at what the company has done in the past in comparison with other companies that you might invest in, but at the quality of its management, the state of its markets, and so on. But Mac seemed to think that the computer couldn't be wrong. Perhaps I am just jealous of the machine; maybe I'm afraid that it's going to grab off my job some day.

CONTROLLER: That's funny. You say he's working up new programs for you. But there are a couple of programs the supplier has that I believe would extend the use of the computer in my department, and he told me he didn't have time to get them and train his people to use them. Yet they were pretty routine stuff, and it shouldn't have taken him too long to get them going.

VICE-PRESIDENT, R&D: I think that's one trouble with him. He knows his stuff, and he feels he's a little above the routine applications. We have some of that, and he does give us computer time when we need it and work out programs for us when we insist. But I think he feels his real mission is to advance the state of the art.

ADMINISTRATIVE VP: You know, I think you've put your finger on something that indicates I haven't made his objectives clear enough to him. EDP is a service department; if it doesn't provide the service you fellows want and need, first of all, it's falling down in an important way. If we can go on to more exotic applications, well and good, provided they pay their way. But first things first. The way we make money on our computers is by doing things faster and more accurately and at less expense than we could otherwise. Would you all agree, then, that to some extent Mac needs to come out of the clouds and get down to earth on the routine applications? (*There is general agreement.*) I think, though, that we should give him credit for keeping abreast of his field and trying to see how he can be of more value. After all, we don't want him to just keep on doing the routine stuff and never suggesting anything new. One of the troubles may be that at MBB he was head of an experimental group whose sole job was to develop new applications. He didn't have to bother about routine applications at all. When I hired him I explained, or thought I explained, that we were strictly a bread-and-butter company, that we couldn't spend money on frills that might or might not produce a commensurate return.

DIRECTOR, R&D: Actually, the application I was interested in really wasn't too routine, but it was good only for my department, and he was mainly interested in things that would affect top management decisions. What I wanted was a data bank on the properties of certain materials we are working with. It would save my engineers an enormous amount of time if they had that.

ADMINISTRATIVE VP: I'm glad to know that. That's the sort of thing that will help the equipment to pay for itself. I'll speak to him about it. When we get these services to the departments going, then he can work on top management decision-making programs if he wants to and has the time. Now, about his handling of the people under him. I think he's trained them well. Some of them were transferred from other departments, and he taught them programming. One or two weren't even college graduates. Does everyone agree with that, or have any of you seen any evidence to the contrary? Bill?

CONTROLLER: I agree. But I do think that once he has trained them, he leaves them alone too much. After all, they're comparatively new at the work, and they still need a lot of help. Some of them have come to me with questions about accounting applications that they should have gone to him with. Ken Jenkins, for example. He's a good man who used to be a bookkeeper in my department; now he supervises the clerical help in Mac's group. He's not exactly brilliant, but he's very conscientious and accurate. I asked him why he didn't get Mac to help him, and he said Mac was concentrating so hard on some new work he was doing that he didn't like to disturb him.

ADMINISTRATIVE VP: That's bad. He's supposed to be a manager, and he should be paying more attention to his people. They like what they're doing, I know; and they want to keep on learning. People like Ken worry when they're not sure they're doing things right and Mac should be there to help them.

CONTROLLER: I'm no OR man, but I did take a couple of courses in computers, and I have more or less general understanding of them. But, although I was able to answer Ken's questions, I think Mac could have helped him more.

ADMINISTRATIVE VP: Is he pleasant when you go to him to discuss possible applications? Or does he act impatient?

CONTROLLER: He's pleasant enough, but he acts almost too patient. I feel as though he's holding onto himself, trying not to show that he feels I'm interrupting his really important work.

DIRECTOR, R&D: I get the same impression.

SECRETARY-TREASURER: So do I.

ADMINISTRATIVE VP: Gosh! That's something I didn't know. He always seems eager to talk to me, but of course I'm his immediate boss. And since all of you are on a higher level than he is, he's not likely to be openly impatient with you. I wonder if he snaps subordinates' heads off if they interrupt him.

CONTROLLER: No, I don't think so. I think he adopts the same attitude he does with us. I know Ken pretty well—he worked for me for five years—and I didn't get the impression he was afraid that Mac would light into him if he asked for help. But that tightly controlled impatience would naturally disturb him more than it would me because Mac is his boss. As a matter of fact, he admires Mac tremendously and feels that it's a privilege to work for him because he can learn so much from him, has, in fact, learned a lot in the time he has been in the department. But because he admires him, he doesn't want to annoy him. Let's say, he's rather in awe of him.

ADMINISTRATIVE VP: It seems to me it boils down to this. Mac has somewhat the wrong conception of his job. Primarily, he's there to be of service to you people, to give you the service you want and ask for, not what he thinks you ought to have. Is that about it? (*There is general agreement.*) Then I think we can say that so far as the technical parts of his job go, he's excellent. He doesn't need any more training in that respect. I also think he keeps up with his field well, and I don't need to do any prodding there. As for relations with his employees, they're good in many respects, and he's done a wonderful job of training people. But he needs to unbend a little and realize that he is the man they have a right to look to for help. In his current job, he must be a manager, not just a technician. I think I can convince him that he'll go much further by being a good manager than by confining himself to technical matters.

A FIRST-LINE
PRODUCTION SUPERVISOR'S
APPRAISAL

The second excerpt is from the appraisal of a first-line production supervisor who is in charge of a group of twelve machine operators. He is a college graduate, an engineer, and is young and ambitious.

The appraisers are his boss (the production manager), the assistant production manager, the plant engineer, and the head of the methods department.

PRODUCTION MANAGER: You all know Al Malloy, and you all have contacts with him. He's been with us two years, and he seems to be trying very hard. I have, of course, more contact with him than most of you, but there are a lot of things I don't know about his performance, and I think you can help me there because what he does affects the performance of your own groups. Now, as you know, I'm slated to become manager of the new Patman plant, when it's opened next year, and Jim here [his assistant] has been promised my job then. Now Al might be able to do Jim's job, and I'm wondering whether he should be considered for it. He's the only graduate engineer among the foremen, and he would be a logical candidate for it. The other foremen don't want it. They're older men who have come up from the ranks, and some of them will retire in a few years; the others don't seem to be interested in advancement. They're happy where they are; they know what they're supposed to do and how to do it; and they feel they've done pretty well in getting to be foremen. I know! I sounded a couple of them out, and they didn't seem to be interested, particularly since it would mean taking some courses on their own time. But the first thing to consider is how Al can do his present job better. Now I know Al doesn't always meet production schedules, but he seems to have been plagued with a lot of absenteeism in his group. I am wondering whether this is due to something he does, or whether the absenteeism was just one of those things that happen to the best of us occasionally.

PLANT ENGINEER: I wouldn't think he's unpleasant to his people—at least he's always very pleasant to my mechanics when they work in his department. And I find him very cooperative.

ASST. PRODUCTION MANAGER: There have been no grievances in his group since he took over. His predecessor was an old-time foreman— you all remember Link—he ran the department with an iron hand and we had a lot of trouble with the personnel department over him. There were even a couple of wildcat strikes over what seemed like very trivial things.

HEAD OF METHODS DEPT.: Al's very intelligent, I know. He made a couple of suggestions for improving methods that worked out very well.

PLANT ENGINEER: Yes, some of his suggestions for modification of the machines have made it possible to cut downtime. But one thing I notice is that when my mechanics work in his department they don't seem to finish as quickly as they could. Doing a job in his department seems to take longer than doing the same job in another department. I don't know why that should be, and I can't send a supervisor with the craftsman every time there's a little job to be done.

ASST. PRODUCTION MANAGER: I think I know why. There's a lot of conversation that goes on; and Al doesn't seem to notice it. Also, I've found that when one of his own men comes in late, Al doesn't say much.

PRODUCTION MANAGER: Maybe he's too easygoing. Because Link caused so much trouble with the men, I stressed the importance of good human relations to him when I hired him. But I didn't mean that he should ignore the rules, or put up with a lot of lateness and unjustified absenteeism. He seems to think that good human relations means being lax. Sometimes you've got to be a little tough—not necessarily disagreeable about it, but firm at least.

ASST. PRODUCTION MANAGER: Yes, he gives the impression that he's more anxious to keep everyone happy than to get out the work. But the trouble is that he appears to feel no sense of urgency, and that feeling is transmitted to the men. So they take a day off whenever they happen to feel like it. Of course they have their wives call in to say that they're sick. But, funny thing, they seem to get sick oftener during the hunting season than at other times. Also, when it's a particularly nice day, there are usually one or two men out.

PRODUCTION MANAGER: As long as he continues that way, I don't think he's promotable to Jim's job. But he has several months to change, and I know he's ambitious. He's a good engineer, and I think the suggestions he's made indicate that he's got good ideas and should eventually go pretty far.

METHODS MANAGER: Yes, I'd like to have him in my department, but as a technician, not as a supervisor.

PLANT ENGINEER: Same here.

PRODUCTION MANAGER: Well, we might sum it up this way: Jim is a good engineer, an excellent idea man. He has a pleasant personality, but he's not firm enough for a line manager. I'll talk to him about his laxness with the men—it may be that he just doesn't understand how important it is to keep them up to the mark. If he can't improve in that respect, he'll have to be transferred to some kind of technical job—that's all there is to it. But I think he wants to be a line manager; and I think he'll make an effort to change when he understands where he's falling down.

**A REGIONAL
SALES MANAGER'S APPRAISAL**

The example which follows is only several indicative portions of an appraisal of a regional sales manager, Arthur Winfield, who is in charge of sales in ten states along the West Coast and east through the Rocky Mountain area. It is the largest region the company has in point of square miles, and second in population. The product is pumping equipment of all kinds. The company is forty-eight years old, and Art has held this job for about thirteen months at the time of this appraisal, his first on the present job. His seniority is relatively short, as he had been a district manager for Alabama in the Southeastern region for eighteen months and a salesman in Florida for nine months before that. His salary has risen by leaps and bounds in his approximately three years with the company. He has six district sales managers reporting to him, and together they have about seventy-odd salesmen in the six districts. This first year, his region—which is one of eight—accounted for approximately 16 percent of the gross income of the company.

His boss, Gene Whitehouse, is vice-president and general sales manager. Mr. Whitehouse has asked Melvin Barnard, the financial vice-president, George McBurney, the production vice-president, and Peter Villems, the personnel vice-president, to participate as appraisers with him.

The men have just started the appraisal as we cut into the tape.

MR. WHITEHOUSE: As you say, George, he is demanding on the plants. I think I'd agree with you that he urges his men to promise the customers faster delivery than your plants can always seem to produce. I wonder if that is bad, though, because the facts show that the plants usually come through very close to the promised date—at least I get no complaints from customers:

MCBURNEY: Yes, I guess that's so. But I mentioned it just to let you know that I get considerable rumblings about it from my plant people. In fact, there was a case three weeks ago, that Arizona irrigation job, where we were told that their whole project would be held up if we couldn't get those four CD 108s to them by the promised date, and we were two weeks behind on them. We made it, all right, but we had two weeks of full overtime for two shifts to do it. I'm sure that the profit will be cut on those four.

MR. WHITEHOUSE: Perhaps so, but that Arizona job is a huge one; they will be spending over 2 billion dollars on the whole plan, and we want our share of it.

MCBURNEY: OK, if you say so. I just wish I'd been better informed so I could have explained it clearly. I don't think my folks would have grumbled so. I get the feeling that they think Art is a bulldozer, and for his own benefit only. As far as that goes, Gene, you might keep me better informed on these important rush jobs yourself.

MR. WHITEHOUSE: Probably I should, and I'm sorry I've neglected to. I'll try to let you in on the background of some of these jobs.

MCBURNEY: Fine, but the fact remains, Art still treats every job as though 2 billion dollars depended on it.

VILLEMS: Gene, I think Mac is right about that. Art has made a lot of enemies in production. Sure, he's a nice guy, a hard worker, and all that, but I've even had phone calls from wives of some of the plant supervisors. They are objecting because their menfolk have to work so much overtime.

BARNARD: Tell me, Gene—do your other regional men do like Art does on this scheduling?

MR. WHITEHOUSE: No, except in very rare cases.

BARNARD: Maybe he's gunning for your job. (*A hollow chuckle or two*)

MR. WHITEHOUSE: Oh, I hardly think that; he has too much of a wanderlust. I really don't think he'll be here that long. He has itchy feet. He told me that when I promoted him to this job.

VILLEMS: You know, Gene, I don't think that's to our credit, giving a man that high a job when he even announces he may not stay, or rather he implies he may flit on to another job soon, and maybe take some accounts with him. Does he say why?

MR. WHITEHOUSE: No, just that he wants to sample a lot of different companies.

VILLEMS: Doesn't he profess any loyalty to the job?

MR. WHITEHOUSE: Yes, he said that he would do a good job, as good as he could, while he was here. I think the dollar sign is very important to him, and the quick dollar at that.

BARNARD: If he's so financial-minded, maybe he should be in one of the financial departments.

MR. WHITEHOUSE: No, no—no, Mel, I don't think so; he's a typical salesman. He's loaded with ideas and gets in on all of the big sales himself. I've cautioned him on that, and I think he's letting his district boys and their salesmen assume their rightful duties now.

BARNARD: Gene, as we've been talking here I get the feeling that you are milking this one fellow for all you can get out of him for as long as you'll be able to keep him. What about your other regions?

MR. WHITEHOUSE: No, not really, though I guess you could say it looks that way. Maybe you are right, at that.

VILLEMS: It would seem to me that you should make an effort to keep him, make him a part of your team. What do the other regional boys feel about him? Take Tom in Southeast.

MR. WHITEHOUSE: He seemed to like him all right, but he also seemed anxious to get rid of him.

VILLEMS: Why?

MR. WHITEHOUSE: I don't know, though one time soon after Art started with Tom as a salesman Tom mentioned that he was a pusher and that he seemed to irritate the other salesmen. That eventually had something to do with his being promoted to district manager in Alabama.

VILLEMS: You remember, Gene, that there was some concern among the Alabama sales force then. Some of them didn't care for him.

MR. WHITEHOUSE: Yes, but he overcame that in a few weeks—at least I felt he had.

BARNARD: I heard about a little commotion from my auditor down there. I don't think he really changed; I think the men just decided he had to be accepted. Do you know what his nickname is?

MR. WHITEHOUSE: No, what is it?

BARNARD: Maybe I shouldn't say. It isn't too favorable.

MR. WHITEHOUSE: Come on, out with it. If I'm to help him to improve as a result of this appraisal, I've got to know these things. What is the nickname?

BARNARD: Oh, let's skip it. I'd really rather not mention it.

VILLEMS: I'll tell it then; it's not a mean one, but it is a revealing one. In fact, it tells us a lot about him from the viewpoint of his salesmen. They call him "old pushy pants."

MR. WHITEHOUSE: Is that all? I thought it was serious.

MCBURNEY: I think it is serious, Gene.

BARNARD: Yes, I do, too. It has implications that could tell why he's changed companies so much. He may cover the real reason that he feels that he is disliked—by saying he likes to move.

VILLEMS: Yes, that's so, and he may not really know what the real reason is. I think that here is a man loaded with potential and he is lost to every job eventually because he has this one personality quirk that no one has tried to help him with.

MR. WHITEHOUSE: Perhaps so. I've made notes of all of these things for the appraisal write-up.

BARNARD: I'd say he is basically a blusterer. Not that he goes around blustering. What he's doing is rather in the nature of putting up a front and hiding behind it.

MCBURNEY: That's funny, 'cause anyone as outgoing as he is you'd hardly call a big-mouth, but that could be the real reason he puts up such a clear front—he really just isn't too sure of himself.

MR. WHITEHOUSE: All of these things may be so, but in my book he's a good marketing man. His region has the highest gross sales. I don't think I can write him off as easily as you fellows seem to want to.

BARNARD: Don't misunderstand me, Gene; I agree that saleswise he has done a remarkable job, but it seems to me that if he's so good, then his talents should be made available to all the districts, or regions, that is.

MCBURNEY: And have my plants on overtime all the time? No, thank you.

VILLEMS: If you could help him to overcome these personality traits that make his salesmen either dislike him or fear him, he'd be a good assistant to you. You could use him to train all your regional people.

MR. WHITEHOUSE: Wait a minute, not so fast. That may be a good idea, that assistant bit, but not yet. There are too many things for him to learn before I could do that.

VILLEMS: He won't have the time; he'll move on before that unless you can convince him of some very basic things we've been talking about and help him to change his ways . . .

The appraisal continued as the men really put their minds to the task.

Here were top-level people helping each other to improve the performance of one of the subordinates of the chairman of the appraisal session. The things which Art's boss has learned can be clearly seen; so can the changed opinions of all the others. These new ideas will help them in the direction of the section of the company for which each has responsibility.

One of the outcomes of the appraisal was the agreement that Art would have to go to his boss for approval of production overtime beyond a rate to be determined in his interview. If he wanted to push production, it would have to be done through his boss so that the production vice-president would be better equipped to inform his plant managers of the importance of the particular job. This would improve the relationship between marketing and manufacturing.

The notes for the appraisal, which were to be placed on the appraisal form, were simple. The chairman had made them as the meeting progressed. He had two blank sheets in front of him. On the first he had written "Results" at the top, and about halfway down had placed "Methods."

On the second sheet he put "Personal qualifications" at the top and "Actions" halfway down.

Results

Overshoots his planned quota. Tops in regional sales by all scales. Hung on to Arizona Irrigation Project.

Causes lack of understanding between himself and production.

Creates a feeling of unfairness among his salesmen.

Methods

Often promises what appear to be impossible delivery dates.

Demands plants produce. Is a driver.

Oversells importance of some small sales.

Appears to be running away with his job. Uses his good ideas.

Tends to hold on to duties which should be delegated.

Personal Qualifications

Hard worker, drives himself.

Seems to give appearance of blustering.

Irritates his men and entire production department.

Quiet about personal affairs. Fights off questions, energetic, loaded with ideas.

Reticent with subordinates. Reluctant to accept criticism.

Action

Have all contacts with production through vice-president of sales.

Keep production better informed of needs of sales.

Explain need for long-term loyalty.

Point out long-range benefits.

Give help in getting better acceptance from subordinates.

Try to get him to accept that his good points should be shared.

Ask him for help in determining causes of his so-called wanderlust.

The other parts of the appraisal included discussion of his most noticeable weakness, his strongest single qualification, and his current status, all for inclusion on the appraisal form.

CHAPTER TWENTY-SIX

Higher
Management
Control

APPRAISAL SESSIONS take about two hours. Thus, a department head who has ten subordinates will have to spend the better part of a week on them —though he will not necessarily have to conduct them all in a single week; they may, in fact, be spread over several weeks if the pressure of other work makes it advisable. Nevertheless, twenty hours, more or less, seems like a lot of time to many executives—an inordinate amount of time if they do not believe the appraisals are important. In addition, there is the time they must spend taking part in appraisals conducted by other departments.

Now there is no magic in the group method, per se, that ensures that *all* executives will make appraisals regularly. Many, of course, will recognize the value immediately because so many definite ways in which they can help their subordinates to improve become evident to them when the group method is employed. But, if the matter goes no further, inevitably there will be some who will appraise their subordinates once or twice, put the reports in a file, and then forget about the matter.

The answer to this problem is higher management control. Higher management must demand a report on the appraisals, and further, a report on what the superior is doing to help each man improve in the direction that the appraisal has shown he should improve. It is not enough for higher management to *expect* that appraisals be made; it must inspect what has been done in the way of appraisals, and equally important, in the way of follow-up development.

One company president who professed himself heartily in favor of appraisals complained that the department heads just wouldn't keep on making them.

"Do they do the other things you ask them to? Watch budgets, and so on?" he was asked.

"Yes, they do. But they can't seem to become interested in appraisals."

"What do you talk about in your executive committee meetings?"

"Oh, we talk about production and sales, costs, things like that."

"Do you check up on department performance in those areas?"

"Yes, of course. Where would we be if we didn't watch our costs and our sales volume? We go over all the results regularly."

"And the results of the appraisals?"

"Well, we haven't any formal program for that, but when there's an opening coming up, we ask to see them. Then we find that they aren't complete or up to date. For a little while after something like that happens, people start appraising again. Then the same thing happens. Once the heat is off they forget all about it; they let the appraisals go again. I've *told* them I want them to appraise their subordinates, but I can't seem to make it stick."

Higher management review of the results of the appraisals and of the development work undertaken in consequence of them is an essential part of the appraisal plan advocated in this book. When this is undertaken regularly, getting the department heads to make the appraisals presents no problem. They know they will be asked about the results, just as they will be asked about budget variances; and they consider appraisal and development a normal part of their jobs.

The higher management review also produces other benefits. It is, in fact, a means of development in itself. As a man talks about his subordinates—what they do well and the development they need—higher management often learns a good deal about the man himself—his conception of what his group should be achieving and how they should be going about it, and his own strengths and weaknesses. Thus the higher managers can get him back on the track if he has misconceptions about company policies or objectives and can determine what help he needs to improve in other areas.

Second, it is often extremely difficult for top management to know what is going on down the line, aside from the information that may be expressed in figures, which, of course, can never tell the whole story. The enormous amount of space devoted to "communications" in management literature is evidence that managers are very conscious of how difficult it is to ensure that their ideas are transmitted in ungarbled form, all the way down the line, and how much more difficult it is to make certain that upward communication takes place to the extent necessary if they are to know what is really going on.

There may, for example, be a good deal of work going on that is completely unnecessary—forms being filled out and reports being made that no one ever looks at. Someone in a higher position once wanted them, because he was checking up on certain phases of the work with a view to instituting new systems, but he left the company before he came to any conclusions, and his successor felt that there were easier ways of accomplishing the same result. Or there may be important things that are being neglected because top management has no way of finding out about them. If higher management does not know just how its subordinate managers are spending their time, it does not know how the company is really operating.

It is well known that formal organization charts may not give a true picture of the way an organization structure operates. There is often an informal organization, or more likely several informal organizations, with spheres of influence that have no resemblance to the relationships prescribed by the formal organization chart or the organization manual. Sometimes these informal structures do no harm; they may even facilitate cooperation between people on the same level in different departments. If this is so, it may indicate deficiencies in the formal structure that make cooperation difficult unless people circumvent the formal relationships to some extent. On the other hand, the existence of an informal organization that is acting as a brake on company efforts (and such harmful informal structures do exist) may indicate a need not only for a change in the formal structure, but for changes in top management policies.

Ordinarily, it is not easy for top management to discover these things. Generally, it remains in ignorance of them until growth or merger makes it necessary to have a general reorganization and realignment of duties all down the line. But higher management review of appraisals gives the top men an insight into matters like this that they would find it almost impossible to obtain in any other way.

The higher management review is conducted by a group of three to five managers on a higher level than the man who is to present the results of his appraisals. One of them, of course, will be his immediate superior. The sessions may be conducted in an office, provided it is large enough and has a table big enough to accommodate all the participants. If this is not available, a conference room may be utilized. In either case, there should be no interruptions. All the participants should have left word that they will not take telephone calls, barring an extreme emergency, during the time the review is in progress.

The reviewers sit on one side of the table, and the man whose appraisals are to be reviewed sits on the other. The latter, who may be referred to as the "department chief"—although he may be any second-line (or higher) manager—brings with him the department appraisal book containing the two most recent appraisals of each subordinate, a position description for each person he is to report on, and a personal data sheet, showing service record and rates of pay, for each one. He may also bring a large organization chart showing the names and positions of the managers under his supervision, color-coded to show the current status of each: "promotable," "promotable with further training," "satisfactory," and so on. This can be attached to the wall where everyone can see it.

When the group enters the room, the department head gives the appraisal book which contains the personal data sheets and the position descriptions as well as the appraisals to the review board. Since the appraisal and development of his immediate subordinates is considered one of his major responsibilities, he is expected to be able to talk about each one without referring to records or notes. If he doesn't realize this, the higher managers can impress its importance on him.

In one company that had just started the appraisal plan, a department head had had copies of the appraisals made and surreptitiously withdrew them from his briefcase and held them in his lap. The higher managers had noticed the briefcase when he came in, and his boss suspected that he planned to use notes in the discussion.

The department head looked at the top appraisal sheet, and began: "I want to tell you about Anderson. [He had the sheets in alphabetical order.] I think there is considerable room for development there."

"Then let's leave him until later on," said his boss. "Suppose you talk about Mitchell first."

Mitchell's appraisal was somewhere in the middle of the pile, and the department head couldn't shuffle the sheets in his lap without making it obvious that he had them.

"Mitchell's a pretty good man," he said. "He does very well. I think he'll be promotable with further development."

"What kind of development does he need?" asked the boss.

"Well, I'm kind of thinking about that now. I haven't quite made up my mind."

"What weaknesses does he have?"

"He isn't really weak at all. He's a good man."

"Has he suggested any new ideas? What, for instance?"

At this point, the department head began to sweat. Every time he made a general statement, the boss asked him for specifics. Eventually the boss told him to come back the next day when he was better prepared to talk.

He took the appraisals home with him and studied them thoroughly, and made plans for development that would really meet the needs. Because he had devoted thought to each of them, he had no need for notes the next day.

That story may make it appear that the higher management review is a painful process for the department head. But the case was an exceptional one because the department head had not, up to that point, thoroughly accepted the idea that appraisal and development of the managers under him was an important part of his job, and he needed a short, sharp lesson on the matter. Further, he had ignored the advice of his coach, who had warned him what could happen.

Ordinarily, the review board views its job as one of helping the department head in concrete ways. It does not want to embarrass him or find fault with him. It handles him as carefully as he should handle his own subordinates in the appraisal interview.

Ordinarily, also, a department head who has used the group appraisal had learned enough about each of his subordinates to be able to discuss them intelligently without using any notes. He has been forced to put his own ideas into definite forms, to think of specific training needs, and the thought he has devoted to doing so has impressed the facts about the man's performance and potential on his memory. And if his fellow appraisers have told him things about a subordinate he did not already know, these are likely to stick in his memory, if only because they have surprised him.

The process is best illustrated by quotations from review sessions.

**A SECOND-LINE MANAGER'S
REVIEW SESSION**

In the first instance, Howard is a department chief in a medium-sized company who has several executives under him. Seated opposite him at the table are the controller, who is Howard's immediate boss, the assistant to the controller (a staff man), and the production manager, who is on the same level as the controller.

Howard has set up his chart and handed his appraisal book to his boss, the controller, who acts as chairman of the session.

CONTROLLER: (*Looking at chart*) I see you've made some changes since last year.

HOWARD: I have several.

CONTROLLER: I'm glad to see that Rigger has made out all right on the new job. Remember you weren't too sure when you put him in.

HOWARD: He's coming along fine.

CONTROLLER: Suppose you tell us about him.

HOWARD: Well, I think we can work with him a little while more. As a matter of fact, his problem is that he's just too good. Too much of a perfectionist, perhaps. He's a hard thinker, trains his people well, and gets them started on the job. But after he has them trained, he is a little impatient if they make the slightest mistake.

ASSISTANT TO CONTROLLER: What are you now doing about that?

HOWARD: Well, we've had one talk. I tried to get his ideas on what a mistake means—I was, of course, trying to get him to realize a mistake is an opportunity to work with a man rather than something to condemn, something that strains the relationship between them.

PRODUCTION MANAGER: You say he is impatient. What, specifically, does he do?

HOWARD: He wants his people to keep up to schedule, and they do. But he seems to feel that because he has done a good job of planning and scheduling and has trained his people well, there should never be any hitches. Someone makes an error, and right away he's all upset. Everything is bad.

CONTROLLER: Do you know how the employees feel about that?

HOWARD: Only to the extent that the last time it happened the girl he talked to left right after that for the restroom and looked pretty bad.

And that three people have quit in the last six months. Three out of eleven—that's not too good.

CONTROLLER: What explanation did he give you for that?

HOWARD: Well, as a matter of fact, he sort of throws the blame our way. He said we expect accomplishment and he expects to give it to us. We want those things handled and handled on time, and he doesn't think mistakes have any place. He sees no reason for them.

CONTROLLER: That poses an interesting one, don't you think, Howard? Are we expecting you to enforce standards of performance that are too high?

HOWARD: No—I don't think so. The thing that bothers me is that he seems to think so.

CONTROLLER: Do you suppose this would help? I remember a few years ago we had Miss Jones in charge of the new series of ledgers for the temporary accounts we had to set up. She had four or five girls working for her, and those ledgers had to be balanced every day. And every time a ledger was balanced they had to run an adding machine tape that was probably 15 feet long. Miss Jones insisted that if the ledger didn't balance with the control, the girl had to run a whole new tape instead of merely finding the mistakes and correcting the total. We didn't know that for a long time. We just kept losing employees. Maybe there's something like that.

ASSISTANT TO CONTROLLER: If I remember rightly, Miss Jones thought we wanted her to run a new tape. She thought she had to.

PRODUCTION MANAGER: Does he have enough people?

HOWARD: Yes, I think so.

CONTROLLER: You don't know? The thing is this: We don't want overstaffing, but we certainly don't want to run a sweatshop deal. There's always a possibility that a new supervisor may try to work understaffed just because we talk a lot about cost control. You state here in this appraisal that he's cost-conscious. That's good. But supervisors should understand that we're not trying to cut costs below good operating standards.

HOWARD: We've analyzed the job demands, and these people have about as much work to cover as the unit has always had.

PRODUCTION MANAGER: How often do you review that?

HOWARD: We haven't done it for two years now. I did mention that point to Rigger, though.

CONTROLLER: (Looking at the appraisal) Under "Methods" you say he is slow in delegating responsibilities to employees until he considers them fully qualified. What was the thinking in back of the statement?

HOWARD: It comes right back to this same thing. He wants the job done right, no matter how much work it takes. If he thinks an employee can't do it perfectly, he won't delegate a job to him. In that way he has some of his people loaded down, and others who aren't doing too much.

CONTROLLER: Well, I gather there's only one thing wrong with Rigger, and that's this "requesting too high a standard of performance," which is making for bad feeling. In his next appraisal, I'd be interested in knowing what you've done to help him on that. However, I recall that when you were filling that job you asked all the applicants: "If you get this job, what do you feel you should do to improve the way the group operates?" You finally picked Rigger, I believe, because he was the only one who seemed to have any ideas on that. Now in this appraisal I don't see any evidence that he's applied any new ideas or even attempted to.

HOWARD: We didn't note it down in so many words, but one of the things he has done is apply very effective induction and training ideas, and his people are good. The only thing is, they're naturally not perfect, and he expects them to be.

CONTROLLER: (*Referring to appraisal again*) I'm a little worried about this lack of cooperation with other departments.

HOWARD: Yes, his predecessor had the same problem. Part of it's the nature of the job.

ASSISTANT TO CONTROLLER: Yes, every time he picks up the telephone to call somebody, he has to find fault with their work, or indirectly show that they have made a mistake. What can we do to lick that?

HOWARD: Well, of course, the resentment he arouses may be due to his own attitude.

PRODUCTION MANAGER: Is he scared?

HOWARD: That's what I'm wondering now. He may be viewing us as standing over him demanding perfection.

CONTROLLER: You have his potential here, and you feel that eventually he's going to be the kind of a man who will go places. I don't quarrel with that; I assume you have some evidence. But, frankly, I don't see the evidence in this appraisal. I think you should come back here and talk about him in about—oh, say, two months. I don't mean make a new appraisal; just work with him and come back and tell us what you have accomplished. Here's a new man, and we have a chance to make something of him. If you want to talk about him sooner or have something to suggest, why, come back and tell us. I'm leaving it up to you to decide just what you should do. Let's get on. Let's look at Adams. Last time he was promotable to Dudley's job, wasn't he?

HOWARD: Yes, we thought he would be.

PRODUCTION MANAGER: Now he's only "eventually promotable." What happened?

HOWARD: That was the first round. I think we've learned a lot since then.

PRODUCTION MANAGER: How old is he, and how long has he been here?

HOWARD: He's forty-nine, and he's been with us twenty-two years. He's had this job for nine years, and he's doing it very well. He has five men working for him, and they're all lawyers. It's very technical work.

CONTROLLER: Under "Personal qualifications" you say he is thorough and dependable, very capable, qualified for his job by training and experience. What training? He was trained as an engineer, not a lawyer, wasn't he?

HOWARD: Well, I was thinking of the management aspects of it. But the combination of law and engineering seems to have disadvantages. He overworks, does things that aren't needed. It's a kind of weakness in judgment.

ASSISTANT TO CONTROLLER: Have you noticed how he overexplains things?

HOWARD: That's just the point. In Dudley's job he'd drive you insane faster.

CONTROLLER: By all means let's not let him do that. I can see now why you don't think he's immediately promotable.

HOWARD: Well, I'm not saying he can't improve. When he writes a report, he takes ten pages to say what he could say in two. He works on it nights, puts in all the details, and checks them over and over again. He has pages of tabulations. In a way he's something like Rigger—too much of a perfectionist.

CONTROLLER: Did we pick the problem children to discuss here first?

HOWARD: Pretty much. Anyway you picked two of them.

PRODUCTION MANAGER: You do say, though: "It is apparent that in the last year he has shown a noticeable improvement in overcoming some of these negative habits." I'd like to know what evidence you have for that. The last time I called to ask him a simple question, I couldn't get him off the phone for an hour.

HOWARD: Well, now, let me see. I don't think I stated that just right. Actually, it's only within the past two months that he's shown some improvement. Let me put it this way: When we appraised him the first time, he seemed to be more than satisfactory. But the first six or eight months of this year things seemed to pile up. This going over things, saying "I'm not ready yet," and "I'll have to check that," seemed to be more in evidence. Finally I talked it over with him and pointed out that we trusted his judgment, and needed only enough detail to know what the thing was all about. On the last two reports he's turned in he's left out some of the detail.

ASSISTANT TO CONTROLLER: I'm wondering how much of these reports he does himself. Does he delegate the work? After all, there are five other trained people in that department.

HOWARD: The load is pretty heavy down there.

CONTROLLER: But we don't need more than two cases to prove a point. Why do we have seven on a particular brief?

HOWARD: The really tough jobs he keeps for himself.

ASSISTANT TO CONTROLLER: That must be about 90 percent of them.

CONTROLLER: Do we hire him to do the work himself?

HOWARD: No, I don't think so. He's the manager of the group.

CONTROLLER: I see that under "Results" here, you say more than 400 opinions have been prepared in the past year. That's a good heavy load. But they might be overprepared. These five men and Tom Adams might be doing more than they need to. Do we have to have every opinion stand up completely? Would it really make much difference if 1 or 2 percent weren't quite so perfect?

HOWARD: I'd hate to think what would happen.

PRODUCTION MANAGER: What would happen?

HOWARD: I don't know.

ASSISTANT TO CONTROLLER: Actually, nothing very expensive. I think it costs us more to have this 100 percent perfection than it would to have one or two mistakes. After all, these are pretty high-priced men who are spending all this time.

HOWARD: I guess perhaps we should take a gamble.

PRODUCTION MANAGER: I notice that his initials are on every report. Does he go over everything his subordinates do in detail?

HOWARD: He's never been wrong. We put a lot of trust in his judgment.

CONTROLLER: That's just the point. He's got to trust his subordinates if he's ever going to develop them. He may have to watch a few for a time, but he should be able to trust some of them to handle a complete job without supervision on details.

PRODUCTION MANAGER: Yes, from the point of view of developing them, hadn't you ought to take the risk of having something wrong once in a while? After all, the chance is small. Most of them are pretty good men.

ASSISTANT TO CONTROLLER: Some of them have a sort of hangdog look, though. It seems to me I would, too, in their place—detailed supervision and never any credit for what I did.

HOWARD: That's always been our policy. The man responsible for passing on the work has to sign it.

CONTROLLER: Perhaps we could change that policy. There's no reason why the names of the others should not appear there.

HOWARD: It's all right, then, if I convey the idea that in the interest of developing these people we would like to see him put a little more confidence in them?

CONTROLLER: You're asking us that? Whom does he report to?

HOWARD: He reports to me.

CONTROLLER: Well, then—I'd like to add this. You know, of course, that we're going to appraise you, and I think by now you probably recognize some of the areas we're going to cover. I wasn't too concerned about the first round of appraisals; we were all learning the technique. But I think now we owe it to the management people who report to us to do the best development job we can. And we're going to be very interested in what you do from now on to develop these people. In fact, I'd like to discuss some of these things rather often— especially Rigger. Now don't misunderstand me. I honestly think you're doing a good job. But all of us can always *do better*.

Here is an example of how a failure in communication can be spotted in a review session. Howard complains that the men under him are too fussy about unimportant details, too frightened of having the slightest mistake chargeable to them. As he talks he begins to realize that perhaps his own attitude has something to do with this—he hasn't made it clear that perfection of detail is not the highest good. Similarly, his superiors cannot but realize that they have failed, in some measure, to communicate their objectives to Howard. His question, "Is it all right, then, if I go ahead?" indicates some misunderstanding of the job of a manager, a misunderstanding that is at least partially cleared up in the session. His superiors get across the idea that the sky won't fall because of some slight percentage of error, and impress upon him the fact that he has not only responsibility but authority to develop the men under him.

Suppose, on the other hand, the situation revealed had been exactly the opposite. Instead of too great of spirit of perfectionism, suppose the department appraisals had shown that mistakes were too frequent. This would have led the members of higher management to different counsel. They might have suggested reexamination of procedures, the institution of more checks, perhaps a new survey of the workload to determine whether or not more staff was indicated, or further technical training for some of the staff.

In either case, Howard gains greater insight into what his superiors expect of him, is encouraged to devote greater effort to developing the men under him, and receives some pointers on how to go about it.

Members of the review board, too, have learned a great deal, not only about Howard's subordinates, but about Howard himself, his personality and his methods. They may even have gained some new understanding of themselves. If not only Howard, but other department chiefs as well, report that the common failing is too much perfectionism and too little delegation, the controller and his assistant may well be forced to ask themselves whether this is not a reflection of their own attitude, their own unreasonable impatience with mistakes. ("I keep seeing myself in these appraisals," one company president commented.) If they are capable of growth, they, as well as the department heads, should grow a little as a result of the review sessions. The review session is thus an integrated part of a development process that extends up and down the line.

No rating form devised by psychologists, no expensive formal training program, can take the place of this personal interest and intensive effort on the part of the higher managers themselves. This is a positive demonstration that they consider the improvement of management performance a basic part of every department chief's job.

ON A HIGHER LEVEL

In the second example, the administrative vice-president is reporting on the performance and potential of those under him. They include four fairly high-level managers: the electronic data processing manager, a portion of whose appraisal was quoted earlier, the head of the organization department, the personnel director, and the head of the legal department. The review board consists of only two men—the company president and the executive vice-president—since these are the only two positions in the company higher than that of administrative vice-president. In this company the group appraisal system with higher management review has just been started. Below is a portion of the discussion.

PRESIDENT: Joe, since this is the first time we've ever done this, we're all feeling our way as we go along. I'm particularly interested in your findings. Since your departments are all service departments, the group system should be particularly valuable to you. You undoubtedly know how capable your department heads are so far as their own specialties are concerned, but if the other departments aren't getting everything they need, they may not always let you know about it. Of course they'll squawk if things are really bad, but they won't mention the little annoyances unless they are asked about them. Also, they may not give out with the compliments when they are deserved. So did you learn anything new?

ADMINISTRATIVE VP: I certainly did. Which one would you like to hear about first?

PRESIDENT: How about Mac, the head of EDP? We're spending a lot of money on his department nowadays, and it looks as though we're going to be spending more and more. I'm sold on computers; but I don't know as much about them probably as I should; and of course, I'm not yet ready to turn my own decisions over to them. I think eventually they'll be able to help me by providing information I can't get in any other way. But at present EDP is supposed to be helping people further down the line. When it was under Bill Mayhew [the controller] he got a lot of help from it, but we felt that other departments could use it, too. That's why we put it under you. However, you know all that. Now Mac hasn't been with us too long. How is he shaping up?

ADMINISTRATIVE VP: Technically he's extraordinarily capable. He's also ambitious and anxious to go ahead and be of more use. But the point the appraisal brought out is that he's a little too interested in working out higher-level systems. Let's say he's trying to go a little too fast.

EXECUTIVE VP: How do you mean? Is he doing too much, or what?

ADMINISTRATIVE VP: First, perhaps, I ought to mention that all the financial and clerical jobs that were being done when the department was under his predecessor are still being done, well done, and done on time—Bill had no complaints on that score. But I found out that Mac's not too anxious to take on new work unless it's one of these so-called exotic applications. Bill wanted some more routine reports, and he didn't get them. Mac said his department didn't have time to work out all the programs. R&D has had the same problem. Yet Mac has been working like a demon on systems that no one asked for.

EXECUTIVE VP: Have you talked to him about that?

ADMINISTRATIVE VP: No, not yet. Frankly, I didn't know about it until we had the group appraisal. But you can be sure I'm going to. As someone said during the appraisal, he thinks his mission is to advance the state of the art, not to help us make a buck.

PRESIDENT: It's pretty hard to change a person's attitude so drastically. Do you think you can do it?

ADMINISTRATIVE VP: I can make a good try. I think if I show him that he can get along much faster and win much more status by doing what we want him to, he'll try. I don't think I can revolutionize his thinking in one interview, but I'm going to watch things carefully and talk to the other appraisers occasionally and then discuss the matter further if I need to.

EXECUTIVE VP: How is he as a manager? Has he trained his people well? Do you think he motivates them properly?

ADMINISTRATIVE VP: He did an excellent training job in the beginning. He took people who didn't know a thing about computers and made them into fairly capable systems analysts. But he doesn't seem to realize that he must keep working with them. Some points were brought out that showed he's not always as approachable as he might be. His group doesn't dislike him; in fact, they admire him because he knows his stuff so well. They want to learn from him, but he doesn't always have time for them. It's all part of the same thing. He's too much of a technician and not enough of a manager. But he has the managerial ability, I'm convinced, if he can be made to realize that it's just as important as the technical side.

PRESIDENT: Do you think that all he needs is a good talking to?

ADMINISTRATIVE VP: Primarily, but not just one. I have to keep impressing on him that the managerial part of his job is important, and that he must provide the services people ask for, not just those he thinks they should want. I also think I have a good talking point in that we do plan to extend the uses of the computer, and that we'll get around to some of these more advanced applications in due time. He's very intelligent, and he'll go along, I think. He was, so to speak, brought up wrong at MBB—all they wanted from him there was the pure science stuff. I also think we might have him serve on a task force or two when the opportunity presents itself—some group that is working on something that has nothing to do with EDP. He's so intelligent I think he might contribute outside his own field, and it would give him some feel for the realities of business life.

PRESIDENT: That's a good idea. But don't give him any busy work.

ADMINISTRATIVE VP: I'm not planning to; however, I'm going to watch out for opportunities to broaden him.

EXECUTIVE VP: One more point: Do you think we should buy the new-generation computer?

ADMINISTRATIVE VP: I'm not sure.

PRESIDENT: I think what you've said here indicates that we should hold off for a while. We need to get all the good out of the present generation before we start upsetting things by introducing a new type of computer.

EXECUTIVE VP: This session has saved us some money, then, if it hasn't done anything else, and I think it's done quite a few other things.

ADMINISTRATIVE VP: So do I.

PRESIDENT: Good. I think we know a lot about Mac now and what you're going to do to develop him. Now, what about Alan Allen, the head of the organization department? I don't think much of his parents for giving him that name, but I don't hold that against him.

ADMINISTRATIVE VP: Allen has only a small department, just four people, which I think is as large as it should be for a company our size. He's something of an empire builder, however, and he always seems to think his group should be larger.

EXECUTIVE VP: What do you do about that?

ADMINISTRATIVE VP: I don't allow it, naturally. But I must say the men from the other departments seemed to like him and to be getting a good deal of help from him on their organization problems. Another thing that's good about him is that he doesn't force his ideas on them; he presents them with more than one possibility and goes over their problems carefully with them.

EXECUTIVE VP: You say *he* goes over their problems with them. What do the other four people in the department do?

ADMINISTRATIVE VP: They draw charts and write up manuals.

EXECUTIVE VP: Are they just draftsmen and writers, or are they organization specialists too?

ADMINISTRATIVE VP: They're supposed to be organization specialists.

EXECUTIVE VP: Do we need that many people to do that? After all, we have a drafting department that could spare a little time to draw up the charts if somebody roughed them out. When we had the big reorganization two years ago, we hired three extra people for Allen, but the question is whether we need them now.

ADMINISTRATIVE VP: Perhaps we don't, at the moment. But as we all know, there are some mergers in the offing and we're going to need them then.

EXECUTIVE VP: What does Allen know about finance and corporation law? Anything?

ADMINISTRATIVE VP: He was with a CPA firm—Goosenslop and Goosenslop—before he came to us, and he worked in the management department, helping companies with reorganizations.

EXECUTIVE VP: That gives me an idea. What do you fellows think about having him delegate this routine organization work, and having him do a little work on acquisitions?

PRESIDENT: I like the idea. My assistant has been doing a lot of that, but he's overloaded. He could use some help. Working on those things should help to satisfy Allen's ambition. But he's got to learn to delegate first.

ADMINISTRATIVE VP: That's the first thing I'm going to work with him on. I'm going to tell him to send one of his men when a department calls on him for minor help. He must let them learn about organization problems firsthand.

EXECUTIVE VP: Do you think the other departments will get mad if they don't get a chance to talk to Allen himself?

ADMINISTRATIVE VP: I think we can say he may go and see them, but just once. Then he'll have to send someone else. He can train his people, tell them some of the questions he wants them to ask. That will be good for him, too.

PRESIDENT: You know one of the reasons we set up the staff departments under you in the reorganization was that they were tending to proliferate unduly. When they reported to me, I didn't have time to ride herd on them, and they got away with murder in the way of adding people.

ADMINISTRATIVE VP: I know. I've been pruning some of them down a little. I haven't been firing anyone, but I've let a little attrition take place. I don't like to do too much of that, however, because people get somewhat disgruntled if they see their departments shrinking.

EXECUTIVE VP: Yes, I agree that we can't do too much of that, and since we're growing, the overstaffing will take care of itself eventually. In the meantime, I think we've got to make sure we're using the staffs on work that really needs to be done, not busy work. Further, I think we should be more cautious about adding people to take care of temporary situations than we have been in the past. We can always use consultants for the temporary jobs. Of course, consultants tend to try to hang on like everyone else, but they're a lot easier to get rid of than regular staff members.

ADMINISTRATIVE VP: I'll bear that in mind.

CHAPTER TWENTY-SEVEN

The Appraisal Interview

THE APPRAISAL INTERVIEWS are best held after the higher management review, for at that point the superior has better knowledge of what those higher in the organization want from him and from the groups under his jurisdiction. If possible, his own appraisal and appraisal interview should be held before he conducts the interviews with his subordinates. He is on surer ground, then, when he transmits directions and advice to his subordinates, and there is less danger that he might transfer misconceptions of objectives and policy down the line.

In addition, the knowledge that higher management has already reviewed and accepted the appraisal will make a subordinate more convinced of its validity. He knows, then, that his value to the company will be enhanced if he makes an effort to improve along the lines suggested—and that managers up the line will know that he has improved.

An appraisal interview is, of course, a delicate matter. The subordinate is not to be told brutally of criticisms. At the same time, he must not be led to think that he is currently perfect if there is room for improvement, and there practically always is. The aim is to avoid discouraging the man, on the one hand, and inculcating overconfidence on the other.

How does the superior conduct the interview? How much of the appraisal should he reveal?

First of all, he should not hand the appraisal sheet to the subordinate, or simply read it off. He must reveal everything that will be of help in fostering self-development and nothing that will not contribute to that end. He should bring out each important point and discuss it with the man, get his ideas on why he has been falling down, if he has been doing so, and learn of any difficulties he may have been having.

In the beginning, he should, in all cases, reveal who the appraisers were, but he should not attribute any of the remarks to any specific one of them. He will be able to fend off queries on this point by truthfully pointing out that nothing was recorded on the appraisal sheet unless everyone in the group concurred.

In the old JRT (Job Relations Training) course developed by the Training Within Industry group of the War Manpower Commission for use in expanding industries during World War II, supervisors were taught that before reprimanding an employee, they should ask themselves the question: "What do I really want to accomplish?" In other words, "Do I merely want to make the man *feel* bad, or do I want to help him to *do* better?" The superior should ask himself a similar question: "What do I really want to do to the man?"

One of the things he should endeavor to avoid, of course, is raising expectations that are quite likely not to be fulfilled, at least not in the immediate future. Thus, he should not directly mention the man's current status ("promotable" or "unsatisfactory" or any of the other divisions of the scale). If the subordinate asks him a question about, say, promotability, he will, of course, answer it truthfully but point out that he cannot promise anything because there are no higher jobs open at the time. The superior might also ask the subordinate what higher jobs he thinks he might be capable of doing, now or in the future, and so gain insight into his ambitions. When the superior knows what the man wants to do eventually, he has a clue to methods of motivating him.

The superior can still talk about "potential," but in the sense of potential for improvement in the current job. He does not have to bring up the matter of raises when he does so, for everyone is conscious that the man who improves is more likely to get a raise than the man who goes along doing things in the same old way, particularly if he has been told definitely and specifically what higher management wants in the way of improvement.

The interview may be conducted in the boss's office, or in the man's own office if he has a private one. It may be better, in fact, for the boss to drop in on each man in turn, rather than summon them to him, for the subordinates may be more at ease in their own surroundings. A certain amount of nervousness on the part of the subordinates may be inevitable when the appraisals first start. It should, however, diminish steadily as time goes on and the subordinates realize that what actually occurs is a two-way discussion in an effort to explore opportunities for improvement jointly.

As in the case of all the techniques described in this book, no one can tell the boss exactly what to say. He must be natural, and he should not find it hard to be so since the only things he will have to discuss are matters directly related to the job. He doesn't have to probe into the man's private life or confuse him with generalities about needing more "vision" or tell him he lacks a sense of humor. He talks only about what the man has been doing and should be doing in the future *on the job,* not about what the man *is.* Thus the discussion should be no more difficult for him than it would be to say in the normal course of business: "You did a good job on that assignment," or "What happened in your department to delay those reports last week?"

Again, illustrations are in order. They are not presented as "models," and no boss should attempt to use the same wording in his interviews—they are given here only to promote understanding of the technique. The sample discussions that follow are portions of appraisal interviews.

THE TAX MANAGER'S INTERVIEW

Below is the appraisal interview conducted by the chief accountant with Jim, the tax accountant.

CHIEF ACCOUNTANT: You know we've just started these appraisals, and so we're still feeling our way. I recognize that you may be sort of wondering what goes on. I wondered about my own appraisal until I had my appraisal interview last week, but I found it a very helpful thing—I learned a lot of new things about what is expected of me, things I hadn't given too much thought to in the past. I have a notion we all will, and more and more as time goes on. I believe I've already told you who the members of your appraisal group were. We were able to get Anderson and Smith, the ones you suggested. And as I told you in advance, nothing went down on paper unless everyone agreed to it. Now I'd like to tell you that the first thing that came out of your appraisal was this: We were all highly impressed with your technical knowledge and skill. We recognized your loyalty to the job and to the company. And I'm not sure that I've given you anything to be loyal about—but that's something I intend to correct. We were all agreed that every one of the 753 tax returns you filed each year were 100 percent accurate.

JIM: Well, that's very gratifying to me because I've tried hard, and I'm glad people realize it.

ACCOUNTANT: Yes, as I said, there was no criticism of your devotion to duty—everyone recognized it. Nor of your skill as a tax man. But there's another side to it, too—the management side. One of the things I've been learning since I've been making appraisals and talking to Mr. Bigg about them is that technical ability doesn't necessarily make one an excellent manager. If you're so concerned about accuracy that you feel you have to do everything yourself, you aren't making full use of the group under you—and after all, the manager's job is to get things done through other people.

JIM: You certainly have to have the respect of your group—and you won't get it unless you're competent.

ACCOUNTANT: That's true enough, but it doesn't mean you have to do everything yourself. Here's what I'm trying to lead up to. We get the feeling that you're doing too much yourself, and that you're not giving us the kind of management performance we really think you're capable of. And frankly, I don't think that's your fault, and I said so in the appraisal meeting—I think it's mine. As the discussion went on, I saw that clearly, and it bothers me. Never once in all the nine years you've been supervisor of this group have I stopped what I was doing to tell you about this. So you see, it's not your fault.

JIM: I felt that maybe you had faith in what I was doing.

ACCOUNTANT: I have had. I'm not censuring you in this. It was only when Mr. Bigg talked to me during the review session, and during my own appraisal interview, that I really thought about this at all. But now I want to do something about it. That's why I'm talking to you about it now. It was really embarrassing when I found I couldn't tell them that I'd worked with you to help you utilize your staff better.

JIM: Well, they certainly work every minute of the time.

ACCOUNTANT: I know that, but the point is this: How many of those people have full responsibility for any given report? Your name is on every tax report that goes through—you prepare every one of them. Of course I know you don't do all the legwork, but as nearly as I can figure out you're the one who has all the responsibility for the actual preparation.

I think it's fine that you're so competent technically, but supposing you're on vacation—and don't think I'm not aware of the fact that you never go out of town because they might need to consult you. Incidentally, what does your wife think of never going out of town for a vacation?

JIM: Well, I think she realizes that it's my responsibility to run the department, and she's sort of adjusted to it.

ACCOUNTANT: Wouldn't you honestly like a real vacation once in a while? Don't you think your wife would like it?

JIM: I guess I would. But I find that . . .

ACCOUNTANT: Are you afraid of what your people would do?

JIM: I'm not sure yet that they really know enough to do the job.

ACCOUNTANT: Two of them have been there at least eight years. How long did it take you to learn to do these reports? You've been on that job eight years, but you can't tell me that many of the tax reports haven't changed in that time. You've had to learn as you went along.

JIM: I'm not saying that they're not capable. They are capable. It's just that I can't seem to find the time to work with them and teach them.

ACCOUNTANT: You're too busy making out the returns yourself?

JIM: I suppose that's it.

ACCOUNTANT: That leads us to another thing. We discovered . . . Frankly, I just found it out four or five months ago when I came in here on Saturday afternoon and found you working, and you told me you came in almost every Saturday. I was amazed that you were putting in so much overtime. That bothers us. It's against company policy.

JIM: I don't expect any overtime pay.

ACCOUNTANT: I know you don't. But it's company policy to pay exempt employees for overtime if it's necessary. But we don't think it should be necessary very often. We're not trying to run with a minimum staff and work everybody to death. But let's not worry about that now. The thing I'm concerned about is that your whole appraisal points to one very important thing. You probably know more about taxes than anybody in the country, and technically you've done a remarkable job. But if you're the only one who knows how to make out the returns, you're going to be stuck with doing them the rest of your life. Unless we can free you from some of the work load, how can we hope to give you the kind of experience that will help to make you one of the men to be considered when higher jobs open up? Does that make sense?

JIM: It does. Do you know, I never realized that. I always thought you wanted me to go on the way I have been going.

ACCOUNTANT: It's my fault, as I said. That's the value of these appraisals—they help us all to realize how far off the right track we've been getting. But let's make a resolution now that we won't leave ourselves in a situation like this. Now let's see what we can do. You spend about three days a month on the sales tax return, don't you? And that comes up next week.

JIM: It's a big job.

ACCOUNTANT: I know it is. Now I'm going to ask you to do something for me. If you feel it's impossible, I'll try to adjust it some way. But I hope you'll be willing to give it a try. Today is Tuesday. Now I'd like to have you come to see me on Friday, say at 10 o'clock. Can you make it?

JIM: Yes, I think so.

ACCOUNTANT: This is what I want you to do. When you come in here Friday morning I want you to be able to tell me whom you are going to turn over the filing of the sales tax return to. Don't figure it out now. That's too fast. I want you to think it through, determine who can do the job by going over the qualifications of everyone in the group. Then Friday morning when you come in I'm going to ask you why you picked that particular person. And I give you fair warning. I'm going to ask as many questions about it as I can think of. So it shouldn't be a random selection—you'd better have reasons. Does that make sense?

JIM: Yes.

ACCOUNTANT: OK. And the following week, you're going to work with him on that tax return. After that, you're never going to do it yourself again, no matter what happens.

JIM: That's going to be pretty rough.

ACCOUNTANT: I don't care how rough it is. It's your future that's at stake, and to some extent it's mine, too. I want you to teach him how to do it.

JIM: Oh, we can do it together then?

ACCOUNTANT: You've still got three days, and you can do anything you want to with them. But this is the last time you do it. Then, when it's finished, you let him sign it but you put your initials on it. That's what I do with your reports. Did you ever stop to think what would happen if I didn't trust you? I'd have to sit down with an adding machine and go through the whole thing myself—there wouldn't be much point in having two of us. But I don't do that because I trust you. Now I'd like to see you, as a management person, trust your subordinates in the same way.

JIM: Come to think of it, I should get rid of my calculating machine. You don't have one.

ACCOUNTANT: That's a good thought. Now for another one: I'm willing to see a mistake once in a while. But if you're a good manager, you can stimulate your subordinates to take as much pride in accuracy as you do and there won't be much danger. I know that next month you're going to have to spend a little time on this sales tax report—be available to answer questions and so on. But it won't take you any three days. You can drop over to the man's desk and discuss it with him, and then walk away. This may be difficult for you to do. You may find it's almost more than you can bear.

JIM: I'll have to sit on my hands.

ACCOUNTANT: And control your tongue, too. Don't tell them exactly how to do their jobs. Now just think what this will do for the morale of the person you pick. In the past your subordinates have really been doing the most menial work we could assign to them—just putting figures together and filing papers.

JIM: I have found a lot of inaccuracies in their work, but maybe that's because they know I'm going to check it anyway.

ACCOUNTANT: You get much better work out of your employees if you give responsibility. Now you needn't assign any of the other reports as yet. We'll go gradually on this, but inside of a year I don't think you'll have to do any of them yourself.

Now another thing. We subscribe to $9,000 worth a tax services a year. But in the appraisal all we could find in the way of new savings ideas was the accruing of vacation costs and that $16,000 on the Clinton deal which you have suggested. It seems that the tax services ought to provide ways for further savings—maybe we should cut them out. Do you read them?

JIM: No, I don't have time to. But I think we can get a great deal of good out of them if I assign them to someone.

ACCOUNTANT: Good. I think we should give each one to one of the people in the department and ask them to indicate the things that apply to us. Then you can look at the sections they have indicated and see whether we can use them or not. You see, what I am looking for is a way for you to manage this group of employees in such a way that they will be as interested in their jobs as you are in yours. We want you to pass your skills on, not to do the work yourself. And don't be afraid you'll work yourself out of a job. You'll simply put yourself in a better position for consideration for a higher job. Right now if a better job opened up, we'd have to say: "We can't take Jim away from the taxes; there's nobody else to handle them." So you see this thing can pay off for you in the long run as well as for the employees.

JIM: I'm kind of wondering how to do this. You suggested starting with one return, and I think that's good. But I just wonder how the men will react. I don't know how they will feel about it.

ACCOUNTANT: No more than I knew about your feelings when we started this talk. Do you ever sit down with them and talk with them about their jobs? Or have you been as bad about that as I have been with you?

JIM: Well, I haven't had much time, I guess.

ACCOUNTANT: I didn't think I had the time, but I've discovered that I can make it. If you can farm out this technical work, you can have the time to be a manager—which is what we're really paying you for. Now if you're concerned about how they feel, I think we can hazard a guess. How do you feel about being a better manager? Along the lines we've been talking about?

JIM: Quite frankly, I always thought I was doing a good job before.

ACCOUNTANT: But do you see the validity of the points we've gone over?

JIM: I have to admit that my props have been shaken a bit. I know I haven't been doing some of the things you've talked about here.

ACCOUNTANT: And please understand we're not criticizing you. We're trying to help you to be a better manager, just as I'm trying to be. The whole point of this is that we want to help everybody to improve and progress.

JIM: I was a little afraid of the whole thing in the beginning—I thought it was kind of like being blackballed . . .

ACCOUNTANT: No, it's the other way around. I got blackballed for your appraisal, not you. But that's not going to last. It's going to be on your shoulders from now on. Do you think we're on the right track? Do you resent what I've told you?

JIM: No, I don't think so.

ACCOUNTANT: Well, then, how do you think your employees will feel?

JIM: I just hope I can talk to them the way you've talked to me.

ACCOUNTANT: You won't have any difficulty on that score, because you're going to talk sense to them—and give them an opportunity to take more responsibility, become more valuable.

That leads to something else I want to bring up that may help you. I've been learning a little about methods of instruction, some very simple principles that may help you out with your subordinates. I'd like to pass them on to you. Monday or Tuesday I wish you'd give me about an hour or an hour and a half, at some time convenient for you, to go over them. Because you have a big teaching job coming up if you're going to get all these tax returns off your hands. I think I can be helpful.

And that leads us to still another thought. There's this assistant position in your department that isn't filled. You had two assistants in quick succession, but they both left because they couldn't see any future there. I think we know why now. They didn't get a chance to do anything.

JIM: I never really felt I needed an assistant.

ACCOUNTANT: Do you feel that way now? Remember you're going to take vacations; you're not going to work Saturdays; you're going to go to lunch. And you're going to spend more time finding out how we can save on taxes. And probably I'm going to find some new assignments for you that will give you a better knowledge of the company as a whole.

JIM: I must admit that I always thought the person who had an assistant was admitting he couldn't run the department himself. But the tax law *is* getting more complicated every year.

ACCOUNTANT: Perhaps you're right about the assistant business. My own assistant and I do many of the same things.

JIM: I didn't mean you.

ACCOUNTANT: Well, we can let the assistant business rest for a while anyway. The first thing to do is to get the sales tax return assigned, and then to start work on assigning the others. With all this teaching you're going to have to do, you may find you need some help. But, of course, better supervision doesn't mean that we need more people to do the same amount of work. In fact, we should do it with fewer—or do better work with the same number, rather.

Now there's just one other point. Two years ago you came to me and said the Tax Executives' Institute was having a conference in Los Angeles and that you'd like to go. I asked you to bring me a copy of the program, but as I remember you never did, and that was the end of it. I didn't think much about it then, but it bothers me now. Perhaps you thought I didn't want you to go. The only reason I asked to see the program was that I thought Mr. Bigg might want to know where you were. I wanted to be able to say you were at the conference, hearing so-and-so talk about such-and-such. That was all. I didn't want to have to say that you were at a conference, but that I didn't know much about it. Are you a member of any professional groups?

JIM: Not now. I was with TEI for a while, as you know, but I've kind of dropped out of it.

ACCOUNTANT: Why?

JIM: To be very honest, it was on the basis of what happened about that conference. I thought you didn't consider the organization worthwhile. I used to get some new ideas from it, though. I paid for it myself.

ACCOUNTANT: You now know how poorly I've been communicating with you. When you get less immersed in detail, I hope I'll be able to do better. That's one of the aims of this whole thing. I know of no better tax organization than TEI, and I don't think you should have to pay for it out of your own pocket. If you really want to belong, the company will pay the full fee, and it will pay for the dinners if you attend the monthly meetings. We feel this way: Unless you rub shoulders with other men in the field, you may miss out on some of the things you should know—or at any rate you won't get the necessary stimulation to initiate new ideas. When you get some more of your work delegated to other people, you should have time for the meetings.

Now here's what we do: As soon as we get through this little business of going over the principles of instruction, you start on your sales tax teaching. Then, within the next three or four weeks, I'd like you to make me a list of the reports that are coming up, and we'll sit down together and discuss whom you should assign them to and how fast. I'll give you all the help I can—though it won't be much because I don't know your people as well as you do. Now I can't say that you'll get a raise or a promotion as a result of all this, because I don't know. But at least you'll be in a better position to fight the competition if an opening does occur.

JIM: Actually, up to this time, I never thought I might be considered for any other job. I thought I'd gone as far as I could.

ACCOUNTANT: Frankly, nobody ever did consider you before, because we thought we had to keep you on where you are. We're proud of you as a tax man—your returns, your relationships with other departments, are all good. People respect your advice. But they always see you, not your people.

JIM: You don't think they'd mind if I sent someone to answer their questions instead of going myself?

ACCOUNTANT: No. Your subordinates can often talk to their subordinates. It isn't always necessary to go through channels. I don't say you shouldn't talk to people, and they appreciate what you do. But they do have this comment: You're so busy that you're in and out before they have a chance to ask you all the questions they have in mind. Perhaps you could talk to them about their problems, and then assign one of your subordinates to work with them. That will help to develop the subordinates, too. You can guide the men you assign, of course; that's the manager's job.

All I want you to do, Jim, is to acquire enough supervisory skills so that you will be able to do a development job on these subordinates of yours. Then, if a chance to promote you occurs, we'll be able to take you away with reasonable confidence that there won't be entire chaos in the tax department when you go.

JIM: I might drop dead, too.

ACCOUNTANT: We're not thinking of that. But it is true that all this work you're doing, this eating at your desk, skipping vacations, and so on is the very thing that causes coronaries. It's smarter to be a good manager and get the same results through other people without driving yourself too hard. I mentioned promotion in passing, and it's always a possibility if you can learn how to manage. But I don't want to put any emphasis there, because the possibility is too nebulous—

there are no higher jobs open now, and we don't expect any in the near future. And, of course, there'll always be other people who may be in line for them when they do occur. But here's an immediate factor that makes it absolutely essential that you start delegating: You're doing just about as much as one man can do right now, and yet the job is growing all the time. If you don't train the people under you to take some of the load, you're not going to be able to keep up your record for 100 percent accuracy and always meeting deadlines. Briefly, this appraisal adds up to this: We realize that you have tremendous technical skill and knowledge, but we feel that you should pass it on to other people. As head of the department, it's your job to see that the work is turned out—not do it all yourself. The way it is now, we're wasting talent—the talent of the people under you who, I'm sure, are capable of doing more than legwork. We also feel that you are very loyal to the company, and to me—though why you should be loyal to me I don't know because up to now I've done nothing to help you to be a better manager. And perhaps your subordinates could say the same about you. But I think with the program we've outlined we can both change. We could go on and talk about a lot of things—your vacation, for instance—but I think they'll take care of themselves.

JIM: I'd enjoy a vacation, all right; but I wouldn't want to take one unless I was convinced that everything would go smoothly while I was away.

ACCOUNTANT: We'll see when the time comes. Well, thanks for spending all this time with me. I hope I haven't put you behind too much. But I think when we get going on this development, we'll be ahead instead of behind.

JIM: I've appreciated this talk. I think I expected something quite different. I think what you've told me will help.

ACCOUNTANT: I know it will. I'm going to make it help.

JIM: Well, it's worth working on.

THE EDP MANAGER'S INTERVIEW

In the following appraisal interview, the administrative vice-president is counseling Mac, the EDP manager, who was appraised in Chapter Twenty-five and reviewed in Chapter Twenty-six.

ADMINISTRATIVE VP: You remember when I hired you that I told you we were planning on starting a series of appraisals, right up and down the line, with a view to seeing whether we couldn't get better management all round. You'll be appraising your people, too. And you probably know, also, that during the past few weeks, we've been conducting group appraisals of the heads of the staff departments under my jurisdiction. The day before yesterday, I presented the results of the appraisals to McCullough [the company president] and Argyle [the executive vice-president], and they and I agreed on the various types of improvement needed in the groups under my jurisdiction. Not that I haven't a lot of good people—you included—or that top management felt we were falling down. We simply talked matters over to decide how we could do an even better job.

MAC: Would you object to telling me who the appraisers were in the first place?

ADMINISTRATIVE VP: Not in the least, I intended to tell you. I was chairman of the group, and it included Bill Donnelly, Johnson, and Henry Allard. I chose them, of course, because you provide service for each of them, and I thought they could help me to determine how we could be of better service to them. I must add, however, that nothing went into the appraisal record—good or bad—unless everyone concurred in it, including me.

First, I must tell you that all the other departments said that you were getting the regular reports to them on time, and that those reports were accurate. There were no complaints on that score. But there were some about new systems.

MAC: But I've been suggesting new reports to them, and they just didn't take any interest.

ADMINISTRATIVE VP: That point came up. It seems that the new reports were a little too rich for their taste. What they wanted was more or less routine, not these applications that they considered exotic. They weren't ready for the more advanced ideas.

MAC: When I came here, I understood that the company was interested in using its computers for all sorts of new things. Has policy changed on that?

ADMINISTRATIVE VP: No, it hasn't. But we have to go more slowly, and take care of the easier things first. You know your department was originally under Bill Donnelly because the only applications we had were accounting applications, and it was placed under me in order to broaden its scope. Now my title is "administrative vice-president," but perhaps it should be "service vice-president" because all the groups under me are set up to provide service to other departments, the service they want, not the service we think they should have. We have to give them credit for knowing what they are supposed to accomplish and how we can best serve them. If they're mistaken, it's not our place to tell them so. They'll find out soon enough because all the department heads will be appraised, too.

When we are giving them everything they ask for, then we can make suggestions for new applications, and they'll be more receptive, I imagine.

MAC: There was that data bank that R&D wanted. Do you think I should begin working on that?

ADMINISTRATIVE VP: What do you think?

MAC: Yes, I suppose I should. But I've got so many good ideas for other things.

ADMINISTRATIVE VP: I know you have. Everyone agreed that you were highly intelligent and that you knew your stuff backwards and forwards. Would it help if you made notes about your new ideas, and talked them over with me? We can go into them together and see whether the time is ripe to present them to other departments. By the way, can any of your staff help you with the development of some of the new routines?

MAC: Not exactly. They're pretty good at making necessary changes in the regular programs, but when something's entirely new I have to do it myself. You know, many of them had no experience in programming until I trained them.

ADMINISTRATIVE VP: Yes; and everyone had high praise for the way you've trained them so far. But training isn't something you can do once and for all. You have to keep bringing them along.

The consensus was that your staff admires you for your knowledge and for the way you've enabled them to learn these new skills. Because you've done so, they now have better jobs than they had before the computer eliminated their old ones. But we have a feeling that they're a little in awe of you, and sometimes, apparently, they're afraid to ask for extra help. Do you suppose they're afraid you'll think they're stupid if they do? It could be that you're always so busy on these new ideas that they don't like to interrupt you.

MAC: I never criticize them for interrupting me.

ADMINISTRATIVE VP: No, not in words. But apparently you do give the impression that you're impatient; and even though you think you are controlling yourself, they must sense it by your expression or something. Maybe you have to decide whether you want to be just a technician or a real manager. Nobody questions your technical ability, and no one can be manager of a department like yours without a high degree of technical ability. And your ability to initiate new ideas is an extra bonus for the company. But technical ability and initiative are not the only qualifications for management of an important department like yours.

MAC: I want to be a manager. I'm not just saying that because it's the answer you evidently want. As I told you when I came, the reason I wanted to leave MBB was that I was just a technician there. The work was interesting, but I do think I have managerial ability, and

I think the way I've trained some of these people who had no previous experience shows that.

ADMINISTRATIVE VP: Yes, it does, but I'd like to see you spend more time on managing; that is, be more accessible to your people. Suppose when you go to discuss this data bank with R&D, you take one or two of your better people with you, and later talk over with them how you're going about building it up. That will be good training for them, and perhaps you'll be able to get some real help from them. If not immediately, certainly later on.

You know, if things keep on as they are going, your department is going to become more and more important, and probably larger. Then you'll eventually have to delegate more and more of the technical work, and if you don't have anyone you can delegate it to, you're going to be swamped. You simply won't be able to get everything done.

But one thing we've got to remember is that this company has to make a profit. We can't get anything more in the way of new equipment or personnel unless we're going to get a return that will be at least equal to what we could get by investing the money somewhere else. That's simple business arithmetic.

MAC: Yes, of course. But doesn't the company sometimes have to make investments that won't pay out until later?

ADMINISTRATIVE VP: We do, but counting on a later payout is always risky; you don't know what the future holds. The fact is that I'm a little doubtful whether the new equipment we have gotten in the last year has begun to pay for itself yet. But if you could work out those new routine applications accounting wants and the data bank suggested by R&D, I think it will pay off in a big way. Then we can think about the new generations of equipment. Some of the software you can get from the supplier, and you and the supplier's experts can help your people to learn to use it.

MAC: Well, that's probably right. I'll get to work on it.

ADMINISTRATIVE VP: Now to sum up: There are two things I definitely want you to do. First, get these new applications that the other departments have suggested going, and spend more time developing your people. When you do that, we'll be getting a real payout from your department. Leave the advanced applications for a time, aside from making a few notes on possibilities that I'll be glad to discuss with you at any time, and we'll decide together whether or not it is time to present them to other departments or to top management.

Second, I want you to be more accessible to your people. Ask them about what they're doing more, and see whether they need any help. For the time being, consider that your primary job is helping them to become more skilled. And at the same time, you should be more accessible to people from other departments who need help from your group. Let them know that you're there to be of service to them, and you're glad to have them make suggestions. Perhaps the things they want won't always be feasible, but don't start with the idea that the advanced applications are more important and that the things they want aren't worth spending time on.

Do you think you can accomplish those two things: Work out the programs already suggested by the other departments, and be more accessible both to your own people and to people from other departments?

MAC: I think I can. I don't want to be just an ivory-tower guy. I admit I am tremendously interested in the technical side, but I really want to advance as a manager.

ADMINISTRATIVE VP: I warn you I'm going to check up, and not just when the next appraisal time comes around. I'm going to talk to you more often about what you're doing and why, and about how much your people are learning. I haven't done enough of that in the past. I assumed because people didn't complain and no one in your department seemed to be anything but busy, that things were going along pretty well. Now, I could, of course, tell these other departments to make all contacts with your department through me, and then keep after you until you've satisfied them. But I don't want to do that. I want to build you up as a manager who can take the responsibility yourself. You certainly have the ability; it all depends on what you want to do and on how you see your objective.

MAC: I'd say now that my objective is to provide the service the other departments really feel the need of, and to make greater use of my own people in providing it. I can do both, I know.

ADMINISTRATIVE VP: That's my objective, too. The departments I supervise are all service departments, and when my boss appraises me, he's going to judge me by the service that's being provided and the extent to which the departments are paying their way. It's easier to provide financial justification for your department than for the others, and for that reason I'm anxious to see that we have it. If accounting and R&D can handle their increased work loads with the same or fewer people, we'll be able to show a real payout on the equipment and personnel we now have. Well, that's about it. Do you want to discuss anything else?

MAC: No, I've found this very helpful.

ADMINISTRATIVE VP: Now you know what I expect, which is what my boss expects me to get. We'll have another talk soon about how things are coming on.

CHAPTER TWENTY-EIGHT

Improving Performance

WHEN AN APPRAISAL INTERVIEW predicated on a group appraisal has been held, the stage is set for the superior and the subordinate to use the findings of the appraisal in the normal day-to-day operation of the business. It goes without saying that unless the information is used on the job, the value of the whole process, including the interview, is reduced nearly to zero.

The boss must be entirely conversant with the findings of the appraisals of members of his group so that he can bring up any pertinent examples that will prove points, favorable or unfavorable, mentioned in the appraisal. In the interim between appraisals specific cases should be called to the attention of the appraisee, for they will help to make clear exactly what the appraisers meant by the statements they made.

Mentioning specific cases is not awkward and it does not need to be time-consuming. Certainly, the discussion of the incidents should not take the form of a harsh reprimand. Merely recalling any incidents to the appraisee's memory will help to make him accept a judgment that he may be inclined to dismiss from his mind because he does not wish to regard it as valid.

This might, in itself, be called management development, for accepting the need for improvement is the first step in making an effort to improve. Other more formal methods of development, one or more of which may be used in a specific case, are outlined later in this chapter, but first let us look at the way in which the mention of a specific case can be used later on in day-to-day development on the job, even if the appraisee does not fully accept the judgment during the interview.

DEVELOPMENT ON THE JOB

In one case, the company president, in the course of an appraisal interview with his production vice-president, pointed out that members of the marketing department did not feel that they were getting enough cooperation from production. He cited two instances in which production had lagged behind promised delivery dates and the production vice-president's immediate subordinates had refused to commit themselves to new dates. Instead, they had cited a series of incidents which, they said, were responsible for the delay, and implied that the new delivery dates would depend on when their problems could be cleared up. Apparently, they felt no real responsibility for ensuring that the deliveries were made on schedule as long as they could produce a "good excuse" for missing the dates. They also tended to pass the buck for this attitude up the line, which indicated to the president that they were merely copying the attitude of their boss, the top production man.

During the appraisal interview, the president felt that he had made his point, but he also sensed that the production man had not fully accepted it, apparently hoping that it would be forgotten later. Now if the president had believed that he could do the whole development job in the interview, there would have been little or no improvement. The president knew that he must make it plain that he considered delivery dates of great importance, not only in the interview but in subsequent on-the-job discussions with the production man.

The ideal time to bring up such a matter, of course, is the next time a similar instance arises. In this case, it was not long before the president received a letter from one of the company's biggest customers canceling an order for construction hardware. The letter stated that this step was being taken, despite a long and generally friendly association, because the customer had found that the company could not be relied upon to meet promised delivery dates, and this time there would be a large penalty if the construction were not completed on schedule. The letter further stated that all attempts to get a new delivery date had met with failure, and the customer simply could not take a chance that delivery would be made soon enough for him to meet his own schedules.

"We know," the customer wrote, "that suppliers sometimes have difficulties that make it impossible to meet promised dates exactly on time, and we have a certain amount of leeway in our own schedules for this. However, we must have some idea when the material will actually be here; we can't make the necessary adjustments in our own schedules unless we know whether the delivery will be delayed by a week or a month. And we have been unable to get even approximate information on this from your firm."

Upon receipt of this letter the president asked his sales vice-president and his production vice-president to meet with him immediately. When they came into his office, he read the letter aloud to the two men, then asked for comments.

The sales vice-president said that he had received a copy of the same letter in that morning's mail and had worked out the dollar value of that contract and of all other outstanding contracts with the same customer that he was afraid would be canceled also unless something could be done. The canceled contract had totaled $92,000, and the total of the others was well into the six-figure category. He mentioned no reason for the failure to meet the delivery date, but because of the facts learned in a group appraisal the president knew exactly what had occurred.

When the president turned to the production man, the latter was silent for a time. And it was a humble man who finally said he guessed it was his department's fault.

After some further discussion, a new delivery date was set, and it was agreed that the two vice-presidents would draft a letter for the president to send to the customer in the hope that some of the damage could be repaired.

As the two men started to leave the meeting, the president asked the production man to remain for a while to discuss further ways in which production could be speeded up. In the subsequent conversation, he was able to point out that the incident illustrated exactly the point he had mentioned in the appraisal interview—the tendency of production executives to shrug off responsibility for meeting delivery dates whenever they ran into difficulty.

It was not necessary for the president to be vituperative or harsh; the serious results of production's attitude were only too clearly evident. Instead, he received a promise that the vice-president would attempt to clear up the situation and make it plain to his own subordinates that he wanted, and meant to get, a complete change of attitude.

It was only a short space of time before the whole situation was taken care of, and production began meeting schedules as a matter of course. Needless to say, the production vice-president found it a bit difficult to straighten out his own subordinates because their attitude had been only a reflection of his own. But he frankly admitted that he had been remiss in this respect, and he succeeded in producing the needed change.

Thus this incident that occurred in the course of the daily work was used to reinforce a point made in the appraisal interview and was used to improve the performance of two levels of management. In addition, of course, the discussions enabled the company to keep a valued customer it would probably have lost if nothing had been done.

There is a rather hard-boiled school of thought that advocates dismissal of the man responsible in a case of this kind, and there are many companies that would fire him, almost as a matter of course. In this case, however, the president knew that the production man was fundamentally good at his job, and that it would be wasteful not to salvage him. In using the incident, not as an excuse for a firing or grand bawling-out, he was doing his own job better by working on the development of his immediate subordinate himself.

A simpler example which indicates how the appraisal may be used to improve day-to-day performance is the case of a first-line supervisor who, the appraisers had agreed, had one major fault: a tendency to interrupt whenever another first-line supervisor, a subordinate, or even his boss was attempting to explain something to him. The man didn't accept the criticism at first; in fact, he interrupted the boss as the boss was explaining the point—which gave the boss a chance to show him that the point was valid.

At that the man began to accept the idea, but since he was not always conscious of the fact that he was interrupting someone else, he soon lapsed back into his old habit. But in the course of the day-to-day work, the boss pointed out (courteously but firmly) that he had interrupted every time he did so in the course of their daily discussion. In addition, if the boss overheard the man interrupting someone else, he told him so later in private. Finally, the man was able to break an annoying habit which was damaging his relations with everyone with whom he came in contact. If the boss had merely mentioned the matter in the appraisal interview and not followed up later on the job, there would probably have been no change, because it is difficult to correct a long-established habit without constant reminders.

These examples are only indicative of the way in which the points brought out in the appraisals can be used to improve day-to-day managerial performance. And the knowledge gained through the appraisals can be used positively as well as negatively: to emphasize strengths as well as to correct weaknesses.

SOME TRAINING TECHNIQUES

In many cases, also, other measures will be advisable. Having a good diagnosis of the areas in which a man needs to improve, the boss will be in a position to judge which of the more conventional techniques will be of benefit in a given case. The following techniques do not cover the whole field, but they may suggest other possibilities, for each manager may have ideas of his own on training methods.

Advanced Management Courses at Colleges and Universities

More and more educational institutions are offering courses of this nature. Some companies go so far as to detach men from their jobs and pay their salaries for a year or more of full-time university training.

"Assistant to" Positions

A young executive of promise may be made an assistant to a member of higher management, again with the idea of broadening his view of the company as a whole.

Special Courses at Universities or Elsewhere

These courses may deal with anything from technical specialties to human relations, rapid reading, and public speaking.

In-company Training Schools and Courses

Like the special courses given outside the company, these may deal with techniques or with broad subjects like human relations. Sometimes they are conducted mainly by means of lectures and visual presentations; more often the conference method is favored. In the study of human relations, the most usual technique is to present a problem—occasionally real but more often manufactured—to illustrate a point and allow the students to work out a proper course of action through discussion. An alternate technique is "role playing"—in which two students extemporaneously act out a discussion between boss and employee while the rest of the class watches; then the fellow students comment on the way the "boss" conducted himself.

Multiple-management Plans

A "junior board of directors" may be created to discuss overall company problems and make suggestions to top management.

Job Rotation

The trainee is assigned to different departments for periods ranging from two weeks to two years, to broaden his understanding of the different functions of the business. Sometimes two executives or supervisors are required to switch jobs temporarily.

Special Assignments

Executives may be assigned to make special investigations—of a new plant site, for example, or of the prospects for a new product—that will enable them to practice new techniques and broaden their knowledge of economics and business practice. Or they may be given committee assignments for the same purpose.

Attendance at Meetings and Seminars outside the Company

Executives may be encouraged to attend meetings of professional societies or of management groups, such as the American Management Association or the National Industrial Conference Board, or to take part in seminars conducted by management groups, consultants, or universities.

Distribution of Reading Matter

This may range from the routing of special articles to arrangements for correspondence courses. It may include publication of a management newsletter, provision of subscriptions to special business services, or distribution of the company president's favorite book to everyone above a certain level in the organization.

BLANKET TRAINING IS USELESS

All these techniques may have value, and any one or a combination of several may be indicated in a particular case. But many companies are using them on a come-one, come-all basis, without any clear idea of just what they can hope to achieve by their use. The following incident illustrates one attitude that is all too common in industry today.

A professional management consultant who had made a speech advocating improvement of managerial performance by management development techniques met an old friend, a personnel manager who had been in his audience a few weeks earlier.

"Joe, I want to tell you," said the personnel manager, "we are really making strides in management development in our company now. Our president has finally agreed to really participate in a course for all our management people."

"What course is it?" Joe wanted to know.

"It's a communication course with emphasis on public speaking. We have convinced our president that the idea is good and he's going to attend when he can. Except for the four weeks he'll be in Europe, he's planning to attend every one of the fourteen two-hour weekly sessions. We are using the ballroom at the hotel, and we're going to serve everyone a dinner before each meeting."

Joe, who had once been a college professor himself, thought of the two-hour, one-semester course in public speaking many colleges require freshmen to take. He knew that many of the teachers would be only too glad to give it outside at $100 a night. Fourteen hundred dollars, he reflected, would be a nice addition to any professorial salary and very little effort would be required since the course material was readily available. He thought also of the cost of hiring the ballroom and providing the dinners. But he knew better than to throw cold water too suddenly on his friend's enthusiasm.

He asked his friend: "Will you find out how many of the persons taking this course have had the usual elementary public-speaking course in either high school or college? Also, how many of them may have had advanced courses?"

A few weeks later the personnel manager called up and told him somewhat sheepishly: "Well, I have the bad news. Out of the eighty-five management people we enrolled in that course, there were only five who hadn't had the elementary course before, and twelve of them had had more advanced courses. In fact, two had actually taught public speaking previously."

"Are they all coming yet?" Joe asked.

"Well, the first week the old man was there, and everyone came. But the next week he started his European trip a week early and couldn't make it. So we were down to seven people last week."

"Did the seven include the five who you felt really needed to take the training?"

"No, none of them seemed to realize they needed it. We're going to pay off the professor and forget about the whole thing."

"Human relations" courses are the commonest of all when they are blanketed over all management people. It is a rare supervisor or executive who has not been exposed to one or more of them. Do they all need the training? It is safe to assume that many of them may have studied psychology in college and read enough books on "getting along with people" to know as much as any classroom or discussion group can teach them. Whether they use this knowledge is the real question to be answered. Another large group may be so naturally endowed in this respect that they need no further training. Of course no one will be harmed by the course; some may even get one or two new ideas. But couldn't they spend the time in some more profitable way? Is the course actually worth the money being expended on it?

Another overworked subject matter is rapid reading. It is quite customary for companies to subject hundreds of executives to courses in rapid reading that have been widely publicized, without stopping to learn how many are really slow readers, or whether those who are slow readers are actually being handicapped by the disability to the extent that training in rapid reading is one of their primary development needs.

A manager may benefit from one or more of these forms of development or he may not require any of them. All development plans must be based on individual needs, as shown in the appraisals. And these needs differ widely, as shown by the following.

In two companies the appraisal forms required the appraisers to list each man's strongest qualification and his greatest weakness, and tabulations were made in each category.

In one of the companies, fifty-five executives were evaluated, with the following results:

Strongest Single Qualification	Number of Executives
Knowledge of the job	28
Ability to get along with others	20
Organizational ability	5
Dependability	2
Judgment	1
Energy	1

The most noticeable weaknesses of the same executives were:

Complacency	15
Making other people feel ill at ease	11
Neglect to keep people informed	7
A laissez faire attitude	6
Avoidance of problems	5
Difficulty in writing reports	4
Being socially effusive	3
Inability to pace explanations	2
Distorting facts and difficulty in presenting them	2

EXPERIENCE VERSUS PRECEPT

Learning managerial skill and making it usable are matters of conditioning as well as of learning the techniques intellectually. People are conditioned to do the things that produce favorable results in the environment or climate in which they find themselves at work. It is well known that the child who gets what he wants by throwing a tantrum tends to have recourse to the same technique the next time he is thwarted. Conditioning in business goes on every day, whether superiors realize it or not; and if the formal training runs counter to experience on the job the lessons of experience will win out every time. This has been borne out so many times, when members of a group training course say, "If only the boss would take this course."

When the boss demands an unreasonable quantity of work and never questions how it is obtained, his subordinates are being taught by each day's experience to drive employees under them. This goes on even if the resultant turnover costs more than is saved by the increased production.

When the boss is unable to allow the slightest error, his men will go over every detail themselves, actually waste their own time repeating the work of their own employees. Certainly they may have learned in a course somewhere that "delegation of work" is an important part of the manager's job, but the current pressures make that "truth" seem unrealistic.

A basic value of the appraisal system with review by higher management is that it forces executives at all levels to work on the development of the men under them. Normally, the executive is looking upward. He studies his boss, makes himself familiar with his superior's moods, pet foibles, and idiosyncrasies. He seeks to learn how he can "sell" himself to those who have the power to further or hamper his career. His subordinates get little or no attention. His general impression of the capabilities of each subordinate tends to remain unchanged over the years, regardless of what they may be doing now or how well they may be doing it. Pressure of work, and his eagerness to know what his boss thinks of him, keep him from using development techniques on those who work for him.

It is in the appraisal process that he is forced to bring his thoughts to bear on each of his subordinates. Is his general impression really accurate? If so, what facts does he have to back it up? Do others have the same impressions? If not, why not?

Again in the appraisal interview, he is forced to concentrate on his subordinate. Does the latter know what is expected of him? What difficulties has he encountered in attempting to improve his performance? How can he be helped?

And, lastly, the higher management review really puts proper emphasis on the matter. The superior knows that he himself will be judged by how well he appraises his men, that he will be asked to back up his judgments with facts. And it will not be enough to state that a man writes poor reports, is unable to delegate work, has good or poor "human relations." He must be able to substantiate his remarks with the type of information he can supply only if he has been studying the people under him day by day.

Moreover, he must be able to suggest intelligent ways by which they can overcome their weaknesses. And these suggestions cannot be perfunctory because the next time around he must report on results and justify his report with facts again. He himself will be judged on the actual development of his subordinates, not on the number of training programs he sends them to.

In the same way his superior is concerned with developing him, because the superior's own boss will inspect what he does in this area. In consequence, there will be a general tendency for *all* to help the men under them.

If a department head has become honestly convinced that development of the men under him is a part of his daily job, not just a matter of asking them to attend courses, how does he go about it? The methods are as various as the needs.

Much management training today uses the technique of "learning by doing" by placing the learner in a situation as nearly like an actual job situation as can be reproduced in a classroom. But the *real* training by the immediate superior is done in the *real* job situation, not in a replica of it. Role playing is good practice, but in business people are playing for keeps and they know it. They know they must learn to perform, not merely be able to give the right answers. The crux of the whole matter lies in the normal day-to-day contacts on the job. Subordinates treat their subordinates as their boss treats them; they are motivated to self-development by his willingness to teach and to explain the broader aspects of the work; they emphasize the parts of the job he inspects most carefully. No matter how much formal training the company provides for its management people, the boss cannot dodge his own major part in the development process. And if he is really a manager, he will not want to dodge this part. We might say that the central core of the management development process is this daily conditioning, tempered by well-planned day-to-day contacts. Everything else is secondary to it—the special courses, the suggested reading, the development assignments, and all the rest. The good manager must work every day at developing the personnel, management or otherwise, who report to him.

PART SIX

In Conclusion

CHAPTER TWENTY-NINE

The Concept of the Coaching Role

THE COACH has been mentioned from time to time throughout this book. The use of a coach is recommended, for he can help line managers to develop skill in conducting meetings with their subordinates, whether the meetings deal with the major segments of their job (the preparation of performance descriptions), the areas of responsibility and authority, or the standards of managerial performance. In addition, the coach can help the line managers to prepare themselves for the group appraisals, for the review sessions, and the subsequent appraisal interviews, and help them to improve the way in which they handle all three.

The coach has several roles to fill: (1) He serves as a teacher of the technique; (2) as use of the technique proceeds, he provides specific help to each level of management so as to ensure that no major variations in it are allowed to creep in down the line; (3) he acts as private critic of the line managers' performance in using the technique and so enables them to increase their skill; and (4) he absorbs a great deal of knowledge about the actual workings of the organization that will assist him in helping the management.

There is general agreement that the coach may be either a line or a staff man. But in either case he fulfills a strictly staff role when he is serving as coach. It must be understood that the terms "line" and "staff" designate two distinct types of functions, and the differences between them should never be allowed to become blurred.

First, a line organization includes only the people who carry on the two primary functions of a business: producing either a product or a service and selling it. In simple form, the line organization might consist of a group of production workers under a foreman, a group of salesmen under a sales manager, and a boss to whom both the production foreman and the sales manager report. As the company grows, other layers of supervision must of necessity be inserted. When the number of foremen becomes so great that the head of the company can no longer personally direct their work, he delegates that responsibility to a production manager; when the organization becomes even larger, a few general foremen may be placed over the first-line foremen and under the production manager. Similarly, extra layers of supervision may be added in the sales department—sales managers in charge of groups of territories or groups of products. In each case, however, the form of the organization is *line:* A straight line of authority, at least on paper, runs from the head of the company to the worker at the bench and the salesman on the road.

The original *staff* in this organization will probably consist of the president's private secretary and perhaps a bookkeeper. These people have no place in the line of authority. They report directly to the company president, but they do not direct the work of those down the line. As the company grows, there may be an accounting department instead of a single bookkeeper and several staff departments performing a variety of specialized functions. These may be such groups as methods men, organization experts, and the personnel department, people whose job it is to help the *line* to manufacture and sell goods or services. They themselves are not to engage in actual production or selling the services or product.

In theory at least, these people have no actual authority over the members of the line organization. If they do, one of the primary rules of modern management is violated: the principle that each person should have only one boss. Each manager in the line organization is already responsible to his line superior; if he must also be directed by a staff man in regard to certain areas—personnel practices or methods, for example— allegiance as well as authority is divided. The staff person's responsibility is to provide the line superior with the information he needs for sound decisions. In fact, it is probably correct to say that the personnel expert who is a true staff person will do nothing that the line should do for itself, but will do everything possible to *help* the line to do its own job.

The situation is complicated, however, by the fact that the staff man may have higher status than many of the line people. Thus his utterances may become "the law of the company" merely because he is attached to or reports directly to a high-ranking management person. Then the staff man's knowledge and experience, coupled with the stature of his boss, tend to give "added verisimilitude" (to borrow a phrase from Gilbert and Sullivan) to an otherwise bland and innocuous opinion. Such a staff person must constantly be on guard to keep his advice and opinions from taking on an "official" flavor.

The staff personnel man usually is a specialist in his field. He is expected to possess knowledge of and know-how about the technical aspects of his specialty. If he is a personnel man, he is able to give his full time to consideration of the needs of the people reporting to his superior, and he often has a number of definite functions to perform. He carries out the orders received from his superior. He advises his superior of steps that should or could be taken, he investigates conditions and the needs of his superior's work groups, and he offers plans to bring about needed results. He assists management in developing the general personnel policies of the company and in translating these policies into workable procedures that become a part of daily routine. He reviews the use of particular practices and helps management to ensure that they are understandable, workable, and uniformly administered.

A staff person and a line manager *must* be aware of the same things and have many of the same skills, but in varying degrees. Both must know about company policies, practices, and procedures, and both must have recognizable skills in communications. Further, both must know what affects employee morale. And, of course, both need to know all the other factors that are important in getting quantity and quality of production. But each has a different understanding and interest in the daily applications of these factors.

The line man is expected to be able to perform in a multitude of areas, some of which he plunges into and others that he merely dips into. And if line supervisors are directly responsible for the work production of their groups, it follows that they must also be responsible for the basic elements of sound administration. They participate in the selection, induction, and training of their employees, keep employees informed of things that concern them, handle complaints and grievances, and recommend employee pay increases and job promotions.

But the line man of necessity is a "jack of all trades." He has to be ready to go from one job to another. He may without any advance warning have to go from the inspection of a machine breakdown to the settling of a potentially explosive union grievance. And when he experiences difficulties in the performance of any of his responsibilities, he must know that he can look to his boss for help. And during the course of a particular job or on its completion, he must inform his boss of the things he has accomplished.

In the work situation, however, the boss is not always available immediately, even though theoretically he is said to be. The fact is that many times he just cannot be available.

Since a man cannot always see his boss when he wants or needs to, or he cannot consult him on every problem that arises in a working day, his training must equip him to handle each of his responsibilities as they arise. And, if the training is to be really effective, it must come from his immediate boss, who must make a determined effort to train his line subordinates in all aspects of their duties so that they can function effectively when he is not available for consultation. The superior's main concern, therefore, is to train his subordinate managers to use the basic elements of sound administration as a part of their daily duties.

All this is perfectly clear in the abstract, and few personnel men would dispute it. In practice, however, the personnel man, perhaps more than any other staff executive, is subject to temptations to assume line authority, which can be of the "growing" kind. Since management is the direction of people, his special sphere of knowledge touches almost every phase of the line manager's work. In addition, he deals with intangibles, and it is difficult, if not impossible, for him to "prove" the value of his work in dollars and cents. Hence he may feel a need to institute activity for activity's sake—to take over responsibilities that are not properly his. This is especially true of the training man; he often feels it necessary to justify his position by the number of persons who have been through his training sessions. And since he is higher on the organization chart than many line managers, he can sometimes ensure that they all attend his courses.

A rather usual procedure for a personnel staff man who is "on the make," so to speak, for greater importance within the company, is to "sell" his boss, who may be the company president or the top line man of a division, on the idea of introducing a new activity. This may be anything from a management development technique to specifications for a survey. As soon as he has gained his superior's blessing, he announces a new "program" to the line, using the name of the top man to ensure acceptance.

If the staff man really wants to increase his value to the company, he will resist every temptation to oversee the line. He will endeavor to make the jobs of the line executives easier, rather than harder, seek to win confidence instead of acquire power. If he does this, he will not need to "prove the value" of his work; it will be recognized by everyone.

Such a procedure is often a slow process. The fact that the superior has hired a personnel staff man does not necessarily mean that he is convinced of the value of personnel work in any broad sense. He may have decided to have a personnel group merely because other companies have one, and he has a vague idea that it is "a good thing to do." He may regard the personnel man as a mere record keeper and have no intention of consulting him on broad policies.

In the latter half of the twentieth century a conception has crystallized in the minds of top executives of companies of all sizes, from the smallest with the three-level management teams to the multilevel organizations, that personnel staff men or departments are necessary to handle certain technical aspects of the personnel functions. But it is not these basic activities that are being considered here; rather, it is the basic relationship between each man and his boss.

No matter how many ideas the personnel man may have for improvement, he should be willing to wait until he has won the confidence of the line—of his own superior and of the line managers further down. Even if the superior is already convinced of the importance of the personnel job, the staff man will do well to be patient, for he must win acceptance as a person.

First of all, he must understand his superior's viewpoint and long-range aims, and he must be in general agreement with them. If he isn't, he should get another job. The staff man who thinks he has all the answers and is certain that he must revolutionize management thinking in the company is in the wrong organization. The superior will eventually be open to suggestions on better ways to reach his goals, but he is unlikely to change those goals appreciably at the urging of the staff man.

The problems on which the staff man is consulted may be only minor ones at first, but if his suggestions prove sound, his superior is likely to turn to him more often. In this way the staff man will build the line's confidence in both his function and himself as a person.

Similarly, the staff man must work at establishing good relationships with other line executives. If possible, he should keep himself comparatively free of detail work and take time to circulate, to talk with the line managers, and to gain insight into their problems. If he notices that their personnel practices are not of the best, he should not correct them or carry tales about them; he must prove to them that he is there to help them, not to police them. Once he has convinced them that his own attitude is friendly and fair and that he is not out to aggrandize himself at their expense, they will talk freely to him and ask him for suggestions. If those suggestions make their work easier, they will consult him on more important matters, and his stature will grow.

This is the only way in which the staff man can really accomplish anything worthwhile. At the end of a year or two, he may not be able to point to a dozen new "programs" he has installed as "proof" of his value, but he will not need them because the line will not be questioning his worth. Line executives will be getting help when and where they need it.

As the staff man gains a firm footing, he can gradually introduce some of his own ideas in his conversations with his superior. Timing is important here. If the superior is worried about a problem in finance, he is not likely to be receptive to the idea of a clarification of organization responsibility or the institution of an appraisal system. If a line manager has just had a heart attack, and the superior has no idea who should take his place, a tentative approach may well be advisable.

But the personnel man should not push any idea too hard. He should wait for his superior to take the initiative. He should never allow any of his techniques to be adopted with merely the approval of his boss: "Well, if you think that's the answer, let's get started on it." If the idea gets only that much support, he has not done a proper job.

The staff man must be certain that the decision is not made until the superior has recognized the problem and is himself convinced that the technique is the answer to it. The superior must have a thorough understanding of the plan and be not only willing but eager to install it himself.

The personnel staff man is an adviser, a coordinator, a designer of plans and procedures, an assistant to the line in a specific area. If he cannot accept this role, he should transfer to the line.

Perhaps the most important proof of good coaching is evidence, sharp and clear, that the line personnel who have been coached are now thinking for themselves in regard to their own supervisory conduct. This will be most apparent when they no longer talk about their people problems in a frustrated or "so-what" manner, when they will approach and attack their managerial problems in a matter-of-fact way and develop solutions that are fair, obviously good, and productive. When they do so, their decisions will be accepted as valid by their subordinates because the subordinates have recognized the validity of their methods and have participated in furnishing the boss with the facts which he uses in making the decisions. Thus the results will be generally acceptable to all parties concerned: the subordinates, their boss, and appropriate and affected higher management. Subordinates will also sense that in facing the problem the boss was not just going through the motions, that he was not using a given technique only because he had a report to make on some statistical aspect of the problem.

A caution might be inserted at this point: The improvement achieved as the result of the coaching may be only slight. But the statement, "It is better to have the right man do a poor job than the wrong man do a good job," is particularly applicable here. Even if the improvement in the performance of the "right" person is very small, with continued coaching and practice there will be a little bit more improvement, then a little bit more, and so on.

Both superior and subordinate should show gradual improvement. When the boss spends a little more time and effort on helping a subordinate improve his performance, he himself is developing more skill in management. He has less need to lean on someone else in performing the basic managerial duty, the direction of the people under him.

SELECTING A COACH

Unequivocally the good staff man, probably (but not necessarily) a personnel man, makes an excellent coach providing he has an open mind and is willing to assume a pure coaching role when he helps to teach the techniques to the members of the line organization. With these attributes a coach can subjugate his "superior knowledge" to the needs of his students, the line members.

The choice of the coach is up to the head of the organizational unit that needs a coach. An amenable, knowledgeable, and technically trained staff man may be very successful in the role. On the other hand, the top man may want to use the coaching job as a training measure for one of his line men. If so, he can designate the person to function as a coach, either part time or full time depending on the number of persons to be coached. Such an assignment requires working closely with *all* members of the organization's line team. But if a line person is selected to do the coaching, there is a good probability that the coaching will occupy only a portion of his time, leaving him free to continue his regular work, if only on a limited schedule.

The coach may, in some cases, be placed in an entirely new relationship with some members of the management team—he may find himself attempting to coach persons higher in the hierarchy than he himself is. If this is so, it will be necessary for the top man in the organizational unit to make it completely clear that he has selected the man for sound reasons and to delineate the limits of his activity so that there will be no hidden fears about him.

One knowledgeable high-level manager once asked the question: "How can staff people become accepted as coaches by the line people?" This is a difficult question to answer because so much depends on relationships between line and staff in the past. If a staff man has become *persona non grata* because of the way he handled past assignments, then winning acceptance as a coach will be a long procedure. Further, it may be necessary for the staff person to change his whole philosophy—from one of *doing* to one of *helping* others to do their own jobs. This is doubly complicated since it involves a reversal of both philosophy and action. Usually it can be accomplished only after a long period of time. If, on the other hand, a staff man is freely accepted by the line as an individual, he still must confine his activity to coaching rather than be trapped into *doing*.

COACHING TECHNIQUES

Some of the techniques for coaching managers in conducting sessions dealing with performance descriptions, statements of responsibilities and authority, standards of performance, and making evaluations will follow, with specific attention to the meetings discussed in Parts Two through Five of this book.

To a great degree the success a boss achieves in the meetings with his subordinates depends on his attitude and skill. Even if he has had considerable experience in leading meetings, working either as a chairman or a boss, he may not get the best results without some guidance, for the meetings he will be called upon to conduct in using the techniques described in this book may be somewhat different from those he had led in the past. For this reason he usually has a unique need for the help of a coach, both before and after the meetings. The coaching should be from an objective observer who understands the purposes and processes of the meeting to be conducted.

There are three basic kinds of coaching which apply to all the activities in this book:

1. Premeeting coaching
2. During-meeting coaching (if the coach is observing the meeting)
3. Postmeeting coaching

The second type is not always feasible, because the boss may feel that having the coach in the room will make him self-conscious or inhibit the response of the group or individual concerned.

Premeeting Coaching

In this kind of coaching the coach primarily tries to make the person to be coached feel comfortable in the process. He can go over the purpose and techniques to be followed, the three-step technique mentioned earlier if it applies to the particular meeting the chairman or boss is about to conduct. He must never attempt to dictate what the chairman will actually say, but he may want to ask the leader to "practice on him" various ways of starting the meeting. While this may seem a bit like child's play to the reader, experience has shown that many management people of all levels actually enter into a sample rehearsal with seriousness, and as a result, have much better first meetings.

The coach can also point out how the wording of a question or the attitude of the questioner may determine the answer. He may even have the leader suggest "neutral" phraseology. The literature on public opinion polling affords many suggestions on this matter, and the coach will do well to familiarize himself with some of it.

In helping the leader to be "comfortable" in the type of meeting he is to conduct, the coach must neither underplay the naturalness of the technique nor overplay it. It is true that leading the meeting is basically simple, natural, and normal because it deals with subject matter that both the leader and the members of the group normally discuss with each other. But there is danger that the leader will think his job will be so simple that he does not need to prepare himself; then he will inevitably end up with a poor performance. Conversely a leader who regards his task as immensely difficult may struggle so hard to do a good job that he forgets to be natural. A middle-road approach must be used, and a wise coach will know what the middle road will be for each of the management people he coaches.

During-meeting Coaching

If the coach is present at the meeting, he must, as a general rule, keep his mouth shut while the meeting is in progress. He should answer only when called upon, and in the premeeting coaching he should insist that the leader *not* call on him except in the rarest of cases, not one of which I can think of now.

The coach is there to observe the leader and make mental notes to discuss with him later; these will cover things he might have done differently, words he might have used, or actions he might have taken. The word "mental" is used advisedly, for a coach who takes written notes may be suspect in the eyes of one or more of the participants, and the meeting will lose some of its value. If written notes must be made, they should be unobtrusive and minimal.

After a boss has conducted two or three meetings of a given type, it is seldom necessary for the coach to attend the subsequent meetings. Sometimes either the leader or the coach will feel that it would be helpful for the coach to attend a few more, but generally all that will be needed is a "once-in-a-while" visit to a subsequent meeting to help the leader to stay on the beam or get back on it.

Postmeeting Coaching

The third of the three types of coaching is perhaps the most difficult and yet the most rewarding from the standpoint of the coach. It is in this postmeeting session (which, incidentally, should be held right after the meeting) that the action of the leader is reviewed. The best coaches ask the leader to tell them how he felt the meeting went. Invariably the leader will mention almost all the things the coach planned to bring up because, if the premeeting coaching was good, the leader himself will recognize any poor choice of words on his part or mistakes he may have made and comment on them. Then the coach can merely suggest things he might have said or done instead. If, however, the leader does not bring out most of the breaches himself, the coach will have to inject ideas into the discussion so that the leader can profit by them in the next meeting.

Above all, however, it cannot be too strongly emphasized that the coach's role here is not to tell the leader how well he did or did not do but to let the leader tell him. If the leader appears too satisfied with mediocre results, the coach can venture to prod him a little by such questions as: "Did you learn much from the group that you didn't know before?" or "So-and-so didn't enter into the discussion much, I wonder why?" There may be an occasion where the coach will have to point out specifically that there was too much domination, but this is usually the exception rather than the rule.

These three types of coaching will be treated specifically for each of Parts Two through Five in the next few pages.

Part Two had to do with the technique by which a boss prepares performance descriptions with and for his subordinates. Dividing the coach's role into the three kinds of coaching mentioned, let's look at the premeeting coaching.

At this point it should be realized that the first time coaching is done for a specific meeting, it must be predicated on any general overall coaching already done on the overall use of the technique and go as far, perhaps, as to cover the general approach to one or more or all of the managerial uses of all of the tools mentioned in detail in this book.

In the area of preparing performance descriptions, this first meeting will probably be the only meeting held on the subject.

The coach must point out to the chairman or boss that when he calls the meeting to order he will use his own words, and not something that he, the coach, or someone else has already written; that using his own words, however awkwardly, will do more to make his subordinates realize that he is serious in this venture. Further, his own words will reflect his own feelings.

If it is clear to the coach that the boss is going into this managerial activity against his own wishes and as a puppet, the coach may have to say that there is no real reason to coach him. This is a "tough" approach but it may be a necessary one for some people. Others, the coach may feel, can be coached, since it is clear that although they are planning to prepare performance descriptions merely because their own superior has told them to, they will begin to change as subsequent meetings are held and they begin to realize the worth of the technique.

Since the boss will call first for a recital of the things which the subordinates do, he will, in effect, be nothing but a secretary for the group. The coach cannot stress too strongly the importance of his staying in the secretarial role for the preparation of the first list of major segments. The chairman must confine his utterances to variations of the question, "What else do you do?"

To start this list, there is only one sentence that the boss has to learn: "Major segments of a _____'s job are:" The blank is to be filled in with the general company title for the job the subordinates do, such as corporate officer, or department head, or first-line supervisor, or district manager, or superintendent, or sales manager, or supervising engineer, or what have you.

This beginning phrase that the chairman will write across the top of the blank sheet on the paperboard has been kept short, yet definitely to the point. It is designed so that writing on the paper will not take long, and thus the group can be kept attentive. Some coaches have a tendency to lengthen the opening sentence by attempting to explain what is meant by "major segments." This should not be done. It is better to coach the chairman to explain simply, if necessary, the meaning of the term after he has written the sentence on the paper and has turned back to face the group. However, the shrewd coach can minimize the possibility of confusion by suggesting that they go right into the next thing which is included in step 1 of the technique of conducting this type of meeting, and that is to *write down all they say*.

Here the coach will have one of his most difficult coaching problems. He must impress upon the chairman that he *is* the secretary at this time, and should be vocal only in asking "What else?" Because many managers will be tempted to suggest items themselves or to comment on the items suggested, the coach must point out that for the leader to stop at this time and get into a discussion before he gets a workable list on the paper will prevent the meeting from ever getting very far. Further, if there is need for such discussion, it will occur in good time when the boss goes into step 2 of the technique.

In spite of the best possible coaching, there will be quite a few meeting leaders who will fail to learn the importance of being a secretary rather than a talker until they have really bogged down a meeting by letting it become a verbal brawl on one subject and have not obtained a useful first list of major segments. It seems that many chairmen fail to catch the importance of what might be called a rule until they have tripped themselves in front of their subordinates. The coach must keep at it, doing his best and hoping for the best when the meeting goes on.

Step 1 of the technique must be coached so that the chairman, when he has enough major segments, accurate or inaccurate, good or bad or just bookish, will be able to switch to step 2. Since the purpose of making the first list is only to provide some suitable terminology for the group to discuss, a few pages of major segments will be "enough." Some coaches say that the discussion can be started when at least three sheets have been filled with from five to seven items on each; others say that no more items are necessary when the discussion seems to start spontaneously. Still others suggest that the leader, when he senses enough intense interest stirring, should go into step 2.

The boss can lead into step 2 by saying (whichever is appropriate) something like "Well, here is a good list, certainly not complete but at least one which will give us a healthy number of items as we go on." Or,

"It is clear that we have some controversial items up here, so let's all discuss them one at a time."

The coach can point out that since the group has "come to life," so to speak, the leader will start a clean sheet (the filled ones all having been posted on the wall for all to see) with a repetition of the same sentence which started the first list, but he can shorten it to, "Major segments of your job are:"

Coaching for step 2 now has to point out that the leader reads the first item on the first list and then *asks:* "How about that?" or "Is that something we all do?" or "Is that a segment for general use?" or any natural question which will start the discussion.

The coach must point out that the members of the group will be on the alert to recognize any hint on how the boss feels about a given item. He must further urge the leader to answer all questions with a question, but to help finally in the determination of whether the item under discussion should be put up on the second list, discarded, or rephrased or combined with another major segment. When the leader has satisfied himself that step 2 (the discussion) has resulted in step 3, that is, that all the members of the group *understand* the terminology used and *agree* that it be used, discarded, or modified, then he writes the agreed-to segment on the new list.

Coaching on such things as lack of 100 percent agreement, and the "hold out," or the chronic troublemaker, must be based on past experiences, and the boss should be helped to deal with them in such a manner that dissenters are eventually *won over*, not coerced or bulldozed.

This step 2-step 3 combination is continued through each item on the first list until the second list (usually much shorter) is agreed to.

The coach must point out to the leader that most of his own ideas will show up, without his injecting them, and even if they don't there will be time to get them in future meetings if some one of the group doesn't eventually suggest them.

The coach will point out that it is the duty of the leader to make any appropriate remarks at the end of the meeting, offering to give all members of the group a copy of the results of their discussion (typed) and mentioning that the list will provide the items for which standards for their own performance will be set in the future.

If the coach is present at the meeting, he will merely observe, not contribute. If it seems wise, the leader can explain his presence by saying that he is there to help him, the leader, get to be a better leader.

The postmeeting coaching should be done immediately following the meeting. It is at this time that the coach determines by questions how the leader felt the meeting went and offers any suggestions for improving future meetings.

**RESPONSIBILITIES
AND AUTHORITY**

Coaching on preparing statements of responsibilities and authority follows the pattern just described. However, since there are two possible final results, statements of responsibilities and statements of authority, the coach must point out that the leader has an additional duty; he must use his knowledge of company practices to set limits and yet get all the ideas of the members of the group so that he can, if necessary, recommend broadening (or narrowing) specific company practices.

The coach can point out that the list in this case may be shorter than the list of major segments. This is natural, and probably good.

The working through steps 1, 2, and 3 in this subject both for pre-, during-, and postcoaching is practically identical with that for the performance descriptions.

PERFORMANCE STANDARDS

Preparation of managerial performance standards involves roughly the same type of coaching, and the coaching a manager needs is relatively simple. Presession coaching is necessary and involves, primarily, explanations of the techniques mentioned in earlier chapters.

Presession coaching is divided into three parts. The first, and perhaps the most important, is devoted to making certain that the leader has a complete understanding of the purpose of standard setting. This means that the coach must review what the leader learned from his own boss when he was directed to set standards with, and for, his own subordinates. It is *not* the function of the coach to sell the individual on the merits of the process. That is the job of the man's own boss. Once the coach is convinced that the man has a good grasp of what his boss wants, he can then amplify the instruction.

The second part of the coaching session is spent in explaining the actual techniques of setting standards. This calls for a thorough discussion of the best way of conducting the meetings. At this stage it is important to make certain that the leader understands that the process is a natural and normal part of his managerial job. This is a fact, and the coach can state it in so many words. (Unfortunately, too many coaches overcoach and tend to make the whole process appear to be so difficult and complicated that the man becomes afraid to try it for fear he will appear ridiculous before his subordinates.) A natural approach, explaining the normality of the situation, is all that is needed.

The third part of coaching, guidance in meeting leadership, occurs *after* the session. Often the coach is present, but only *as an observer*. Later, by recalling the things that occurred at the meeting, he is able to give the man who conducted the session valuable help in this area.

The coach should *never* do the paper work for the session. That merely serves to shift the responsibility to the coach and detracts from the effectiveness of the session. Unless the boss himself handles the whole session, the subordinates soon write it off as another staff-sponsored experiment.

MANAGERIAL APPRAISALS

The appraisal plan calls for a kind of coaching that is different from, yet additional to, the general approaches already described.

Before the first appraisal, the coach will confer with the chairman and go over the appraisal procedure. To this end, he must be aware of all the points brought out earlier in this book and of all the nuances indicated by the case examples. He will explain that while it is the chairman's job to keep the meeting on the track, he must avoid any indications of domination, and that one of the best ways of doing this is to withhold his own opinion until the discussion is fairly well started. The coach should reemphasize that facial expression and tone of voice can convey an opinion as well as words, and that the chairman should watch this aspect of his behavior. He can also go over with the chairman the areas of performance that should be discussed, perhaps review them with the chairman in the light of the job description of the person to be appraised.

In addition, while the coach should never attempt to dictate what the chairman will actually say, he can point out how the wording of a question, or the attitude of the questioner, may determine the answer and have the chairman himself suggest "neutral" phraseology.

The coach should, of course, be present at the first few appraisal sessions, and he will takes notes to assist him in subsequent discussions with the chairman. But he must resist any attempt to make him the permanent secretary. He must encourage the line manager not to become too dependent on him or to regard the appraisal process as a staff project.

The coach should suggest, also, that the chairman take his own notes during all appraisal sessions, even though he may have appointed his assistant or someone else in the group as secretary for the first or second appraisals. This will help the chairman to become adept in writing his own appraisals later.

During the appraisal session, the coach will not talk except when his opinion on technique is requested or he is asked about a specific point. Generally, he can confine his remarks to questions designed to start discussions of areas the group seems inclined to ignore.

After the first appraisal, the coach sits down with the chairman for a discussion of such questions as: "Did members of the group participate freely?" "Did they keep to the subject in hand or wander off into too much gossip?" "Were there any areas of performance that were not discussed?"

After the first few appraisals, the coach may find it wise to miss a few sessions, and join the meetings only once in a while. In the later appraisals the coach will be wise to keep mum, performing only as an observer.

In the higher management review sessions, the role of the coach is similar except that he coaches both the man who is to report and the chairman of the review session.

To the man who is to report, he explains the review technique, emphasizing that it is a normal business function and that members of the review board will be trying only to find out things they need to know, not to catch the reviewee in mistakes or inadequacies. The coach will also impress on the man that he will need to be prepared to answer any or all questions from the board and to give a reason for any of the judgments the appraisers have made. In addition, the coach will stress that the session will give the reviewee an opportunity to find out what higher management really wants and to get help on some of his problems. As added reassurance before the first session, he may mention that the technique is new to everyone in the organization, that the reviewers are themselves still feeling their way, and that they do not expect perfection from him or anyone else.

To the review board chairman, the coach will explain that the chairman's function is to ascertain how the reviewee really operates. He will point out how this can be done by judicious questioning about different statements in the appraisal. In addition, the coach should mention that the reviewee will naturally be somewhat nervous about the procedure, and that the board should attempt to reassure him as far as possible and let him talk freely without interruptions.

Finally, the coach should remind the chairman to ask for the appraisal book at the beginning of the session. He further should point out that it is not necessary for the board members to read each appraisal word for word. Rather they should listen to the reviewee's summary of the appraisals and use the written reports only as a basis for questioning. It will be very disconcerting for the reviewee if the chairman is reading intently during the time he is talking. Other members of the board may be briefed either by the chairman or by the coach. The former procedure is preferable, since it emphasizes the line nature of the review process.

The coach should make no attempt to guide the review session itself, once it is under way. Since this is a more formal procedure than the appraisal session, his presence will not have an inhibiting effect. He should, however, make himself as unobtrusive as possible and avoid conspicuous note taking.

The criteria for judging a review session are two in number: (1) What did the reviewee get out of the meeting? (2) What did the review board get?

The reviewee should have a fair, honest, and thorough hearing as he presents his evaluations and plans for development, and he should leave the review session feeling that his superiors take his ideas seriously and are vitally interested in his progress. He should also feel that he has a clearer idea of how to proceed with his management work and has gained a fresh slant on the possibilities. If he has been made aware of some of his own managerial shortcomings, he should know what higher management expects him to do to correct them. His ability to communicate should be improved, and his faith in his own managerial abilities should be strengthened.

The review board chairman, who is the reviewee's immediate superior (and to a lesser extent the other members of the review board), should have a clearer idea of the development needs of the organization, of the way in which the managers down the line are operating, and a better knowledge of how to help them in day-to-day work. The chairman should also be convinced of the necessity of flexibility of outlook, of the need to change any preconceived ideas he may have been harboring about functions or individuals if they are not based on fact.

The staff man must coach with these objectives in mind. He must be sensitive to them, be alert to evidence of change or lack of change, and diplomatically discuss them with the chairman before and after each session.

In coaching for appraisal sessions, the coach's aim must be to leave the appraisers on their own as soon as possible. The sooner he works himself out of this job, the more successful he has been. Coaching of review sessions, on the other hand, should be a more or less permanent process, for the review sets the pattern of the subsequent appraisals and the whole course of management development, and it is here that the staff man is able to make his greatest contribution.

But there must be no overcoaching, even before the first session. In general, most chairmen are already responsible members of higher management, and the review procedure involves only a sharpening of a management technique they have been using all along. Keeping this in mind, the coach needs only to make the objectives of the session clear, caution that a realistic approach is essential, and coach only on the formal techniques. Before subsequent reviews, he can point out new facets for emphasis or suggest new ideas for development as experience accumulates.

The work of the coach in the review, and in all other phases of management development, must always be guided by an understanding of the organizational problems and the personalities involved. No 100 percent development is required immediately. Growth must be gradual, and the coach must not suppose he cannot learn a good deal about it from the line men. He must be flexible and willing to act as a sounding board for his superior's ideas on the subject as the latter gains understanding of the process.

THE APPRAISAL INTERVIEW

The third phase of the appraisal and development procedure, the appraisal interview, cannot be guided by rigid rules, and the coach cannot, of course, be present at it. But he can coach the superior before and after each appraisal interview in the first round, and before and after the interview later on if the line man feels in need of help.

In the pre-interview coaching, the staff man will attempt to familiarize the interviewer with all the possibilities, to give him the feeling that he will be able to handle any situation that may arise. The interviewer will, of course, have a general plan regarding the points he wishes to discuss and the order in which they will be discussed, but he cannot know what the man he is to interview will bring up and how this will affect his timing.

One of the ways in which the coach can help the interviewer—especially before his first interview and subsequently before especially difficult sessions—is by affording him an opportunity to practice in advance. Under this plan, the coach takes the part of the man being interviewed, and he and the superior run through the session with the coach giving unrehearsed answers to the superior's comments.

This is often extremely effective, because the situation is closer to a real one than one would suppose from a mere description of the technique. Those who have tried it testify that they never fail to become emotionally involved in the situation they are discussing, to live—for the moment at least—the roles they are playing. Thus the coach does not need to imagine what a man will say confronted by certain facts in the appraisal; he knows because he feels that he is the man, that the statements are being made about him. And, though it is difficult for anyone who has never tried it to realize this—it is not hard for him to imagine that he is a tremendously ambitious man, one who is only anxious to get by, or any one of a number of other types, and to answer naturally as such a person would.

For coaching on appraisal interviewing after the interview, the coach may perhaps use a checklist to help the interviewer evaluate his conduct of the interview. This may include such questions as: "What was the man's attitude?" "Did he talk freely?" "Did he object to any of the comments, and did his objections perhaps have some validity? If not, was he convinced that the appraisal was a fair one, or was he merely silenced?" "Did he get definite ideas about improvement?" "Were any operating problems discussed and solved during the discussion?"

As the superior gains confidence, he will need less and less coaching. He will develop his own techniques, which, even though they may not be exactly those that the coach would suggest, still work well for him. Soon it will not be necessary for him to talk with the staff man before and after each interview, and the coach can gradually withdraw from most of this work. He should, however, always be available for discussion, or to provide help if it is required; and he should circulate enough to keep himself familiar with what is going on.

Above all, he should aim to perform a true staff function: to counsel, to guide, to help with suggestions.

CHAPTER THIRTY

Field Supervision

WHEN AN EMPLOYEE is working on his own, without benefit of the supervision of his immediate boss who is unavailable for consultation or guidance except at the beginning or ending of a day's work, many slips in operation can occur. Even if the boss puts in an occasional appearance at the place where the employee is working, situations will still arise in which the employee is required to make decisions committing the company to some course of action.

This "field" type of supervision at its best is still not good. For example, one company had eighty-four men all under one supervisor to service its rug-cleaning customers. True, that one man was an expert in the field of rug cleaning and could answer almost any technical questions phoned to him by his men. Further, he spent all day lining up the next day's assignments so that the tough problems would be given to the more capable men. In addition, he prided himself on the fact that he assigned a full day's work to each cleaner team and thereby made certain that the company was getting its money's worth from each employee. His boss accepted these things as "plus" factors, and no questions had ever been raised about the supervisor's "span of control"; nothing had been done to investigate whether this was the best way to supervise the cleaners or whether there was a better way. Such laxness on the part of the supervisor's boss is, on the surface, unforgivable from the standpoint of enlightened management. Such laxness on the part of higher management is almost incredible. Yet acceptance of this type of field supervision has been the order of the day for as long as service organizations have been in operation.

Let's look at the genesis and growth of "field" supervision in the average industry. It usually starts with a one-man type of service operation—and this one man is the all-knowledgeable technician in the field. As the business grows and this one service man has to have assistants, they are added one by one, and the "old-timer" becomes the "head man" in charge of all the others. From either inertia or fear his boss allows him to continue, even confers a suitable title on him and improves his monetary rewards as time goes on. This type of supervision can lead only to lax work, short-hour performance, and in general, employees who really are not happy, for they usually have little respect for their lax bosses. Moreover, some surveys have shown that the poorest supervisors are often in charge of the oversized groups.

Now to continue with the rug-cleaning situation. Eventually a new owner took over the management of the company and decided to introduce some more modern management techniques. In pursuit of this end, he asked the departments, including the service manager, to evaluate their first-line supervisors. When he reviewed the evaluations produced by the service manager, it became clear to him that the latter knew little about the day-to-day operation of the rug-cleaning section of his department in which business had been constantly falling off because, apparently, the customers were not getting the kind of service they wanted.

The new owner felt that part of the trouble with the operations was that the first-line supervisor had an impossible span of control, that four or perhaps five new first-line supervisors should be appointed and the group broken up into four or five smaller groups. If necessary, he was willing to have the present first-line supervisor raised to a second-line level and have the four or five new ones report to him. Although he had some doubts of the wisdom of promoting a man he was not certain had earned a promotion, for the time being it seemed to him to be a wise move. He actually was more concerned about giving each of the eighty-four employees a boss he could reach, follow, and accept.

EVIDENCE OF POOR SUPERVISION

After the review of the "old-timer's" evaluation along with the evaluations of the others reporting to the service manager, the owner evaluated the performance of the service manager. Then the owner talked to the service manager about *his* performance, noting, among the other things, the fact that the supervisor of the eighty-four employees, although he was a good technical man, was not giving each of the eighty-four employees the supervision they needed. He stressed that:

1. There was practically no check on the quality of work done by the employees except when customers complained (the manager said that if there were no complaints he had to assume the workers were doing a good job).

2. The employees were given almost no direction about specialized cleaning.

3. There was a real unrest among the employees, as shown by excessive turnover.

4. It was "standard practice" for employees to quit early. In order to do so, they rushed assignments so that they could turn in completed tickets the next day and yet have an hour or two to loaf or do something else. (The owner pointed out to the manager that since few visits were made to the men while they were out on the job, such practices became almost routine.)

5. There was very little constructive comment or chance to hear employees' problems under such a setup (the supervisor was so busy making assignments in his rude or crude way that no one dared to interrupt).

All these items seemed to be new to the service manager, at least he so implied. But he agreed that he should do something about the problem.

It was never really clear whether he was afraid of the supervisor or just didn't believe his boss was really serious about the entire matter. And since his boss did not direct that he make specific changes, he procrastinated, even to the point of failing to talk to the supervisor to get his opinion on what could be done or to point out the things that could be done to improve his group. And after some time had elapsed, he managed to forget all about the points the boss had brought up. The owner, however, did not forget. He allowed about six months to go by before he asked the service manager what he had done to correct the problem. Their discussion was even more to the point—this time the owner said that he wanted the service manager, within four weeks, to bring in his recommendations for five new first-line supervisors. These were to be made with the present first-line's concurrence. He also discussed other factors of the case, its ramifications, and potential problems.

After four more weeks had passed and there had still been no action, he called the service manager in, only to find that when the service manager had broached the subject to the first-line supervisor the man had blown up and refused to make any changes.

CORRECTING THE SITUATION

The owner pointed out to the service manager that it was his bailiwick and that if he couldn't handle the situation then he, the owner, would move in, but the latter course was against his own philosophy of management except as a last resort. The service manager said he would try again.

In a few more weeks the service manager, bringing his supervisor with him, appeared with the recommendations for the five new supervisors. It was a decidedly disgruntled supervisor who glumly gave lip service to the proposed changes. Only after the owner pointed out how important it is for *every* employee to have a boss who is available and able to devote time to supervision of people, rather than just to routines, did the old-timer begin to see the light.

The appointments were made, and the service manager, under the behind-the-scenes direction of the owner, taught the new second-line supervisor how to train the five new members of management.

This opened up a whole new avenue of thought for the service manager, the second-line man, and the new appointees. Things discussed were the time allotments for chats with individual employees in headquarters, each day's time allotted for field visits (each man was to be seen at least once every two weeks, and not on a repeating schedule), the use of clerks to prepare routing slips, the clocking of time used on each job, and so on.

The new second-line man began to feel that all these changes were things he always felt should have been done, and he became a real "mother hen" to his new supervisors. The service manager liked what was happening, especially since telephoned customer complaints had dropped to almost nothing, and customers were no longer falling away. The owner pointed out to the service manager that it was his job to make certain that the second-line man did not revert to type but continued on in the way he was now going. (The former retired three years later in a blaze of glory for having "revolutionized the division in such a morale-boosting way.")

The chief thing to notice, however, is the improvement in the "field" supervision. Giving field forces the same quality of supervision which stationed employees have does not really present a problem. One needs only to correct the span of control and then see that the supervisors actually supervise by properly scheduling their time into meaningful duties.

Needless to say, periodic performance evaluations, properly administered by higher management control, will make certain that field supervision is good supervision.

ANOTHER EXAMPLE

As a further example of the need for better field supervision, I will cite a situation discussed in a letter from a friend in the western half of the United States. The general area is served by a number of different telephone companies; so no aspersions can be cast at any one of them. His letter follows—the comments in brackets are my own.

> . . . I had occasion to call the telephone company to have them fasten the pay station telephone back on the wall. The screws had pulled out of the plaster, and the phone was hanging by its own connecting wires. This was on a Thursday evening. As you know, this phone, while a pay phone, is paid for by my own place since it is an advertised listing and is primarily used for incoming appointment-making. On Friday a service man appeared, a pleasant fellow, but the only tool he brought was a screwdriver. That was not enough, apparently, because he muttered about such things as having to bore new holes and taking the phone apart to rehang it. He said that since he couldn't fix it, he would have another man come the next day to do the job. It was Friday when he said that. On Saturday afternoon, after no one had showed up to make the repair, I called the phone company's service department, explained what had happened, and stressed the pay station angle. I was assured that a man would be there at 9 A.M. on Tuesday, as we would be closed on Monday. No one arrived by 11:30 A.M. on Tuesday. In complete disgust I took the course which a customer recommended and called the president of the phone company [a typical reaction]. His secretary was very nice, and after I told her my story she apologized and said it would be taken care of.
>
> Sure 'nuff, inside of an hour a service man arrived with an impressive bag of tools. He took a few things apart, then made a call. It soon became obvious that it was a personal call, because he talked coyly, laughed a lot, and was timed at twenty-eight minutes before I inter-

rupted to ask him if my phone was going to be fixed. He said, "No, not today"—he didn't have the key to take out the coin box. Then he went right on with his personal conversation. I waited a few more minutes; then, in my most impressive voice, I said, "Sir, this is a business phone. I pay for it to take appointments. I wish you'd do your personal calling elsewhere." [Obviously the man had been informed that the company frowned on personal calls from customers' phones, but since apparently no one had ever checked on his performance he felt he could do as he pleased.] The service man abruptly laid the phone down and left.

That was all I needed. You know me—I was so _____ burned up I called the phone company again and said I wanted to talk to the supervisor of the repair department. Well, you can imagine how sacred that supervisor was. I just couldn't get to him, he was so well protected, but I kept on and in fifty-four minutes by the clock finally reached him. I wasn't too pleasant by then, so I guess my voice was loud. I said things like "What kind of a business are you running?" "What kind of employees do you have?" "How stupid can your operators be?" etc., etc. He, too, apologized and—here's the payoff—said that he knew nothing about it. However, he would check it out and see. When I told him about the fifty-four minutes it took to reach him, he said he was sorry. [Here not only the employees had been apologizing but the supervisors were, too, as well as the president's secretary.]

He still seemed uncertain about the solution, so I said to him that I wanted the phone fixed that day—it being the seventh day of the breakdown. It was 4.45 P.M. by then. He informed me he would do his best. Forty minutes later the last service man who had been there, apparently chastened somewhat, appeared, lugging a replacement phone which he quickly installed, and left.

Well, 'nuff of my woes. Just thought you'd be interested in what happens when a little fellow tries to do business with a big fellow.

Yours,
Jim

NOT ISOLATED INSTANCES

Unfortunately, there are too many cases like this. The supervisory staff is insulated by the work force from knowing what is really going on with the customers, and the effect of all the fine public relations activities and paid advertisements is being nullified. There is really only one way that such types of flagrant abuse of employees' "right to work" on their own terms can be corrected, and that is for every level of management to do its own share of managing. Only if every manager has a reasonable span of control can that be ensured.

It is strange that the people who come closest to the customers are invariably the newest and usually poorest supervised employees. Management people of all levels should think this one through. It is true in so many industries and service organizations: banks, utilities, hotels, mercantile establishments, postal services, and on and on ad nauseum.

To be repetitive, it is safe to say that the company whose supervisors do know what they should be doing as supervisors, know how far they are expected to go in enforcing rules and regulations, know how well their bosses expect them to do their jobs, and are informed as to how well they *do* do their work, will not find so many irate customers clamoring for better quality and rapid service.

The two previous examples illustrating the need for better field supervision have been in the service type of operations. The work of selling a product by a mobile salesman is another area where field supervision should be improved.

There is no question that the marketing methods affect the customers' opinions of a company. And although everyone has had experiences with companies which intentionally operate on a questionable basis, others, decidedly in the majority, are trying to maintain a good reputation, yet many find that reputation undermined by questionable selling techniques used by their sales personnel. Scarcely a person exists in the country who has not had at least one experience of listening to a "spiel" only to find the merchandise other than described. Further, when contact is made with the company, there follows a series of apologies and a rapid but often frustrating attempt to correct the "misunderstanding." If the difficulty is serious, the person answering the complaint often says, "Well, I'm through with that fellow—we'll get rid of him." It might be pointed out that perhaps the wrong person was fired.

What is the real cause of such problems? Of course the higher-ups have been convinced that executive training courses were being used on the salesmen, and also that proper supervision was at work directing the field men. What convinced them? Was it habit, blind acceptance of statements, complacency, or—and I dread to say it but feel that it is so often applicable—plain mental laziness, usually disguised under a cloak of busyness or haste?

What proof do they have that the supervision is adequate, say in numbers? Do they ever analyze the "span of control" to see whether it is logical, or do they assume that since they themselves do not hear too many unfavorable complaints everything must be all right? Have they compared their sales supervisors' spans of control with those of their competitors, or do they use the decades-old howl of "We can't get good people any more"?

Unless management at all levels directs more attention to the long-standing habits of subordinate supervisors, and they, in turn, do a much better (closer and more watchful) job of directing their field forces, embarrassing complaints will continue to occur.

One vacuum-cleaner company in a large city found itself constantly besieged by complaints from superintendents of large apartment houses. The "supers" were complaining of breaches of security in their buildings. Various tenants would complain that vacuum-cleaner salesmen were ringing the bells at their apartment doors when *no one* should have been able to unless he has been passed by the doorman and announced. The tenants blamed the superintendent, who couldn't find any breach of security. Always the salesman had a bona fide appointment with a tenant. However, after the appointment and before he left the building he made rounds of other apartments until caught and thrown out. This sometimes necessitated a call by a tenant to the super and then a search to find the intruder.

After a call to the company, the super found out that the tactics practiced by the salesman were forbidden by the company; in fact, were prohibited in writing in the salesmen's manual, and great stress had been placed on this prohibition in the training sessions for salesmen. The only real thing missing here, and it was actually the most important thing, was the field supervision. The manager of the field division of the company confided that this had always been a major problem, and it was damaging the company image. In fact, even though they had increased their field sales force by doubling it, sales from the group had been cut to less than half. He guessed that it was due to the fact that the old-timers tipped off the new salesmen to the trick. His really stupid attitude showed up when he said that he had about decided to ask for another 25 percent increase in the force to attempt to get more sales. At this point, it seems obvious that no more need be said about improving the "field supervision" in this particular company other than to ask, "Who supervises the field supervisors?"—especially since the problem had been repeatedly laid in their laps.

OUTSIDE SUPERVISION

A constantly recurring source of irritation is the complaints, either oral or written, which reach the chief executive officers of companies. As said earlier in this book, these make for one of the most expensive kinds of supervision there is. Most of the replies to these complaints either start or close with the sentence or two which thanks the customer for bringing the matter to their attention.

Just what ails a management person who thanks his customers for pointing out shortcomings in his own organization's performance when in reality what he is really saying is, "We (or I) can't do our supervisory job well enough so that our customers will be satisfied, so we have to depend on outsiders to do it for us"? What an admission of failure! Such happenings may be inevitable once in a while, and as such should be used to keep the problems from arising again. But when this type of "outside management" becomes a way of operating, then it is deplorable—so deplorable, in fact, that in one company the chief executive himself told me that he welcomed the complaints because he couldn't find out in any other way where corrections, firings, chewings-out, or reorganization were needed. How much more inadequately can he fill the job of the "chief executive"? A study of such complaints in several companies revealed that usually, eight-plus out of ten times, they were due to ineffective field supervision or the lack of supervision. The correlation is high, and the effect is devastating because the ramifications are widespread.

For one thing, many top management people take field supervision for granted. This is disastrous. For a second thing, some aren't even aware that there is a difference between field supervision and the average kind where the boss is usually around. This is embarrassing. For a third thing, many top people fail to relate customer complaints to poor field supervision, and this can be bankrupting.

CHAPTER THIRTY-ONE

Some
Criticisms

No SUCCESSFUL MANAGEMENT TECHNIQUE has been allowed to progress for long before scoffers and detractors level their sights on it. The various processes discussed in this book, some of which have been used successfully for fifty years, have their enemies, or at least their critics who attempt to supplant sound management practices with activities that appear promising merely because they have not been tried on any broad scale.

Because so many of these activities are grafted onto the true managerial job and can be carried on by staff people, they often have a strong appeal to those who are mentally lazy and who are looking for instant solutions to long-term problems that in reality can be solved only when the manager gives them continuous attention and works gradually toward solutions.

Some of the critics are undoubtedly sincere. Emotionally, they feel that managing is, in itself, somehow wrong and undemocratic, since it implies that one person or one group must, to some extent, control another. They appear to believe that people can coordinate their own work with that of others without any direction from above. All history contradicts this viewpoint. No project has ever been brought to successful completion without some type of organization, and organization implies a hierarchy of some sort, although it need not be an oppressive one or one that is unresponsive to the ideas and needs of those on lower levels.

Other critics may be less honest. Controversy is always news, and an attack on an accepted process is likely to produce more publicity than a sound exposition of the same process. Thus some of the most vocal critics have been prompted to make their onslaughts by a request to write an article or to speak before some management meeting. Then there are the unfortunate professors who must publish or perish, and hence are impelled to think up new programs to write about and present them as substitutes for sound and proved practices; and the management consultants and personnel men who feel impelled to innovate to justify their existence, whether or not the innovations themselves are justified by the facts. Hence we have the evanescent "changes in focus" mentioned in an earlier chapter in this book.

CRITICISMS OF APPRAISALS

So far as the techniques described in this book go, most of the criticism—sincere or self-serving—is directed at the appraisal process. All the others appear to be fairly immune from attack, for they cannot be criticized either on the ground that they are "undemocratic' or on the ground that they require the manager to abdicate his authority completely.

One reason why appraisals have come in for heavy attacks has been that the process has been widely misunderstood, and the term "appraisal" itself has been greatly misused to describe what is essentially a "rating" process, that is, measuring a man against a list of factors on a known scale. The latter is essentially a limiting process, for it confines evaluation of human performance by a set number of factors and uses predetermined values. And since the factors are often determined by a priori reasoning, they may have no applicability in a given case; and even if they are applicable, it is difficult or impossible to determine the exact position a human being should occupy on the predetermined scale.

In a true appraisal, the appraisers are called only to examine facts about behavior, and only the facts that have actually come to their attention. The judgments they make are those they naturally make in the course of their work.

Some people, of course, have more ability to make sound judgments than others, and for this reason a group appraisal is preferable to one in which the superior alone makes the judgments. The use of a group ensures not only a more rounded judgment of the subordinate's performance, but is a safeguard against unfairness and favoritism. The higher management review is a further safeguard.

No appraisal method, of course, is infallible. A group can be mistaken, but when every member of it agrees the errors are likely to be minimal. In most cases the group will be right, especially in its appraisals of interpersonal relationships. This is shown by the fact that in a few cases two different groups of appraisers have arrived at practically the same results. There was, for example, the case of the man cited earlier who felt that one of the appraisers was prejudiced against him and for that reason was allowed to pick his own appraisers the next time. In both cases the results were the same. Again, comparisons of appraisal findings on human relations and the results of employee attitude surveys are found to tally.

But, regardless of the soundness of the appraisal method, appraisals have been criticized on the ground that superiors have no right to make them. One writer went so far as to state that there should be no "inspection" of managerial performance.* It is difficult to see how this viewpoint can be justified. To say that there should be no inspection of managerial performance is equivalent to saying that once a man has been made a manager, the company has no further right to judge him or guide him. If all selection methods were perfect, and if it were impossible for people to grow and improve, this point might have some validity. But as a matter of fact, no company has ever taken this attitude. If it did, it probably wouldn't remain in business very long.

Every company has some method of inspection, even if it is only examination of sales and production figures and budget variances. The board of directors is, in effect, inspecting the performance of the chief executive every time it meets to examine how well the company is doing, and every discussion of plans and results between executives on different levels constitutes a form of inspection.

But merely presenting a man with the results of the inspections conducted by means of the figures and telling him that he must do better is unfair. If his boss wants better performance in some respect, it is up to him to counsel the subordinate on ways in which it can be achieved. The subordinate wants counsel of that kind from his boss, who presumably is more experienced and better informed than he is. (If he isn't, perhaps he

* Douglas McGregor, "An Uneasy Look at Performance Appraisal," *Harvard Business Review*, May-June, 1957.

shouldn't be the boss, and appraisal by *his* superiors is one way of finding out.)

It is also unfair to judge a man entirely by the figures that appear in formal reports on such things as sales volume, budget variances, production volume, and the number of man-days lost because of strikes, slowdowns, absenteeism, and tardiness. Only when the methods he is using are inspected can one determine whether or not these things are the result of shortcomings in his performance or of external circumstances and determine whether he should be counseled to change his ways.

The appraisal interviews have also been criticized on the ground that in counseling his subordinates on improvement, the superior is, as the late Dr. Douglas McGregor once wrote, "playing God."*

If the superior presumes to evaluate the man, as a man, by rating him on 10, 20, or as in one case, 516 traits that some staff person has determined are necessary to be a good manager, and tells him how he should revamp his entire personality, he is playing God, and the subordinate would have every right to resent such infringement on his privacy.

MANAGERS LIKE TRUE APPRAISALS

But a true appraisal is an appraisal of *performance,* not of what the man is but of what he is doing, and every manager knows that his boss is constantly judging his performance. Since this is so, he is glad to know what the superior and others on higher organization levels think about the way in which he is handling his job. He does not want to wait until he is fired or passed over for promotion to learn that he has not been performing satisfactorily. As I mentioned in the first chapter of this book, one of the things most managers want to know is how well the boss thinks they are doing, and they would rather be told directly than have to learn from occasional hints, which may lead them to inaccurate conclusions.

It is true that many of the elements of performance that are discussed in the appraisal interview may be evidence of more or less undesirable personality traits, but the terms in which they are discussed—actual performance—relieve the boss and the man of the embarrassment that both are likely to feel if there is a direct attack on the man's personality. Many personal idiosyncrasies are corrected when a man is told of specific instances in which he has irritated others or given them less service than they felt they were entitled to.

* *Ibid.*

I have singled out Douglas McGregor's attack on appraisal systems because it is one of the most sweeping I have seen and embodies practically all the criticisms others have offered. Some other points he made have been answered in other sections of this book. For example, I mentioned earlier that the reason superiors often dislike to make the appraisals and conduct the appraisal interviews is that the whole system has been regarded as something superimposed on the regular work, rather than a normal part of the management job. McGregor mentions this, and adds that appraisals won't work without controls, but as I have emphasized throughout this book, they won't work with or without formal controls unless the top man in the organization unit wants them to work, unless he is concerned with the development of subordinate managers and willing to work at the job of development himself.

If he is willing, his attitude will be transmitted down through the line, and subordinate managers will be willing to work at it too, because they will realize that it is a normal part of their job. And development, not determining who should be promoted or fired, is the primary purpose of the whole appraisal process.

As a matter of fact, the appraisal process described in this book is very much in line with McGregor's well-known Y theory—which holds that people really want to do a good job, for its own sake, and need not be forced to work by threats or manipulation. By sitting down with a man and discussing his potential development with him, the boss is capitalizing on this fact of human nature, for the emphasis is always on improvement on his current job rather than on promotion or the possibility of dismissal.

Since it is the manager's job to manage, to direct the work of other people, his efforts should be primarily to help them do what they are already doing better than they have been doing it. It does not cost any more in time or money to help them systematically than it does to use hit-or-miss methods, which are often largely unsuccessful.

CHAPTER THIRTY-TWO

Trends and Conclusions

It is sometimes said that management is a profession, and if this is so, it should be possible for a man to get the greater part of his training in a professional school, just as lawyers and doctors do.

This concept of management training was doubtless the basis on which an ex-Cabinet officer, speaking on TV in the late 1960s, based the prediction: "The young people of today will be responsible executives in corporations within five years from the completion of their college or university work."

But if the colleges and universities are to prepare managers to practice management as a profession as well as the schools of law and medicine prepare their students for their chosen fields, there will have to be a change in the way management is taught. Teachers in schools of medicine or law are recruited from among the best practitioners in the field, lawyers are taught by those with experience, and so on. Business schools will produce truly professional graduate managers only when the schools of management use a greater number of practicing managers. At present, even though some of the professors may have had practical and successful experience as managers, much of the actual teaching is done by graduate students whose experience—when they have any industrial experience at all—has been in very minor positions in industry, often in positions that could not be called managerial positions at all. Thus they can merely pass on textbook material, which is often abstract and difficult to apply to actual managerial work.

For this reason, real training in management that supposedly well-educated young people receive must be on-the-job training, planned by their superiors personally, not by training departments, and the superior must do much of the training himself. If a graduate needs more technical training, there are many courses—in-company and outside—that will provide what he requires. But training in the direction of people must come from the superior, at least until better academic methods are developed.

I am well aware, of course, that some university schools of business and some formal company training courses attempt to teach the students to direct people by the case method, through presentation and discussion of situations that have actually occurred in business or industry. But although this training has value, it is often difficult for the students to apply the knowledge gained from thorough discussion of these situations to the situations that arise on the job, which may seem, on the surface at least, to be entirely different, particularly since their superiors often do not, and cannot, act according to the textbook rules. Only face-to-face training by the superior can provide the knowledge an executive needs to direct his people properly under the circumstances in which he finds himself.

CAN WE AFFORD PEOPLE?

It is imperative that managers begin to devote more time and energy to the direction of the people under them than they have been doing to date, for wages and salaries are increasing faster than productivity, mistakes are becoming more numerous and more serious, and employees (and even many subordinate managers) appear to be becoming more and more lackadaisical about their jobs.

If this trend continues, some companies may reach the point where they simply can't afford people any more. And if they do, they will have to go out of business, for despite the great technological advances of the last few decades, the time when a company can operate without people is still far distant. Moreover, the jobs that are eliminated by automation and computerization are mainly the jobs that required little skill and training;

there are now more jobs that require a high degree of skill than ever before.

A great many managers—from top managers on down through first-line supervisors—excuse their failure to get improved performance from their people by talking about "the kind of employees you get nowadays." This complaint has been heard ever since World War I and with increasing frequency. Some seem to feel that they can expect to get better performance from their subordinates only in the event of a serious recession that will make people so terrified of losing their jobs that the boss can manage by fiat.

But for a manager to take the attitude that he cannot expect to get the work done correctly because of the human material he has to work with makes no more sense than if he were to claim that he could not make a good product until someone developed a new material for him.

Managers have always had to work with the materials available to them, including the human material. And just as well-managed companies get better results with metals or plastics than poorly managed companies do, so they get better results with the human material drawn from the same labor market.

Of course, managers can point to the fact that they no longer have as much choice about whom to hire as they once did, to the permissive attitude in homes and schools that has encouraged apathy and the belief that benefits should come without effort, and to prosperity, which has made discharge less of a calamity than it once was.

DIFFICULTIES ARE NOT NEW

But there is no use in lamenting these things. The good manager is a good manager simply because he is able to make better use of the resources available to him than the poor manager can. Also, there are some off-setting factors that should make it easier to get good employees and to manage them in such a way that they will do their jobs right—better equipment, pleasanter working conditions, wages and salaries with greater purchasing power, despite inflation, than ever before in history, and a better educated population. In the good old days that some managers regard with such nostalgia, there were factors that made getting good work difficult for the manager. They were different from those that exist today, but perhaps more difficult to cope with than those of today. How, for example, could a manager hope to get interested employees when he could not get raises for them no matter how well they did? When they had to work with poor equipment in many cases? When they knew they might lose their jobs anyway because an order to cut down the staff might come through at any time?

Directing people and improving their performance is no harder and no easier than it ever was. Getting results in this area is simply a matter of working continuously on the directing phase of the management job.

Both production and employee and customer satisfaction *can* reach new heights, but there is nothing inevitable about the process. These things will come about only if managers everywhere begin to realize (and to act on the realization) that:

1. Subordinates must know what they are expected to do.

2. They must know how far they are expected to go in assuming responsibility and exercising authority.

3. They must know what standards of performance they are expected to meet.

4. They must know how well they are meeting the standards and their efforts to improve must be guided by their superiors.

5. People do what the boss inspects.

Index